THE WAR AGAINST CHILDREN

BY PETER R. BREGGIN, M.D.

NONFICTION

Electroshock: Its Brain-Disabling Effects

*The Psychology of Freedom: Liberty and Love as
    a Way of Life*

Psychiatric Drugs: Hazards to the Brain

*Toxic Psychiatry: Why Therapy, Empathy and
    Love Must Replace the Drugs, Electroshock
    and Biochemical Theories of the 'New Psychiatry'*

*Beyond Conflict: From Self-Help and
    Psychotherapy to Peacemaking*

FICTION

The Crazy from the Sane
After the Good War

BY PETER R. BREGGIN, M.D., AND
GINGER ROSS BREGGIN

Talking Back to Prozac

THE WAR AGAINST CHILDREN

Peter R. Breggin, M.D., & Ginger Ross Breggin

St. Martin's Press

New York

To America's children and the next generation of Breggins—
Alysha Josephine
Benjamin Jay
Sharon Jane
Linda Karen

Editor: Jared Kieling
Copyedited by Eivind Boe
Design by Kingsley Parker

Library of Congress Cataloging-in-Publication Data

Breggin, Peter Roger.
    The war against children / Peter R. Breggin and Ginger Ross Breggin.
        p.   cm.
    ISBN 0-312-11065-0
    1. Violence in children—Treatment—United States—Moral and ethical aspects.   2. Violence in children—United States—Diagnosis—Moral and ethical aspects.   3. Biological child psychiatry—Political aspects—United States.   4. Social control.
    I. Breggin, Ginger Ross.   II. Title.
    RJ506.V56B74   1994   94-93
    362.2'7—dc20   CIP

First Edition: September 1994

10 9 8 7 6 5 4 3 2 1

Books are available in quantity for promotional or premium use. Write to Director of Special Sales, St. Martin's Press, 175 Fifth Avenue, New York, N.Y. 10010, for information on discounts and terms, or call toll-free (800) 221-7945. In New York, call (212) 674-5151 (ext. 645).

Contents

5/95

Acknowledgments

The experience of discovering, researching, documenting, and publicizing the danger of the federal violence initiative has been both exhilarating and, at times, exhausting. Thousands of people have phoned or written, offering encouragement and support. People from many walks of life continue to provide support, including scientists, medical doctors, mental health professionals, teachers, academics, media representatives, attorneys, government officials, and community activists. Some have been motivated to protect political liberty, others to rescue their communities, and many to save the future of their own children. The majority have been African-Americans. Whatever their occupation, motivation, or race, we wish to thank all of them.

We are especially grateful for the unwavering support from our entire network of more than one hundred people, mostly mental health professionals, associated with the Center for the Study of Psychiatry. Dozens of producers and interviewers on talk radio and TV, the majority of them African-Americans, have kept the public informed; there are too many to mention, but we much appreciate their ongoing efforts. Many print media reporters and columnists, from *The New York Times* and *Time* to the *Chronicle of Higher Education,* as well as innumerable local and community newspapers, have been covering the violence initiative. We appreciate the effort required to wade through our documentation and to untangle the often complicated issues.

We have benefited from working with and have received help from Congressman John Conyers, Ron Walters, Lorne Cress Love, Sam Yette, Jerome Miller, Seth Farber, Fred A. Baughman, Jr., Steve Goldstein, Margie Jensvold, David Oaks, Barbara Becnel, James Prescott, John George, Maisha Bennett, Janice Boursiquot, Elombe Brath, Ernest H. Smith, Bill Johnson, Milton F. Shore, Troy Duster, Elliott Currie, Richard David, and Richard Rubenstein. Many other contributors are mentioned in the text or endnotes throughout the book. So many people have given significant support to these efforts, it is impossible to name them all.

Ronald David, Bonnie Blustein, and David Cohen read the manuscript in its entirety and offered extensive and helpful commentary. Beyond their editing, their moral support has been much appreciated. Leonard Frank, Chad Alden, Becky Diamond, Peter Braveman, Maureen McGlone, Michael Valentine, Mrs. Helen G., and especially Andrea Eisler read and provided important suggestions on specific chapters.

At critical moments we continue to receive vital information from anonymous sources, and we thank these men and women of conscience. The many members of the psychiatric survivor movement have wholeheartedly embraced our concerns about the psychiatric violence initiative. Your courage and lives continue to inspire us.

We were aided by four part-time assistants over the course of this work, and extend our appreciation to Claudia Delgado, M. A. Cashman, Melissa Magruder, and Kristen Speight. Our children have encouraged us from the beginning. Thank you for your willingness to share us with this work.

Finally, we want to thank our agent, Richard Curtis; our editor, Jared Kieling; and St. Martin's Press for believing in the value of our work and this book.

Peter and Ginger Breggin

A Note from PRB

I am Jewish, and some of our friends expressed fears about how much anti-Semitism I might confront when dealing personally with African-Americans or giving speeches in places like Harlem or Watts. In meeting many thousands of African-Americans in small and large groups, on the telephone and through talk radio, I have endured only a very few episodes of antagonism toward me for being Jewish or white. And during these relatively minor incidents, communication always remained mutually respectful. Instead of hostility, Ginger and I have consistently been greeted with deep appreciation and often with love. This has been one of the most deeply warming experiences of our lives.

In concluding, I want to say a word about the role of Ginger Breggin. When we first got an inkling about the planned violence initiative, I resisted getting involved. I already had too many volunteer reform activities to handle on top of my full-time private practice, consulting, teaching, research, and writing. But Ginger insisted that the government's plans were too menacing to ignore, and that we should make the necessary reallocations of money, time, and energy. The decision required an enormous shift in focus in her life, and throughout the process, she has continued to motivate much of the effort, to provide key insights, and to build the necessary collaborative relationships throughout the nation. She has unearthed, analyzed, organized, and most thoroughly evaluated nearly all the vast amount of data. The extent of the background material is the product of her research. I have enjoyed putting the icing on the cake—much of the actual writing (with her editorial input) and nearly all of the media and public appearances.

Peter R. Breggin

A Note from GRB

In a lifetime largely spent writing, this is my first completed book,* and there are people to whom I owe a debt of gratitude and acknowledgment for their support and encouragement.

First among them is my husband, Peter. You have provided a foundation of nurturing security and inspiration in countless ways and through countless moments.

To my parents, Jean and Phil Ross, thank you both for being present and loving throughout my life. The older I get, the more I appreciate your gifts of time, attention, care, and affection.

To my daughter, Alysha Josephine Breggin, thank you for being so generous in sharing the joys and struggles of growing up. I constantly learn from you, and your presence in this world continues to help me focus on what really matters.

I also wish to thank several friends and teachers: Pam Clay, Sheila Bond Fulton, Veronica Hartman, Yvette Ogle, Elaine Blong, Jessica Neeley, Eric Zencey, and Emilio Viano. Your companionship and mentoring continue to inform my life.

Ginger Ross Breggin

*Although *Talking Back to Prozac* was published first, this book was finished a short time earlier.

Acronyms of Organizations

ADAMHA—Alcohol, Drug Abuse, and Mental Health Administration *(now absorbed into NIH)*

AMA—American Medical Association

APA—American Psychiatric Association *or* American Psychological Association

CDC—Centers for Disease Control and Prevention, Atlanta

CH.A.D.D—Children with Attention-Deficit Disorders

DHHS—U.S. Department of Health and Human Services *(includes the FDA, the NIH, and the CDC)*

DOJ—U.S. Department of Justice

FAES—Foundation for Advanced Education in the Sciences

FDA—Food and Drug Administration

HHS—*same as* DHHS

LEAA—Law Enforcement Assistance Administration *(part of the DOJ)*

NAMI—National Alliance for the Mentally Ill

NAMI-CAN—National Alliance for the Mentally Ill—Child and Adolescent Network

NAPA—Network Against Psychiatric Assault

NARPA—National Association of Rights Protection and Advocacy

NAS—National Academy of Sciences *(also see NRC)*

NASW—National Association of Social Workers

NIH—National Institutes of Health

NIAAA—National Institute on Alcohol Abuse and Alcoholism *(formerly part of the ADAMHA; now part of the NIH)*

NIDA—National Institute of Drug Abuse *(formerly part of the ADAMHA; now part of the NIH)*

NIMH—National Institute of Mental Health *(formerly part of the ADAMHA; now part of the NIH)*

NRC—National Research Council *(part of the NAS)*

NSF—National Science Foundation

PHS—U.S. Public Health Service

WHO—World Health Organization

Authors' Update

As *The War Against Children* was nearing publication, Frederick Goodwin, the director of the National Institute of Mental Health (NIMH), announced his impending resignation from his post and from the federal government. We can only speculate that criticism of his leadership role in the federal violence initiative, a program of biomedical social control described in this book, contributed to his decision. We are sure, however, that his departure will not in itself reduce ongoing programs or ward off future ones funded by federal agencies or other sources.

As this book documents, before Goodwin's announced resignation, a new biomedical social control leadership was already emerging within the National Institutes of Health (NIH). All of the current projects described in the following pages remain in operation and the largest violence initiative program of all, funded in part by the federal government, is now being implemented in Chicago. Meanwhile, the use of psychiatric drugs to control emotionally upset and rebellious children continues to escalate throughout America.

America's children need a dramatic transformation in society's attitudes toward them. Whether they languish in poverty in the inner city or live in relative affluence in the suburbs, children have never been so at risk of undergoing biomedical behavioral control or so in need of more individualized and caring alternatives to help and to inspire them as they mature into adulthood.

Introduction:
Doctors of Social Control

Extreme remedies are very appropriate for extreme diseases.

Hippocrates (460–375 B.C.), *Aphorisms*

Some remedies are worse than the disease.

Publilius Syrus (first century B.C.), *Maxims*

THE MAYOR OF WASHINGTON, D.C., SHARON PRATT KELLY, RECENTLY appealed to President Clinton to mobilize the National Guard for help in controlling the daily bloodshed on her city's streets. This was not a far-fetched request, since Washington, D.C.—like most American cities—is being overwhelmed with escalating violence. Casualties include children, like the four-year-old youngster who died after being hit by a bullet during a shooting spree on the playground of a local elementary school. It's no wonder that some African-American leaders, including columnist William Raspberry, have joined the mayor in wanting the National Guard deployed.

Many have hoped that the problem of violence would remain an inner-city phenomenon. Commenting on the rash of tourist killings in southern Florida, columnist Amy Schwartz observed that "for all the statistics, it's been slow to sink in that this isn't just a problem for other people's neighborhoods." Raspberry put it more bluntly: "The cynics said we should just cool it. After all, it was mostly dope dealers killing each other. It would be over as soon as the turf claims got settled. Meanwhile . . . well, good riddance to bad rubbish."

Now horror stories of children killing or assaulting children can be found in every corner of America. If some of us in the suburbs feel relatively removed from drive-by shootings, we feel vulnerable to terrifying car-jackings and armed daylight robbery in our homes.

Individuals with means turn to security systems—from cumbersome steering wheel bars to elaborate electronic home security units. Communities beef up police forces and band together for neighborhood watches. Most tragically, children have begun carrying guns to school in order to protect themselves.

Almost everyone agrees that self-protective measures will not curb the overall violence, and that more arrests and mandatory minimum sentencing are creating new problems. Prisons are overflowing. The inmates are a mixed group ranging from the most violent perpetrators to those convicted for the sale of small amounts of street drugs, and their incarceration tends to make them into more hardened criminals. State legislators, under pressure from shrinking budgets and threatened state bankruptcies, are being forced to confront rising prison costs.

Now science and medicine have stepped forward to offer a helping hand. Some of the most prestigious and respected scientific institutions in our country are increasing their efforts in response to America's growing desperation.

Scientists and physicians are the miracle workers of our century, having provided everything from electric light against the darkness to a vaccine against polio. Their technical inventiveness seems capable of mastering the physical universe. In America we tend to hold them in high regard as impartial, humane, and, above all, objective. "Doctor-recommended" highlights many advertisements. We expect physicians and scientists to deal with facts—precise bits of physical evidence that are indisputable.

Against this background of expectations and beliefs, scientists and doctors are attempting to address violence as a disease:

- The U.S. Public Health Service has launched a "public health campaign" against violence, focusing upon "vulnerable individuals."
- The most powerful psychiatrist in the federal government has publicly promoted the screening and preventive treatment of inner-city children—those with a presumed biological and genetic predisposition to become violent when they grow older.
- Federal agencies, foundations, and private industry are pouring hundreds of millions of dollars into the search for a biological basis for violent crime and antisocial behavior. Once it is found, drug treatments can be developed and administered to those who are biologically or genetically disposed to violence.
- Supporters of the federal Human Genome Project suggest that science is on the verge of locating genes that

predispose people to everything from poverty and unemployment to alcoholism and crime. Anticipating such discoveries, the Human Genome Project has funded a conference called "Genetic Factors in Crime."

- Researchers and clinicians alike are frequently quoted in the media as citing "genetic predispositions" for every possible psychological and social problem, from inattentive behavior in school to alcoholism, schizophrenia, crime, and violence.

The view that widespread violence can be best defined and treated as an individual disorder ignores other vast influences, including social, economic, educational, environmental, and cultural differences in experience. The reduction of human experience to an expression of DNA or a wholly biological event shows an underlying bias and ideology—even though it is presented as objective research.

Even when an epidemic has an obvious physical cause, as exemplified by AIDS, science can have its limits, and identifying or treating vulnerable or diseased individuals may not offer the ultimate solution. Educating Americans to change their sexual values and habits, for example, may prove most effective in controlling the AIDS epidemic. But in the age of science, how many of us expect salvation to come from a combination of personal responsibility and transformed social viewpoints? The prevailing vision is that breakthroughs must happen in the laboratory.

Science and medicine influence our view of ourselves, and in turn science and medicine are influenced by our social prejudices. Scientific solutions are often laden with their own biases, such as an insensitivity to the value of liberty, and a moral vacancy around the rights and needs of children and minorities.

Resorting to the National Guard, as hazardous as it is, may be less menacing to civil liberties than resorting to the National Institute of Mental Health. If a neighborhood is secured and made safe for a time by a military presence and curfews, the curtailments of liberty are relatively easy to perceive. So are the limits of using military force to solve social problems. But the dangers of medical and psychiatric interventions—cloaked in science and the language of disease and healing—can be much more difficult to discern and to resist. Promises for ultimate success may be uncritically embraced by a public eager to find seemingly humane medical solutions.

The Faustian price for turning to the social-control doctors may not become fully apparent until the "cure" has been put into place. In our desperation to find answers, we could end up with measures that are ultimately more threatening than the street violence we all deplore, and to no avail as well.

A recently proposed federal violence initiative, which we have actively investigated and opposed, epitomizes this technological approach. Perpetrators of violence in the inner city are seen as biochemically and genetically defective, and plans are developed for identifying supposedly violence-prone children before they grow into dangerous youths and adults.

The violence initiative is the most recent example of a long series of attempts to resolve social conflict through science and technology. The controversy surrounding it illuminates the broader issue of the role of biomedicine in resolving social problems.

Is there validity to the science of social control? Do genetics and biochemistry play a role in crime and violence? Do pharmacological, or even psychosurgical, interventions hold any promise?

What is the history of biomedical social control, and is there precedent for fearing its wide-scale implementation in America?

How extensive were the government's recent plans for the violence initiative, and where do they stand after all the controversy?

What interest groups are supporting the doctors of social control? How involved is industry? The various mental health and research associations? Private foundations? The government?

What plans and projects remain in place, and what new ones loom on the horizon?

What groups are targeted by current proposals and ongoing programs?

How vulnerable are minorities? How extensive is the danger to all of America's children?

What can be done about the threat of biomedical social control—and what better alternatives are available?

The answers to these questions will affect the future of every American adult and child.

THE WAR AGAINST CHILDREN

1

The Government's Master Plan?
A Scientific Solution to Inner-City Violence

There is no more threatening and no more degrading doctrine than the fancy that somehow we may shelve the responsibility for making the decisions of our society by passing it to a few scientists armored with a special magic....The world today is made, it is powered by science; and for any man to abdicate an interest in science is to walk with open eyes toward slavery.

—J. Bronowski, *Science and Human Values*, 1965

We've been neglecting children so long we now have kids in crisis at all ages.

—Olivia Golden, Children's Defense Fund, 1992

A PROPOSED "FEDERAL VIOLENCE INITIATIVE" SOUNDS LIKE A THING FROM the past—a beast that was fought and seemingly defeated twenty years ago. Back in the early 1970s, government agencies were indeed funding psychiatrists and neurosurgeons who claimed that the urban uprisings were caused by genetic defects and brain disease in individual African-Americans. Some of these doctors were advocating psychiatric brain surgery—modern forms of lobotomy—for selected black "rioters" and even their "leaders." One independent project in Mississippi was actually performing psychosurgical operations on the brains of African-American children deemed hyperactive and aggressive. Federal funding was being used to establish a string of urban medical institutes devoted to violence research and treatment. The University of California at Los Angeles (UCLA) was scheduled for the first one. Its purpose was biomedical social control, and its initial plans included genetic research and psychosurgery.

Critics at the time compared these programs to measures used in Nazi Germany, and many of the programs were abandoned under pressure or took on other guises. For a time, biopsychiatrists were discouraged from publicizing political aims like the control of urban violence. (See Chapter 6 for details and documentation concerning the history and outcome of these events.)

Then in the spring of 1992 we received information suggesting that the government's highest-ranking psychiatrist, Frederick Goodwin, might be planning something much more sweeping—a psychiatric "violence prevention initiative" that would identify inner-city children with presumed biological and genetic defects, children who supposedly might grow up to be violent. Up to 100,000 of them would be singled out for preventive interventions, and it seemed inevitable that most would end up on psychiatric drugs. The media and the public seemed oblivious to the danger, but that was about to change.

Confronting Pedism

We live on the outskirts of Washington, D.C., and anticipated that the city's children would be among the most threatened populations if the government's latest plans were carried out. Two of our own children were in their teen years, not in the city but in its affluent suburb of Bethesda, Maryland. In a community supposedly immune to the problems of urban America, we had become increasingly aware that nearly all the ills attributed to urban life were afflicting the suburbs as well.

At first we thought this represented a kind of encroachment—a spreading of influences, so to speak, from the inner city outward. That reflected our own initial prejudices.[1] We wondered, for example, if the new subway connecting the city and suburbs was bringing in the drugs and alcohol. It turned out that there was little mixing between Bethesda and the urban ghetto. The problems were originating from within our home town, involving the area's more adventuresome and disaffected youngsters.

The teenagers we began meeting, many from well-to-do white families, often felt neglected and abandoned, and were reacting with hostility to any form of authority. Alcohol and drug abuse had become commonplace, and so had precocious sexuality. While shootings are not yet rampant in Bethesda, there are more and more reports of children bringing guns to school, and fear of physical assault is not uncommon.* The cover of a national news magazine recently declared, "Even suburban parents now fear the rising tide of violence."[2]

Psychiatry was already being called upon to control children and youth throughout the nation, even in suburbs like ours. We found that increasing

---

*While both boys and girls fear physical intimidation and beatings, the girls additionally fear rape and other forms of sexual harassment and assault.

numbers of young people are being diagnosed, medicated, and sent to psychiatric hospitals. Frederick Goodwin's proposals seemed like a menacing expansion of these practices onto a more overtly political level.

In all of this, we were coming face to face with America's growing rejection and abandonment of its children. We were coming to grips with something that had no name—profound prejudice against all children. We decided to call it *pedism*. The essence of pedism is captured in a speech entitled "All the Lonely Children," in which African-American pediatrician Ronald David* cites America's failure to value its children for themselves:

> The child as a child is, at best, invisible to us or useless. Our most positive public reference to children is with regard to their potential. When we speak of and for children it is typically in terms of their usefulness to the political economy. We describe them as "our most precious natural resource," and as "our future." . . . In effect, the child as a child is a burden to us.

Transforming Our Own Lives

When faced with the suffering of children, adults have two divergent choices: transform themselves or suppress the children. We chose to examine our own priorities and to change ourselves to meet the needs we saw around us. We especially saw the need to open ourselves in a new way to our youngest, Alysha, and her circle of friends, and to investigate the reported federal violence control program that jeopardized so many other children her age and younger. In both instances, we were taking on much more than we could have imagined.

Our home became a refuge for many of our daughter's friends. Our minivan became a local on-call bus for youngsters who might otherwise roam the streets. We rearranged our own lives—our time and energy commitments, travel schedules, and nights out—in order to maintain a constant parental presence in our daughter's life.

Meanwhile, our home-office became a center for investigating the as-yet-unpublicized violence initiative. It seemed fitting that two white parents should blow the whistle on what looked to us like a mainstream assault on black children. And we knew the proposed measures would not stop with inner-city youngsters, because in fact the resort to diagnosis and drugs had already begun in the larger community.

The violence initiative that would shortly strike many people as a bolt

---

*A scholar at Harvard University's John F. Kennedy School of Government.

from the blue was, we established, an extension of existing federal programs that are already bringing about the mass drugging of America's children. The National Institute of Mental Health (NIMH) estimates that a million children are taking Ritalin, usually for the management of difficult, rebellious, or aggressive behavior. Untold thousands more are being put on Prozac and other drugs (see Chapter 5).

The federal government has long led the way in promoting the widespread use of medication for children, typically on the grounds that they suffer from "disruptive behavior disorders"—the DBDs. The plan to focus on the inner city gave a political twist to the medical control already being imposed on children of every race and social status throughout America. Affluent communities are among those with the most rapidly escalating use of psychiatric drugs for children.[3]

Orwellian Solutions

We soon discovered that plans for the proposed 1994 violence initiative were being hatched at least a decade ago. In the summer of 1984, as if to fulfill the predictions in George Orwell's novel *Nineteen Eighty-four, The Evening Sun* of Baltimore had published a laudatory series on biopsychiatric "social engineering." At the time, Goodwin was already chief scientist at NIMH and "the government's top research psychiatrist." Jon Franklin reported that:

> Dr. Goodwin at NIMH sees the violence-prone criminal as often suffering from one of many physical brain ailments, making him unable to control his actions.
>
> If those ailments could be diagnosed and treated (and there is research to this end), society might be spared a large percentage of its violent crime. The rising costs of the penal system might also be trimmed.[4]

Goodwin—described by Franklin as "one of the most visible proponents of psychiatric treatment for violent criminals"—suggested that a majority of violent perpetrators might have brain disease. Goodwin explained, "As we become sophisticated about understanding the biology of behavior, the more potential we get for altering behavior biologically."

Goodwin himself thought that the large-scale drugging of criminals was not politically feasible in 1984. But he predicted that worsening crime, plus an increased ability "to diagnose criminals with organic brain malfunctions," would eventually bring about a "more sympathetic public attitude." The result, Goodwin anticipated, would be "revolutionary."

Now, eight years later, Goodwin had apparently decided that the "more sympathetic public attitude" toward his revolution had at last arrived. He was also in a better position to implement his plans. He had become the powerful head of the Alcohol, Drug Abuse, and Mental Health Administration (ADAMHA), an umbrella organization over three federal institutes.*

Rhesus Monkeys and Inner-City Youth

Goodwin was first thrust into the hot lights of national media attention in early 1992 after he allegedly made remarks that compared inner-city youth to monkeys who live in a jungle, and who just want to kill each other, have sex, and reproduce. The statements in question were made at a February 11 meeting of the prestigious National Advisory Mental Health Council. One person in attendance was offended enough to phone the *Washington Post.*

Within a week, Goodwin "made essentially the same comments at an untranscribed meeting in the Office of Assistant Secretary of Health James Mason," according to Senator Edward Kennedy and Representative John Dingell.[5]

Ten days of escalating media debate and criticism ensued, at the end of which Goodwin issued an apology. On February 21, 1992, he said he had "learned all too painfully that the absence of malice or bad intentions does not excuse the insensitivity" of his comments, adding, "In an effort to shed light on the violence problem, I juxtaposed primate research to the problems in our cities in a careless way. I regret this insensitivity."[6]

Media controversy continued,[7] but as yet no one had seen the actual transcript from Goodwin's speech to the National Advisory Mental Health Council.

Goodwin Elaborates

Four days later, on February 25, 1992, Goodwin spoke to the Mental Health Leadership Forum, consisting of the heads of thirty-seven national organizations. Eli H. Newberger, M.D., president of the American Orthopsychiatric Association, and Ernest Herman, the AOA's executive director, attended this meeting. With ten thousand members, the association is one of the largest professional groups in the mental health field. It is oriented toward children and youth, and specifically emphasizes the principle of "prevention"—but with a different viewpoint from Goodwin's.

Newberger and Herman were distressed by what they heard Goodwin

---

*ADAMHA was disbanded in 1992, and its three institutes—NIMH, NIDA, and NIAAA—individually responsible for mental health, alcoholism, and drug abuse—were placed within the National Institutes of Health.

say, and they summarized his statements in a protest letter to Goodwin's boss, Louis Sullivan, secretary of the U.S. Department of Health and Human Services (DHHS):[8]

> At this moment of heightened sensitivity, in the immediate aftermath of his personal apology, Dr. Goodwin elaborated on his position by outlining his proposed federal program for dealing with violence among inner-city adolescents. The plan calls for establishing biological markers for the early identification of conduct-disordered youngsters. It aims to predict by the age five—and at that point to intervene with—those children most likely to become disruptive and violent in adolescence.

This was the first mention of the context of Goodwin's remarks—the program of biomedical social control planned for the 1994 budget. But that detail drew little or no attention.

Goodwin "Resigns"

Two days after his February 25 statements to the Mental Health Leadership Forum, Goodwin resigned as head of ADAMHA. In an interview with *APA Monitor* reporter Tina Adler, he explained that his decision was affected by politics. As head of ADAMHA, he explained, he was an especially visible political appointment, and a potential liability to both Secretary Louis Sullivan and President George Bush, during the presidential election year.

According to the *APA Monitor,* Goodwin's letter to President Bush began by asking to resign his post at ADAMHA to become NIMH director. Goodwin explained, "I have been anticipating this move [to NIMH] as part of the administration's plan for reorganization of ADAMHA."[9] Goodwin's resignation was accepted and he was immediately appointed director of NIMH.

Protests Against Goodwin and the Violence Initiative

In their protest letter to Secretary Sullivan, American Orthopsychiatric Association executives Newberger and Herman called for Sullivan to rescind Goodwin's appointment as the director of NIMH. This was an extraordinarily courageous stand for a national organization to take, because Goodwin was probably the most powerful man in psychiatry. In addition to his personal influence, he directed NIMH, with its vast power and funding capacity. In a real sense, Goodwin was the last man on earth a mental health professional or group would want to offend.

Why take such a risk? In appealing to Sullivan, Newberger and Herman summarized their reasons for opposing Goodwin and his program:

> This proposal for a program that would label and stigmatize poor five-year-olds in the name of prevention . . . confounds punitive and preventive, while advocating a rehash of "preventive" intervention that has been soundly discredited in its prior incarnations.[10]

Several professional and advocacy groups added their voices to those calling for Goodwin's removal as NIMH director, including the American Psychological Association and the National Association of Social Workers. Mark Battle, executive director of NASW, wrote Sullivan, saying "we believe that [Goodwin's] unfortunate comments reflect not only a degree of insensitivity, but also an inappropriate use of data, that are unacceptable for a director of a leading research institute."

Even the American Psychiatric Association registered its disapproval of Goodwin's original comparison between monkeys and inner-city youth, saying, "It would be wrong to defend Dr. Goodwin's remarks. . . ."[11] But the APA then went on to support Goodwin's appointment as NIMH director, an action that "appalled" Robert Phillips, chair of the association's Committee of Black Psychiatrists.[12]

Defending Goodwin

The media coverage of Goodwin's apparently racist remarks was considerable, and Congressman John Conyers, chairman of the Congressional Black Caucus, demanded Goodwin's resignation. But then Conyers came under fire from the *Wall Street Journal* in a March 9 editorial titled "The Speech Police." The *Washington Post* followed with an editorial on March 21, "The Fred Goodwin Case," stating that an otherwise great scientist and psychiatrist had made an unfortunate slip. The newspaper commented, "[T]his is the political high season. When the going got tough, Dr. Fred Goodwin was out."

Discovering the Violence Initiative

In an effort to lend support to Congressman John Conyers, we visited his office on March 17, 1992. There we read the newly arrived verbatim transcript of Goodwin's remarks to the National Advisory Mental Health Council. The transcript not only confirmed Goodwin's comparison between monkeys and inner-city youth, it contained something far more threatening. The government was indeed planning a program of urban biomedical social control aimed at identifying and treating children with presumed genetic and biological "vulnerabilities" that might make them prone to violence in later years.

Goodwin described this inner-city psychiatric intervention as "one of the planning initiatives that is the top priority of the agency now for its planning for the future—and what we mean here is the 1994 budget." He went on to say, "What I am referring to [as] our number one initiative is the violence initiative."

Goodwin emphasized NIMH's unique expertise and role in identifying the vulnerable individual—the youngster who might grow up to be violent. He spoke of "early detection" and "preventive interventions." While he acknowledged that "psychosocial variables" do contribute to crime, he focused on psychiatric concepts of "impulsivity," "biological correlates," and "genetic factors." He said that genetic factors in violence and crime "are very strong."

He discussed the need to identify specific populations for "extensive and expensive productive interventions." Supporting the concept of behavioral modification, he spoke of the use of "highly structured environments with both clear positive and negative reinforcers." He seemed to be referring to combined psychiatric-penal institutions with the capacity for total behavioral management. Because the interventions would be costly, it would be necessary to "narrow your focus on your population that you are going to intervene in" to "hone down to something under 100,000."

Goodwin noted the public's concern over violent crime, and suggested that there would be more political support or "leverage" for focusing on individuals rather than on social reform or "large social engineering of society." He cited gun control as an example of social engineering that would draw less support than focusing on individual criminals.

It was in this overall context that Goodwin had made his comparison between inner-city youth and monkeys in a jungle:

> Somebody gave me some data recently that puts this in a perspective and I say this with the realization that it might be easily misunderstood, and that is, if you look at other primates in nature—male primates in nature—you find that even with our violent society we are doing very well.
>
> If you look, for example, at male monkeys, especially in the wild, roughly half of them survive to adulthood. The other half die by violence. That is the natural way of it for males, to knock each other off and, in fact, there are some interesting evolutionary implications of that because the same hyperaggressive monkeys who kill each other are also hypersexual, so they copulate more and therefore they reproduce more to offset the fact that half of them are dying.

Now, one could say that if some of the loss of structure in this society, and particularly in the high impact inner city areas, has removed some of the civilizing evolutionary things that we have built up and that maybe it isn't just careless use of the word when people call certain areas of certain cities jungles, that we may have gone back to what might be more natural, without all of the social controls that we have imposed upon ourselves as a civilization over thousands of years in our own evolution.

Goodwin went on to say that despite NIMH's focus on "biological differences" and "genetic differences" among individuals, the overall escalating rate of crime was probably due to "the loss of structure in society." So while acknowledging this wider social context, he emphasized that NIMH's contribution remained in the arena of identifying and treating individuals.

In March 1992, immediately after we obtained the transcript of Goodwin's remarks to the National Advisory Mental Health Council, we began to organize a national campaign against NIMH's plans. We started by sending out hundreds and eventually thousands of reports from the Center for the Study of Psychiatry and by attempting to arouse media interest.[13]

Goodwin at the American Psychiatric Association

By the spring of 1992, the DHHS and NIMH were trying to put behind them the flak that Goodwin had drawn over his comparison between monkeys living in a jungle and urban youth. Our efforts to interest the media and the nation in the even more ominous concrete plans for the violence initiative met with little initial success. Then on May 5 Goodwin spoke to the annual convention of the American Psychiatric Association on the subject of "Conduct Disorder as a Precursor to Adult Violence and Substance Abuse." It would be the last time he elaborated in a public forum on his views about violence prevention.

Goodwin began his talk by emphasizing how important it is to focus on the violence "that's tearing at the very fabric of this country." He explained that he delved into this issue at the request of Secretary Sullivan, who asked for NIMH to work up a public health approach to violence. He acknowledged that violence is "clearly a very, very complicated and large social problem," but that it was time for public health agencies to play their role.

Goodwin carefully explained that NIMH considers a broad array of psychosocial, biological, and other issues in examining violence, but that the body of his talk would center on a specific kind of research at NIMH. He clarified that the basic NIMH thrust is "to design and evaluate psychosocial, psychological and medical interventions for at-risk children before they become labeled as delinquent or criminal." He made a case for this by citing a National Institute of Justice study that 7 percent of youth account for 79 percent of all violent offenses.*

After these couching remarks, Goodwin reached his main interest, "focus on the violent-prone individual." He brought up the genetic question and stated, as if it were a proven fact, "There is a genetic contribution to antisocial personality disorder."[14] According to Goodwin, while the genetic factor in crime and violence is not "overwhelming," it is a prerequisite. (The lack of evidence for these assertions is discussed in Chapter 3.)

The Politics of Research

Goodwin went on to discuss the theoretical role of biochemical imbalances in crimes and violence. A number of studies, including several funded or conducted by the federal government, are trying to show a correlation between sluggish transmission in the serotonergic nerves of the brain and impulsive behavior, such as aggression and suicide (see Chapter 5).

There are many scientific grounds for challenging the validity of the serotonin theory. In addition, its political implications are potent and menacing. When discussing the federal proposals at a meeting of African-American community leaders and activists in Washington, D.C., for example, many otherwise sophisticated people showed consternation about research results claiming to have found a "biochemical cause" for violent crime. They felt they could argue against racism and even against genetic theories, but not against "biochemical research."

We were also concerned from the beginning that research on serotonin was driven in part by the hope of using drugs like Prozac, Zoloft, Paxil, and Anafranil for the "treatment" of impulsive behavior. These drugs are marketed on the basis of correcting biochemical imbalances related to serotonin and are among the biggest money-makers for the pharmaceutical industry.

It is hard for a layperson to imagine that research activities orchestrated by the government, organized psychiatry, and the pharmaceutical industry (see Chapter 2) have no greater inherent scientific validity than any other kind of political effort to prove a point. The research is carried out by scientists whose personal, professional, political, and financial ambitions combine to direct them to come up with "positive" results in support of biopsychiatry. Researchers who resist this trend are likely to run into trouble.

---

*Elliott Currie of the Institute for Social Change at Berkeley responded in January 1993 to the "small percentage" argument, pointing out that 8 percent of the male population is about 10 million people and that a problem of that size is especially "societal" when most of those people are "predictably concentrated in certain social locations."

Margaret Jensvold was a biologically oriented psychiatrist working in the Menstrually Related Mood Disorder Program at NIMH when she discovered that women with premenstrual syndromes often suffered from a past history of emotional, sexual, or physical abuse that may have contributed to their disorders. These findings undermined NIMH's biological approach and, along with alleged sexual discrimination, contributed to conflicts that eventually led her to sue NIMH.[15]

In recent years at NIMH, most psychosocially oriented researchers and administrators have been replaced with biologically oriented counterparts. Loren Mosher was chief of the Center for Studies in Schizophrenia from 1968 through 1980. According to Mosher, biological research in schizophrenia had grown 300 percent during his tenure, while psychosocial research remained flat. This was due to the changing orientation not only within NIMH but within psychiatry itself. Despite this huge growth in their share of research, according to Mosher, biological psychiatrists were not pleased with the presence of a psychosocially oriented colleague in such a key position at NIMH. It was a matter of ideological impurity. Eventually, biopsychiatrist Herbert Pardes, then the director of NIMH, removed Mosher from his post.[16]

Psychiatric research reflects politics and the profit motive much more than it does science, and in this regard, it is not alone in the scientific community. Economics professor Robert Bell charges that "the American scientific community is as 'pure' and unbiased as the political machinery that dispenses its patronage and its funding."

The Economics of Drugs, Serotonin, and Violence

The serotonin theory gains its energy less from scientific evidence than from politics: it can be bandied about to gain congressional and private foundation funding for biopsychiatric research. The logic goes as follows: If biopsychiatry can pull off a medical miracle, saving America from violence and criminality, it deserves every penny it can get of the taxpayers' money. Why not devote half the military and justice department budgets to it? The serotonin theory could make them obsolete.

Maybe the theory hasn't been proven, and maybe it sounds like an oversimplification; but when "all" the experts agree that there's something to the theory, then Congress, the private foundations, and other funding sources tend to ante up. And when it comes time to testify before Congress or any other establishment body, "all" the experts *will* agree. Naysayers and skeptics are unlikely to be invited, and those without vested interests won't even hear about the panel or hearing until it is over.

Another profit motive behind the serotonin concept is the sale of medications. If violent tendencies can be blamed on a specific biochemical imbalance, then prescription drug maintenance of inner-city children and youth can be justified, because drugs are the proposed way to try to correct these supposed imbalances.

Before the federal initiative came under public scrutiny, government researchers openly and enthusiastically discussed their hopes for using drugs to control crime and physically destructive behavior. *Washington Post* reporter Boyce Rensberger said in an early 1992 article:

> Some findings, for example, show there are specific biochemical derangements in the brains of certain kinds of violent people—exactly the same chemical imbalances found in violent monkeys—and that these can be corrected with drugs. The same drugs work in both species.

According to the same *Washington Post* feature story, "Some psychiatrists claim they can successfully treat humans with impulsive disorders with drugs that boost serotonin." Government-funded projects and researchers continue to support the possibility of using drugs like Prozac to control violence.*

The promotion of serotonergic drugs fits the needs of one of the nation's biggest enterprises, the pharmaceutical industry. The most profitable psychiatric drug in the world, Prozac (fluoxetine hydrochloride), specifically aims at "correcting" serotonin imbalances in the brain. This drug has now been followed by Zoloft and Paxil, and still others are coming through the Food and Drug Administration (FDA) approval process. As a raft of supportive articles in the *Wall Street Journal* confirms, these new drugs are among the brightest lights in the profit future of America's pharmaceutical industry. Is it a coincidence that NIMH violence research focused on serotonin imbalances as a possible cause of violence in the inner city? We shall find surprising answers to that question. The serotonin theory, meanwhile, opens up the nation's blighted neighborhoods as a vast involuntary "Third World" marketplace for drug company wares.

Drugs for the Inner City?

In his speech to the American Psychiatric Association, Goodwin mentioned that some of the violence-prone children would be referred to psychiatrists and neurologists—specialists who usually recommend medications. Goodwin himself, however, did not specifically mention drugging children. Instead, he

---

*A 1993 government-sponsored report by the National Research Council (Chapter 2), as well as government researchers and ongoing federally funded studies (Chapter 5), continue to connect serotonergic research to the control of violence with drugs like Prozac and Zoloft.

provided the theoretical basis for doing so by presenting genetic and bio-chemical theories that inspire drug interventions. As already noted, Goodwin was considering drug treatment for violent crime as early as 1984, but feared the public's response. Could he have avoided the specific mention of drugs in order to avoid arousing yet more opposition to his biomedical proposals?

Under the Freedom of Information Act, we submitted requests to the government for all documents pertaining to biological and medical research into violence and Goodwin's proposed inner-city interventions. In response we received a large batch of papers in which there was an unsigned, three-page document dated March 9, 1992. It bore no identifying marks or signatures and was titled "Preventing Youth Violence: Physical and Sexual Assault and Homicide on the Street and in the Home—A Summary Overview of a 25 Year History."

This document bears a striking resemblance to Goodwin's May 1992 speech at the APA and may have been a draft that was prepared prior to the outbreak of the controversy. The notes conclude with the following comments:

> Up Coming:
>   Pharmacological:
>   Depo-Provera, Prozac
>   L-tryptophan . . .*
>
> *WHAT NEXT???*
>
> The VT[†] Violence Initiative

This document indicates that as of March 1992 someone at NIMH—very possibly Goodwin himself—was relating the violence initiative to pharmacological interventions, specifically including Prozac. As our investigations continued, we would eventually find more concrete evidence of health agency involvement in the promotion of these drugs for biomedical social control (see Chapter 5).

---

*Depo-Provera (medroxyprogesterone), a long-acting intramuscular-injectable female-hormone substitute, is used in clinical medicine as an anticancer drug and contraceptive in women. Experimentally, it has been used as a controversial temporary "chemical castration" for male sex offenders because it can sometimes suppress the male sexual appetite. The government is funding both Prozac and Depo-Provera studies for the control of violence. L-tryptophan is a precursor to serotonin and, like Prozac, has been used to achieve serotonergic effects.

†*VT* stands for the Violence and Traumatic Stress Research Branch of NIMH, its main center for violence prevention studies.

Was There a Written Plan?

We always suspected that Goodwin's speeches—with their emphasis on individual vulnerability, biology, and genetics—reflected a formal written plan for the 1994 budget. It was not until later in our campaign that a source, who wishes to remain anonymous, provided us with a nine-page single-spaced typewritten manuscript entitled "Violent Behavior: Etiology and Early Intervention." The heading identifies it as a section from "ADAMHA 1994 Planning Documents," and Secretary of DHHS Louis Sullivan confirmed its authenticity as ADAMHA's proposed violence initiative for the 1994 budget.[17] It probably dates from the first months of 1992 or earlier.[18]

The plan's one-paragraph abstract summarizes that "minority populations are disproportionately affected" and then points to "an emerging scientific capacity to identify the individual determinants of behavior—at the biochemical, psychological, and social/environmental levels." The proposal further states, "Although the problem is societal in scope, our solutions must reflect increasing scientific and clinical capacities to isolate and target the individual determinants of violence." It emphasizes, "ADAMHA will focus on individual vulnerability factors."

The 1994 budget-planning document maintains that "the precursors of violent behavior are evident at an early age." As the "precursors of future violent behavior," it lists a broad spectrum of childhood behaviors: "physical aggression, deviant behavior, attention deficits and hyperactivity—manifest early on."

The goal is to develop new treatment approaches for the targeted children—"to tailor clinical as well as population-based interventions to [these] behavioral risk factors." ADAMHA will stress "the importance of individual risk factors . . . in identifying and treating those who are likely to engage in violent behavior." These treatments are linked to a presumed genetic defect in the brain's serotonergic neurotransmitter system, and included in the plan are "neuromolecular studies of genes that play a role in controlling serotonin metabolism and other neurotransmitter changes putatively associated with violent behavior."*

Perhaps most potentially menacing, under the heading of "Youth Violence" the plan proposes to send out requests for applications for "multidisciplinary Research Centers for the Study of Interpersonal Violence."†

---

*As Elliott Currie commented on the ADAMHA document in *The Journal of NIH Research,* "Most strikingly, it repeatedly affirms—without supporting evidence—the importance of genetic predispositions in explaining inner-city violence, as if the assertion of those connections were not controversial." In the March 1993 issue, Sullivan rebutted Currie and Currie answered his criticism.

†Somewhat similar proposals for federally funded biomedical "violence centers" were dropped amid controversy in the 1970s (see Chapter 6).

Apparently referring to the inner-city minority community, it states, "The Centers will permit multiple-use access to a hard-to-obtain subject population." This will allow for "the testing of a variety of interventions aimed at the individual, family and community."

Triage Through Inner-City Schools

From the start, it seemed inevitable that any widespread psychiatric intervention into the inner city would require the use of public schools for screening purposes. How else could it be carried out?

During his 1992 speech to the American Psychiatric Association, Goodwin gave an example of how school screening can be done. Elementary schools in "high impact urban areas" could implement the first stage of a "triage" system for selecting students. Goodwin declared that children as young as two or three years of age could be identified as potentially violent on the basis of "early irritability and uncooperativeness."

Based on the principle of triage,* according to the NIMH director, an elementary school teacher could cull out 12 to 15 percent of each classroom for further psychiatric screening of the family via telephone by mental health officials. That NIMH has considered all the details is indicated by Goodwin's observation that school screening will cost an estimated seven cents per pupil while the first telephone interview will cost seven dollars. A third triage level will require "structured interviews" with the family.

Goodwin states that treatments will include teaching families how to implement behavior modification techniques. Day camps for older children from "very disruptive environments" are mentioned, as well as referrals to psychiatrists and neurologists that are almost certain to result in drug treatment.

The NIMH director does not address enforcement of these procedures, or the ethical and constitutional issues at stake. Under the cloak of science, he proposes a program of social control without so much as an ethical wince.

Goodwin did not disclose the source of his estimates on the cost of school screening, but NIMH is currently funding a wide variety of studies that encourage the diagnosis and drugging of children through the schools. As this book is being completed, one of NIMH's most heavily funded researchers, William E. Pelham, Jr., at the University of Pittsburgh and the

---

*Goodwin uses the word *triage* in his address to the National Advisory Mental Health Council (1992a) and then elaborates on the concept in speaking to the American Psychiatric Association (1992b). Triage is the process of selecting from among the injured or wounded those who most need and can most benefit from treatment with limited resources.

Western Psychiatric Institute and Clinic, has made a stirring call for the systematic education of school psychologists to enable them to participate in the early identification of schoolchildren for pharmacological interventions. (See Chapter 5 for details.)

Goodwin Represents a Tradition

Fred Goodwin is not an aberration within psychiatry. Perhaps the most influential biopsychiatrist in the world today, he has published hundreds of papers and has been described as the most often cited researcher in the profession. He has transformed government mental health programs to conform with biopsychiatry, but in doing this, he has merely brought the federal bureaucracy into line with current psychiatry.

Goodwin was by no means the first to formally propose biomedical screening or school interventions as potential solutions to urban crime. *Biosocial Bases of Criminal Behavior* (1977), edited by Sarnoff Mednick and Karl Christiansen, describes medical screening approaches, as well as elementary school triage based on teacher ratings, for the early detection of future criminals. After turning down a 1983 grant application based on these principles from Mednick and a colleague,[19] the Department of Justice (DOJ) has recently begun funding a surprisingly large-scale version of the violence initiative that originates out of Harvard University and is being implemented in Chicago.[20]

The Federal Government Builds Toward Biomedical Interventions and School Screening

In 1989, the DHHS and the Public Health Service (PHS) issued a report through its Office of Minority Health to strengthen "long-range planning in support of strategies to intervene in minority homicide and violence."[21] The twenty-seven-page plan overviews the causes and prevention of violence, including poverty, unemployment, homelessness, gun availability, and the cultural glorification of violence. But when it comes to "prevention and intervention," the focus is entirely on identifying and modifying individuals and their behavior. There is no mention of environmental factors and no hint that racism plays any role.

In the "Prevention and Intervention" section, there are hints of the future violence initiative. Under "Predisposition to Violence," the report states: "Targeting individuals with a predisposition to, but no history of, violence would be considered primary as in programs to screen for violent behavior."* The report concludes, "A priority in any violence prevention program is the development of tools to facilitate screening out high-risk individuals for early intervention."

Under the heading of "Violence Screening," the Office of Minority Health report states:

> Suggested sites for such screening included:
>
> - hospital emergency rooms;
> - health centers;
> - jails; and
> - schools, especially at the lower levels where "acting out" behavior can be screened, counseling provided, and follow-up measures taken.

Under "Violence Research Areas," the plan highlights "research related to biological causative factors." Only one sentence is given to researching psychosocial programs, such as Head Start.

This emphasis on individual vulnerability and biomedical research was finally given the government's formal imprimatur in the major future planning initiative for all health services, *Healthy People 2000* (1991).[22] Like the Office of Minority Health report, the violence overview focuses on social determinants; but again the research recommendations ignore this orientation in favor of more limited interventions and provide support for the impending violence initiative. The recommendations include determining what childhood behaviors are most predictive of future crime and "Basic research on the biomedical, molecular, and genetic underpinnings of interpersonal violence, suicidal behavior, and related mental and behavioral disorders."[23]

The Controversy Heightens

In the spring of 1992, talk radio and TV shows with large African-American audiences began responding to our educational campaign, beginning with WPFW (Radio Pacifica Network) in Washington, D.C., and culminating in the summer with news stories and two interview shows on Black Entertainment Television (BET).[24] Extensive mainstream media coverage would follow; but African-American show hosts began the process.

Beyond our personal network of friends and colleagues associated with

---

*The proposal to target people who have never displayed any violence undermines constitutional protections and readily lends itself to thought control rather than crime control.

the Center for the Study of Psychiatry, most of our initial support again came from African-American activists, starting in Washington, D.C., and then New York, Chicago, and Los Angeles. Eventually, public support, like the media interest, broadened to include many individuals, organizations, and cities.[25]

As criticism mounted against his proposals, Goodwin told numerous reporters that he was no longer allowed to make public statements about them. Louis Sullivan, the secretary of DHHS, took over media relations. While himself an African-American, Sullivan was also a Bush appointee and a Republican. As secretary of DHHS, Sullivan was a member of President Bush's cabinet. NIMH, the Centers for Disease Control, and NIH are all part of DHHS. In an editorial critical of Sullivan for not standing up more strongly to our criticism, the editor of *The Journal of NIH Research,* Deborah Barnes, complains "much of the time he was campaigning for George Bush."

Before the controversy had surfaced, Sullivan's public affairs department prepared a sophisticated outline of plans to promote the broader violence-prevention initiative, including multiple media contacts, article placements in significant medical journals, continuing speeches, and op-ed articles by Secretary Sullivan that would focus on new developments in violence prevention.[26] But our public disclosure of Goodwin's biomedical plans put Sullivan and the government on the defensive even before they could announce their larger program. Under increasingly heavy attack, as well as escalating media queries, Sullivan publicly attacked his critics in a speech to the annual meeting of the American Academy of Child and Adolescent Psychiatry on October 22, 1992. Defending himself against an unnamed critic—whom he later identified as Peter Breggin[27]—Sullivan said,

> For example, one individual has leveled false and inflammatory accusations against violence-related research and activities at the National Institute of Mental Health and the Public Health Service. He has accused NIMH of funding research that attempts to link race with violent and criminal behavior; and he has accused the Public Health Service of planning a pernicious, race-based social engineering program.

Sullivan then went on to defend research at NIMH, stating that little of it deals with the biology of violence. He never mentioned the ADAMHA 1994 planning document or NIMH director Fred Goodwin's several speeches outlining plans for the 1994 psychiatric violence initiative. Quoting from a report by our Center for the Study of Psychiatry, without identifying the source, Sullivan complained, "They have grossly and irresponsibly mischaracterized PHS's initial planning efforts as a 'massive biomedical social control program planned for full funding by 1994.' "

Consistent with Bush's re-election campaign strategy, Sullivan made no mention of the root causes of crime in the inner city—racism and the systematic political neglect and abandonment of the nation's urban centers.

Will the Real Violence Initiative Please Stand Up?

When we began our criticism of NIMH's *psychiatric* or *biomedical* plans for urban American children and youth, we knew nothing about Sullivan's much broader plans for an agency-wide youth violence prevention initiative. The Bush administration was planning a nationwide "public health program" in response to America's fears of urban unrest and physical aggression. Toward the end of 1992, amid controversy over the biomedical component, Sullivan announced that this $400 million effort would be coordinated by the Centers for Disease Control and Prevention (CDC) with the involvement of every relevant federal agency, from the DOJ to NIH and NIMH. This is the program referred to by James Mercy of the CDC when he is quoted in the December 1992 *APA Monitor*:

> To make sure the violence prevention programs described in the initiative receive funding, PHS [Public Health Service] agencies will each ask for funding for their proposals as part of their fiscal 1994 budgets.

Some of these programs were already started, and many more were in the planning stages. Except for those in the health-related institutes, most would not involve biological research or medical interventions,* and estimates on the projected amount for these more controversial aspects varied widely.[28]

As the criticism mounted, Sullivan at times seemed to deny the existence of any formal violence initiative, even while in the midst of describing the substance of what we were criticizing. He declared in his October 22 address:

> First of all . . . there is no violence initiative with a capital V and a capital I. What we do have is a planning process for a possible *future* initiative. What some are characterizing as a

---

*Most of the federal projects, however, including those at the CDC, would continue the basic thrust of identifying vulnerable individuals or families rather than the larger social contexts, like racism or unemployment.

sinister conspiracy is actually an earnest effort to better coordi-
nate our ongoing programs and to determine areas where additional efforts are needed if we are to reduce the epidemic
levels of violence in our nation.

We had never spoken of a "conspiracy." We were criticizing something
much more overt than that word implies—a consciously planned and developing program for massive psychiatric interventions into the inner city. And
while Sullivan now claimed there had never been a formal violence initiative,
approximately two weeks earlier he had told *Science* that there were "no
plans whatsoever" to cancel it.[29]

As the biomedical psychiatric initiative became fused and confused with
Sullivan's larger "public health" idea, we decided to make two separate criti-
cisms. We aimed one at biomedical programs for social control and the
other at the broader "public health" approach to crime.

Violence as a Public Health Issue

A public health approach to crime prevention sounds scientific and humane.
It gains authority from a respected tradition of lifesaving interventions. But
is the violence initiative really in the tradition of public health?

In reality, public health moves beyond medicine's typical emphasis on
individual vulnerability. It focuses on the broader environmental and social
factors that affect human well-being and disease.

When public health officials realized that foul water can spread disease,
individuals were no longer blamed for getting physically ill. It wasn't the "bad
habits" or "weak heredity" of the poor, but deadly microorganisms in the city
water. Instead of spinning wheels over why some people got sicker than others, water quality and sanitation were improved, with dramatic results.

Smog remains a serious public health threat. While there is considerable
individual variability in reaction to air pollution—some people hardly notice
it and others die from it—the public health strategy attacks the source of the
problem. When air quality improves, all individuals benefit and the number
of severe reactions is minimized.

Recently there have been incidents of food poisoning at fast-food restau-
rants. Some people got sicker than others, and some did not get sick at all;
but instead of focusing on these individual differences, the public health approach led to tighter regulation of the safety of meat.

The CDC's current stand in favor of gun control more closely approxi-
mates a genuine public health approach. By contrast, the National Rifle
Association's stand—that people, not guns, kill people—parallels the violence initiative with its focus on vulnerable individuals.

The government focus on vulnerable individuals actually abandons public health in favor of traditional medicine. It obscures the reality that the high rates of physical aggression cannot be understood outside the larger environmental context. While it is important to hold individuals morally responsible for their conduct, it becomes critical to look for causes beyond the individual when the rate of crime abruptly escalates within an oppressed minority.

Why would the government pervert the concept of public health? Sullivan's violence-prevention initiative was timed with the election year to distract voters from larger political factors impinging on the inner city, such as poverty, unemployment, inadequate or absent health care, the unavailability of housing, the decay of the schools, and racism. It supported the growing political tendency to blame poverty, crime, and other social phenomena on individuals and their families rather than on public policy, economics, and broader social issues. Unhappily, many political reformers have also been seduced by these fake scientific solutions. A change of administrations and the ascendancy of a different political party does not guarantee a reversal of this trend.

Anyone picking up a newspaper can see how much attention is being given to the behavior problems of America's children. Some of our most charismatic political figures, such as Attorney General Janet Reno, are specifically focusing on them. This is not lost on the various profit-motivated industries, such as drug companies, organized psychiatry, biobehavioral psychology, and other groups or individuals who claim expertise in dealing with troubled human beings.

Altruistic motives, including a sincere desire to help, do exist. But all too often, personal, professional, or corporate profit masquerades as a genuine wish to help. Many people are concerned about America's children, but many others see them as a big growth market.

Regardless of motivation, we need to select the programs most likely to improve the situation of our children, and to reject those that will further harm them. We must arm ourselves with the information necessary to assess intelligently the various solutions being proposed. Especially, we must guard against methods that will compound the injuries already suffered by our children. To do this, we must understand how biomedical social control programs have been developed and implemented in the past, including the common denominators that repeat themselves throughout history.

We need to know the players—to recognize those individuals, professionals, and industries that promote and support the federal violence initiative and other methods of "scientific" behavioral management. Once we do, we can examine their underlying—and sometimes hidden—biological and genetic principles, including those that continue to inspire the current widespread diagnosing and drugging of America's children. In the process, we shall see why a change in political leadership by itself will not impede America's headlong rush toward the biomedical social control of its children and minorities.

We turn now to these players. Who are the backers of the violence initiative?

2

Backers of the Violence Initiative:
From Scientists to Drug Companies and Foundations

I'm enthusiastic about science, but there is a growing tendency toward scientism—unthinking acceptance of scientific ideas, and a tendency to discount ideas that science can't address.

—Michael Crichton, physician and author
of *Jurassic Park* (1993)

A society such as American society which breeds a very broad variety and extraordinary quantity of criminality and violence . . . may arguably and justifiably be referred to as a "crimogenic society" . . .

—Amos Wilson, *Understanding Black Adolescent Male Violence* (1992)

As THE CONTROVERSY SURROUNDING THE PSYCHIATRIC VIOLENCE INITIATIVE heated up, vested interests lined up behind it. Institutional support for the federal plan ran deeper and was much more concrete than we had anticipated.

A Blueprint for Biomedical Social Control

While the government was denouncing suggestions that it was promoting medical research or interventions in the field of violence, the National Research Council (NRC) published *Understanding and Preventing Violence,* edited by Albert Reiss, Jr., and Jeffrey Roth.[1] A *New York Times* headline aptly read, "Study Cites Biology's Role in Violent Behavior."[2] Richard Stone in the November 20, 1992, *Science* called it a "400-page treatise on violence research that could easily be mistaken for a blueprint for the proposed initiative." One staunch supporter of Goodwin and his efforts enthusiastically declared, "Many consider it a *de facto* endorsement of the Violence Initiative."[3]

James Mercy, an official who frequently speaks for the Centers for Disease Control and Prevention (CDC), declared that the report would help to set future directions for the agency. "The NRC report is consistent with the kinds of things we're trying to do," he said.[4]

Organized in 1916 by the National Academy of Sciences,[5] the NRC is extraordinarily prestigious and influential. Its endorsement of biological and genetic principles vastly increases their odds of surviving the current controversy.

The NRC report was sponsored by three federal agencies, the ubiquitous CDC, the Department of Justice (DOJ), and the National Science Foundation (NSF), and drew heavily on research from NIH and NIMH. The mandate was to develop future policies in regard to urban crime in America.[6]

Focusing on the inner city, the report points to "ethnicity" and "poverty" as the major demographic variables predicting physical violence. It discusses many supposed biological variables, including biochemical imbalances in the brain, as well as other "biomedical measures" and "neurological markers for violence potentials."[7] Its final recommendations for "Research in Neglected Areas" call for "systematic searches for neurobiologic markers for persons with elevated potentials for violent behavior."[8]

Infants as Future Criminals

Infants will not be exempt from biological research interventions. In fact, they will be a central focus, with many of the studies beginning at birth.[9] The NRC wants to look for "biological and behavioral characteristics of infants that increase their risk of growing up to commit violent crimes."[10]

Studies of serotonin activity are specifically included in the suggested research; but these can be conducted only by means of highly intrusive tests, including multiple spinal taps on each individual through infancy, childhood, and adulthood. (The physical and psychological effects of spinal taps [lumbar punctures] and other intrusive biological studies are discussed in Chapter 5.)

Community Interventions in the Inner City

The NRC report calls for "multicommunity" research projects to study children starting at birth to provide both "causal understanding and preventive interventions at the biological, individual, and social levels." They will yield "unparalleled opportunity to examine the relationships between biomedical variables and violent behavior."[11] Carried out in the inner cities, the suggested studies will involve controlled experiments with random testing of therapeutic interventions.[12]

The NRC recommends collecting data on every aspect of the individual's life by every possible means, from official records to self-reports, from social variables to biological ones. The Brave New World implications of such all-encompassing invasions of American family life are not considered.

Another Boost for Drugs

The NRC report directly and repeatedly advocates further research on drugs.[13] In its summary it declares that "knowledge of neurological activity that underlies violent behavior could assist efforts to develop pharmacological interventions that prevent violent behavior by some individuals."[14] It specifically recommends "systematic searches for medications that reduce violent behavior without the debilitating side effects of 'chemical restraint.'"[15] In its final recommendations, it again returns to drugs, with a paragraph entitled "Preventive Pharmacological Interventions." Among its "promising leads" are drugs "that act on the serotonergic system to reduce certain aggressive behaviors."

Ethical Feasibility

An odd turn of phrase, *ethical feasibility,* is introduced as the only constraint on physically intrusive research techniques. The research will include "neurobiologic measures that are as specific for relevant hypothesized processes in the brain as is ethically and technically feasible."[16] The first dictionary meaning of feasible is "practicable" or "possible." *Ethically feasible* in this context seems to suggest "whatever we can get away with."

The Question of Race

Under "Research Priorities," the NRC lets down its political guard when it offers a list of "Key Questions." Number one is, "Do male and black persons have a higher potential for violence than others and, if so, why?"[17] This contradicts statements made by Secretary Sullivan and others that government research and interventions will not target African-Americans. Since the NRC report shows little interest in males in general, and concerns itself with urban areas and ethnic and poor minorities, black males are the real focus of this research priority.

The NRC explicitly focuses on minorities living in poverty. It cites "socioeconomic status" and "ethnic status" as major crime predictors. For example, it makes the observation that "Blacks are disproportionately represented in all arrests, and more so in those for violent crimes than for property crimes."[18] The data are presented without considering that arrest rates often reflect racial attitudes of police officers or institutional racism within the criminal justice system (see Chapter 8). The report does give passing mention of socioeconomic factors in crime, but does not focus on them.

The NRC presents its report as a scientific consensus rather than a political policy statement. It is in reality a planning document for future government programs. It calls for mammoth spending on violence research—$500 million—and increases the likelihood that the Clinton administration will continue to support this biomedical approach on the mistaken grounds that it is scientific rather than political and even racist. The mental health establishment—one of the most powerful lobbies on Capitol Hill—will push the president and Congress in this direction.

The Blue Ribbon Panel

On October 22, 1992, Sullivan announced that he was creating an independent, outside "blue-ribbon panel" to "conduct an exhaustive review of all our present violence-related research activities and any proposed violence initiative." A rush job, it met in November and December. The president of Howard University, Franklyn Jenifer, was appointed chairperson. Convening only twice, the panel had no investigatory powers, interviewed neither Goodwin nor his critics, and based its conclusions on the partial materials presented by government officials a few days before the meetings took place.

While generally exonerating DHHS, the panel recommended that the government "should diversify and expand its research portfolio by encouraging more interdisciplinary research that considers the total human experience. . . ." It suggested more research into environmental factors such as racism, poverty, unemployment, low self-esteem, and white-collar crime. Despite the blue ribbon panel's intended use as a rebuttal to violence initiative critics, it thus managed to formulate and eloquently express precisely those "larger" social issues, especially racism, that provide the foundations from which crime springs.

The Price of Dissent

Maisha Bennett, president of the Association of Black Psychologists, was a member of the Sullivan blue ribbon panel. In the February 1993 issue of her association's journal, *Psyche Discourse,* she raised questions about the lopsided biological emphasis of the projects as well as a possible cover-up of controversial research.*

When the controversy was first beginning to brew, Bennett did not take a public stand against the government's plans. During that interlude she was chosen by the DHHS as a new member of the prestigious National Advisory Mental Health Council. Immediately after she raised questions, Bennett's newly awarded appointment was rescinded without explanation by a letter from DHHS.

The NIH Panel on Violence Research

During the furor that surrounded NIMH in 1992, it became an institute within NIH. In response to the campaign against the violence initiative, outgoing director of NIH Bernadine Healy opened a political can of worms for NIMH by convening the "Panel on NIH Research on Anti-Social, Aggressive and Violence-Related Behaviors and Their Consequences."[19] The panel met in June and September of 1993 and is in the process of writing its report as we go to press.

The panel's mission is "to assess the adequacy of NIH funded violence-related research to meet the public need and to assure that the research is conducted in a socially responsible manner." With a number of psychosocially-oriented researchers on the panel, it quickly proved an embarrassment to NIMH and Goodwin. In the past, Goodwin's presence would have dominated a meeting like this, but he did not send a message or make an appearance. Materials made available to the panelists for the hearings disclosed that, despite previous denials, violence-related projects involving genetic and drug studies are already being funded by several NIH institutes (see Chapter 5).

Before the initial meeting in June, each panel member was given a large portfolio of three hundred brief abstracts that purported to represent all the relevant research at NIH. According to Richard Stone in the June 11, 1993, *Science,* the panel became "the first body ever to evaluate NIH's total package of violence research":

> [V]iolence research at NIH, as the panel heard, is very much alive. Nine institutes and two centers have funded about 300 research projects totalling $42 million for 1993, with the bulk of the work being done at the National Institute of Mental Health (NIMH). Much of the NIH violence research is aimed at determining biological factors that may underlie violent

---

*Ron Walters, professor and department director of political science at Howard University, also dissented.

behavior. . . . Other studies explore a possible genetic basis for violent behavior, investigating whether families of suicide victims have higher than average suicide rates.

Stone reported that "the panel noted an overemphasis on biomedical investigations, with few inquiries into violence's social causes and consequences." *The Journal of NIH Research* made similar observations and quoted Berkeley sociologist Tony Duster: "Of the nearly 300 bits of [violence-related] research funded by NIH, at least 90% analyze the individual, or cellular and biochemical processes within the individual."[20] Duster pointed out, "But there is good evidence that certain social, economic, cultural, and political factors that transcend the individual are playing a more dominant role."

The panel seemed unwilling to call for the curtailment of biomedical research and will probably make a politically safer recommendation for greater balance through more funding of psychosocial research. The panel was also unwilling to take on the violence initiative controversy that had fueled its creation. As declared in the headline of Nancy Touchette's review in the November 1993 *Journal of NIH Research,* "NIH Panel Sidesteps Concern About Violence Initiative." She observes of the violence initiative, "it seemed as though a smelly elephant was standing in the middle of the room," but no one would recognize or deal with the beast. Discussions were "relegated to the waning hours" of the conference in private committee rooms.

The Psycho-Pharmaceutical Complex

The psycho-pharmaceutical complex inspires and channels the biomedical research conducted under federal auspices. Fueled by billions of dollars from the drug companies, the psycho-pharmaceutical complex includes federal agencies such as NIH and the FDA, various national mental health organizations, parents groups that support the psychiatric diagnosis and drugging of their children, insurance companies, medical schools, and virtually every aspect of the health care system.*

Eli Lilly at the APA

The violence initiative has brought one particular drug company to the forefront—Eli Lilly, the maker of Prozac, the first specifically serotonergic drug marketed in the United States. Violence initiative advocates and researchers have emphasized serotonergic imbalances and the possible use of Prozac and related drugs to correct them.

---

*In *Toxic Psychiatry,* I first examined the psycho-pharmaceutical complex, including how drug company financing has fostered the domination of psychiatry by the biological wing of the profession.

Prozac is by far the world's top-selling antidepressant drug, with estimated sales of $1.2 billion in 1993, according to Elyse Tanouye in the *Wall Street Journal*. Money talks, and Eli Lilly's deep pockets have extraordinary influence in organized psychiatry and government agencies.

Each year the American Psychiatric Association attracts thousands of psychiatrists—and millions of dollars of drug company money—to its national convention.* In recent years the meeting has become a drug company carnival. Wandering through the May 1992 convention at which Goodwin gave his address on the causes and prevention of violent crime, I[†] happened to bump into *Washington Post* reporter Joel Achenbach, who, like myself, stood in awe amid the pharmaceutical splendor of the main exhibit hall. I took him on a tour of the expansive exhibits that towered in the cavernous Washington Convention Center. The most impressive was Lilly's showcase for Prozac. Achenbach quoted me:

> "This is the World's Fair of drug companies. I paced the size of the Prozac section and it's 18 by 36 paces. It's the size of a hotel lobby, with fancier appointments and chairs than a hotel lobby. It's shameful."

Truly like a world's fair, the logo of Eli Lilly, a giant golden sun-like pill, turned high overhead on a pedestal. Couches and easy chairs made the free coffee even more tantalizing, along with free literature, of course, and free notepads and pens with Prozac emblazoned on them. Multiple video displays extolled Prozac with hardly a mention of the brewing controversy around its side effects and adverse reaction reports. And if the videos didn't get your attention, there were beautiful young women. . . . Even the carrying case for the conference registration materials, given by the psychiatric association to each doctor in attendance, sported the same Eli Lilly logo.[‡]

---

*In the 1970s, organized psychiatry, as reflected in votes of the American Psychiatric Association Board of trustees, decided to actively seek drug company support for its activities (Breggin, 1991a). The APA went from nearly broke to affluent over a few years, largely through increased dependence on drug company money. Contributions from pharmaceutical firms help to support most of the APA's activities, including congressional lobbying efforts, media relationships, public relations, outreach programs to gain psychiatric referrals from other physicians, scientific meetings and conferences, journal publications, fellowships at the APA, and the overall publicity campaign aimed at convincing the public that psychological suffering is a biologically based medical problem treatable with drugs and electroshock.

[†]Because I (PRB) have been involved in related psychiatric reform activities for several decades (Breggin, 1991a), it seems appropriate at times to refer to myself. How to do this in a coauthored book has been a problem. We decided to use "I" to refer to me alone and "we" to refer to both of us.

[‡]Lilly is hardly alone. The giant exhibit hall was jammed with similar if somewhat less imposing displays. Nearly everything at the annual meeting, from free coffee and entertainment to many of the scientific presentations, is paid for each year by drug companies. The meeting simply couldn't go on without the drug companies, and neither could the American Psychiatric Association and organized psychiatry in general.

Could Lilly Buy the National Mental Health Association?

Last year Eli Lilly seemingly bought the endorsement of the private, supposedly non-profit National Mental Health Association. Like most organizations dependent upon private contributions, the association had run into difficult times.[21] At a vulnerable moment, Lilly stepped forward to make an offer that the National Mental Health Association should have refused—$3 million to $4 million to fund a national campaign about depression with the name of Eli Lilly stamped all over it.* In addition to the massive campaign, individual state associations would each receive $5,000 from the drug company.

The *Wall Street Journal,* which usually considers the pharmaceutical industry one of its darlings,[22] sported the headline "Critics See Self-Interest in Lilly's Funding of Ads Telling the Depressed to Get Help."[23] It noted, "The campaign is the most recent twist in a controversial trend in which pharmaceutical companies use consumer advertising to drive sales of prescription drugs." The ads, placed in the name of the National Mental Health Association, urge potential patients to see their medical doctors, rather than psychotherapists. This is a sure prescription for higher drug sales. Some of the material circulated by the National Mental Health Association has Lilly's name on it as well. According to reporter Tanouye, the American Psychiatric Association has come to the defense of Lilly's involvement with the mental health association.

Not everyone affiliated with the National Mental Health Association is pleased. Bill Johnson is an advocate with the Mental Health Association of Minnesota. He is also former president of the National Association of Rights Protection and Advocacy (NARPA), an organization devoted to the rights of patients and inmates (see Appendix). Johnson has told us that taking money from Lilly is a sellout, and he sent us one of the ads generated by the campaign. It's a four-page brochure advertising a videotape on depression. The tape, entitled, "Moving Back Into the Light," is identified as a "Prozac Educational Video on Depression."

The printed material does not mention psychotherapy as a possible treatment but instead declares, "Doctors are trained to treat depression with medication the same way that prescription drugs are used for other illnesses." Since the brochure estimates that one in five women and one in ten men will suffer depression "at some point in their lifetime," Lilly is talking about a lot of Prozac. The sponsorship of the brochure is shown by the logos and names of both Lilly and the National Mental Health Association, but it's trademarked "Eli Lilly and Company."

---

*The *Wall Street Journal*'s estimate.

In March 1993, Lilly sent a letter to physicians around the country, proudly announcing the campaign. I got one in the mail, and it included a sample and brochure for public distribution with the names of both the drug company and the mental health association on it. The ad lists very general symptoms, like "I'm so ashamed, I can't face my friends . . ." and "It's my fault. I'm weak. I feel utterly . . ." It advises seeking help from a physician or calling the 800 number for a free brochure from the mental health association—which also has the Lilly logo and name on it.

Do massive "educational campaigns" like this—including national television, radio, and print advertisements—really work? American psychiatry has good reason to think so. An article in the May 1993 *Psychiatric Times*[24] waxes enthusiastic about the Lilly-sponsored campaign that includes a toll-free number at the mental health association. Pharmaceutical companies have also found that financing "educational" efforts that promote their products is a profitable activity. Medical writer Lynn Payer examines the many ways these companies try to sell their drugs in her 1992 book *Disease-Mongers.** By way of illustration, she notes that "from 1975 to 1988, the funding of symposia by just 16 [pharmaceutical] companies jumped from $6 million (adjusted for inflation), supporting some 7,519 symposia, to $86 million, supporting some 34,688 symposia, a 14 fold increase in money spent."

Lilly's Research "Breakthrough" at NIMH

As the first company in America to market a drug aimed specifically and exclusively at influencing brain serotonin, Eli Lilly has a special investment in the outcome of programs for biomedical social control. How farfetched is the idea that Lilly money could also influence federal agencies like NIMH and the FDA?

While investigating the psycho-pharmaceutical complex, we had heard whispers from anonymous sources that the drug companies were in effect legally "laundering money" through a private foundation and directing the funds to selected researchers at NIMH. If the foundation existed, it was kept remarkably well hidden; no one could tell us its name or confirm its existence. Finally we came up with the right questions to ask through the Freedom of Information Act (FOIA), and we struck gold. A mother lode of drug company gold, the Foundation for Advanced Education in the Sciences (FAES).[25]

---

*Payer's book is an important examination of how, in her words, "disease mongering—trying to convince essentially well people that they are sick, or slightly sick people that they are very sick—is big business." Although her focus is mainly upon general medical issues, her discussions apply to the psychiatric field as well.

FAES is a private foundation whose membership consists of NIH employees and "alumni." It funnels millions of dollars to NIH scientists.* The donations come from a variety of sources, including other foundations. The first accounting we received included grants from Pfizer, A. H. Robins, G. D. Searle, CIBA-Geigy, Merrell Dow, Sandoz, Upjohn, Hoffman–La Roche, Abbott Laboratories, Du Pont, Bristol-Myers, and Eli Lilly. Drug company money in recent times has gone to projects directed by a variety of investigators at NIMH and in other institutes. The pharmaceutical firms specify to whom their money is to be given.

How deeply involved are the drug companies in funding their favorite NIH officials and researchers? Under the FOIA, we asked for documentation of all pharmaceutical company monies awarded to NIMH through FAES. On September 28, 1993, we received a letter telling us that it would take each senior administrator or researcher an estimated three days to one week to dig up the information on his or her own drug company grants over a twelve-year period, that our Center for the Study of Psychiatry would be charged $55,000 for the effort,[26] and that not much documentation would surface, because NIH left supervision of drug company funding entirely up to FAES:

> However, you should know that it is unlikely that many records will be found. . . . FAES, an independent organization, had been managing these grants and awards and, therefore, kept the official records.

Clearly, there is no internal oversight on drug company moneys being given to federal health officials, including those at NIMH. Yet the beneficiaries of this money have the power to make or break the reputations and income of their benefactor drug companies. Without an outside independent investigation, the extent of drug company funding at NIH probably cannot be ascertained.

Through an earlier FOIA request, however, we did obtain a few figures relevant to drug company support for biopsychiatric interventions into the lives of children. Biopsychiatrist Judith L. Rapoport has for many years been chief of NIMH's Child Psychiatry Branch and is a key person in pushing the

---

*An FAES annual report (1987) states, "In recent years the FAES has become active as the fiscal agent for grant or fellowship funds given to scientists at the NIH by outside sources, including private foundations, voluntary health organizations and business groups. FAES, as a non-profit corporation, serves the donor as official recipient of the funds, and then disburses them in accordance with the provisions of the grant." The report also says, "During the past fiscal year the FAES administered five hundred fifty grants totaling several million dollars." FAES supports biopsychiatry and NIH researchers in other ways as well, for example, by putting on an expensive ($400 per person tuition) two-day conference in November 1993 on "Psychopharmacology in Practice," featuring five of NIMH's ranking biopsychiatric researchers: David Pickar, Robert Post, William Potter, Daniel Weinberger, and Richard Wyatt.

use of drugs on children. Rapoport has a current grant account balance of $48,119 from "CIBA-Geigy/Eli Lilly," the makers, respectively, of Ritalin and Prozac.[27] The money is channeled to her through FAES, and as yet we have information only on the 1992 balance.

As we go to press, we learned that the government has changed its policy toward grants given to individual federal researchers through FAES. Due to problems described as conflict of interest, the government decided that these grants should be considered gifts to the federal government rather than donations to individual investigators for specific purposes. In the future the money would be given to a federal agency for dispersal, rathar than via FAES or other foundations to individual researchers for use as dictated by the contributing drug companies. According to the FAES president's message in the 1993 Annual Report, the government's policy change resulted in a 50 percent decrease in new grant donations to FAES. The FAES president explained that the donors "do not want it to be thought that they are giving money to the government." The real change, however, was the donor's loss of control over how the money would be used by individual researchers.

The Government Helps Promote Lilly

Lilly has found additional ways of influencing federal health agencies and receiving promotional support in return. In the 1980s, NIMH developed a massive PR program for biopsychiatry called "D/ART—Depression/ Awareness, Recognition, Treatment." The idea was to get more unhappy Americans to see their psychiatrists and especially to take drugs.[28]

To support the D/ART program, the agency Frederick Goodwin headed at the time—the Alcohol, Drug Abuse, and Mental Health Administration (ADAMHA)—produced a mass-mailing pamphlet for D/ART called "Depression: What You Need to Know." There is a discussion about treatment with psychotherapy, electroshock or electroconvulsive therapy (ECT), and medication. There is special mention of serotonergic drugs and, at the time, Lilly's Prozac was the only one available.

When the pamphlet was put out, NIMH was a part of ADAMHA. NIMH's name is prominently displayed on the front side of the multicolored pamphlet. On the back side of this government-produced pamphlet is the prominently displayed logo for Dista Products Company, a division of Eli Lilly, plus the name Eli Lilly, and its address.* A note says the pamphlet is "Printed and distributed as a public service" by the drug company. The back side also gives the name and address of ADAMHA.

---

*The Lilly logo and address is printed into the format of the brochure itself. It is not stamped on as if added by the company at a later time.

Could Lilly Buy a Top NIMH Scientist and Administrator?

Steven M. Paul was scientific director of NIMH in March 1993 when he wrote an op-ed feature for the *Wall Street Journal* announcing that he was moving on to become a vice president of Eli Lilly. Although still employed by NIMH, he wrote the column to defend drug companies against the criticism directed at them by President Clinton. Clinton, of course, was making the well-known observation that the drug companies had grown disproportionately rich under the Bush administration. But from the perspective of the scientific director of NIMH, these companies are beyond criticism. No wonder Lilly hired him.

Drug companies don't hire vice presidents out of the blue. What was Paul's evolving relationship with Lilly while he was at NIMH? How did he get to develop such a relationship of trust with a drug company? These and other important questions remain unanswered because the Freedom of Information coordinator for DHHS has written to us that "As a Commissioned Officer, grade 06, Dr. Paul was not required to file a public financial disclosure report."

Coincidences?

Eli Lilly directly funds researchers and major "educational" projects at NIMH and ADAMHA and now has hired away Steven Paul, one of the men most responsible for directing federal mental health research. Is it a coincidence that Fred Goodwin, as the head of ADAMHA, came vigorously to the defense of Eli Lilly and Prozac when the controversy over drug-induced murder and suicide hit the press?[29] Is it chance that NIMH is now spending taxpayer money on research that could end up supporting the use of Prozac for violence control, in effect conducting drug testing on behalf of Lilly? (The research projects are discussed in Chapter 4.) Perhaps most significantly, NIMH is providing Lilly with the priceless imprimatur of federal research aimed at supporting broader sales, opening what could be the greatest market ever for any drug—violence prevention and control.

Could Lilly Influence Bush, Quayle, and the FDA?

In *Talking Back to Prozac,* we have already written about how Lilly's Prozac was approved under the most suspicious circumstances. We suggested that the FDA's rush to approve the drug—without requiring warnings about obvious dangers—might have been influenced by Lilly's lengthy, close association with President Bush and Vice President Quayle. *The Nation*[30] agrees:

After he left the C.I.A. and before he began to run for the 1980 Republican nomination, Bush worked for Lilly. Later, he dropped the Lilly directorship from his resume and failed to disclose his holdings in Lilly stock. As Vice President, Bush continued to lobby on behalf of Lilly, whose first Washington lobbying office was set up by Dan Quayle's uncle, back in 1959.

Lilly's headquarters is in Indianapolis, and synergy with the Indiana-based Quayle clan was inevitable.*

Julie Kosterlitz in the *National Journal* adds information to the Lilly-Bush link. Bush was on the Eli Lilly board of directors for two years before becoming vice president of the United States. Before his holdings were placed in a blind trust, he owned $90,000 worth of Lilly stock and $50,000 worth of another drug company, Bristol-Myers. The *National Journal* reports that as vice president, Bush "repeatedly intervened to help the [drug] industry," among other things by easing the first stage of the FDA approval process. Perhaps those eased regulations contributed to the 1993 deaths in association with an Eli Lilly anti-hepatitis drug that had just passed from stage one to stage two testing at NIH.[31]

The Nation reports that in his role as head of the Council on Competitiveness, Quayle asked Lilly to participate in plans to revamp the FDA to make drug approval swifter and easier. Given Lilly's capacity to affect the entire future of the FDA, it would be surprising if the agency could conduct an objective evaluation of its products.

When adverse publicity forced the FDA to hold hearings on Prozac-induced physical aggression and suicide, the committee was stacked with people who had obvious conflicts of interest. As described in *Talking Back to Prozac,* many had ties to drug companies, including Eli Lily.

The FDA, L-tryptophan, and Drug Industry Profits

In 1989 more than 1,500 cases of a rare and potentially fatal disease, eosinophilic myalgia syndrome (EMS), were abruptly reported in association with ingestion of the food supplement L-tryptophan. The amino acid L-tryptophan is a naturally occurring precursor in the brain's manufacture of

---

*When a plane crash killed Michael A. Carroll, vice president for community affairs at the Lilly Endowment in Indianapolis, it was noted in the press that he was a former assistant to Quayle in the Senate. We assume these various connections are but the tip of the political iceberg.

serotonin. The protein is found in foods such as milk and turkey* and has been used since the late 1960s as a relatively safe and inexpensive alternative to psychiatric drugs for the treatment of insomnia, depression, and anxiety, as well as a variety of other disorders.[32]

When Lilly and other drug companies began promoting their expensive and potentially dangerous serotonergic agents, millions of people had already been using L-tryptophan for many years. Following the outbreak of EMS, L-tryptophan was taken off the market and then banned by the FDA in March 1992. Since then, the problem has been traced to a specific contaminated batch of L-tryptophan produced under inexplicably unsafe conditions at a company in Japan. Yet all L-tryptophan remains banned.

Critics of the FDA and the psycho-pharmaceutical complex have suspected that the ban on this safe and inexpensive natural substance is maintained to force consumers to substitute the dangerous and costly serotonergic products of Eli Lilly and other influential drug companies. Dean Manders, for example, has observed:

> [O]ften dangerous chemical serotonin "enhancers" like Prozac and Anafranil[†] are sold and used widely at the same time that L-tryptophan, a safe nondrug serotonin producer is unavailable to people. . . .

He concludes "the present, continuing FDA ban of non-contaminated L-tryptophan . . . seems unwarranted, harmful, and biased in favor of the pharmaceutical industry."

Could Lilly Buy Influence with the American Justice System?

Lilly has also begun to intervene vigorously with its money and know-how in both the civil and criminal justice systems. The commotion surrounds the many reports of patients committing suicide, murder, or bizarre, impulsive acts while under the influence of Prozac.[33] The most famous case was that of Joseph Wesbecker, who went on a killing rampage in 1989, and then committed suicide. Wesbecker's family and widows of the victims are suing Lilly.

In regard to malpractice suits, Lilly has guaranteed to fund the defense of any doctor if Lilly finds that he or she prescribed the drug properly.[34] This is a big promise. Many malpractice suits have been brought against physi-

---

*It has been suggested that the high concentration of L-tryptophan in turkey is what makes people so relaxed and sleepy after Thanksgiving dinner.
†Another antidepressant with serotonergic properties. It has been especially marked for obsessive-compulsive disorder.

cians who prescribe Prozac. Guaranteeing financial support and expertise to doctors who are sued is Lilly's way of reassuring doctors not to worry. It helps to prop up sales in the face of some very bad publicity.

In many ways even more ethically questionable, Lilly has been offering to help the prosecution in criminal cases in which the defendant uses the "Prozac defense."[35] When the defendant claims that Prozac contributed to his or her violent acts, Lilly contacts the prosecution to offer experts, research materials, and other funding help.

An angered attorney commented on the Lilly strategy:

> Not only am I fighting the prosecutor, now I'm fighting the resources of Eli Lilly. That isn't fair when I'm trying to defend someone on a limited budget in a capital case.

Another declared:

> Permitting a multibillion-dollar private enterprise to join in a consortium with a government prosecutorial agency raises very strong constitutional issues relating to a defendant's right to a fair trial.

Cases have already reached plea bargains that seem influenced by the defense that the individual was "involuntarily intoxicated" or otherwise under the influence of Prozac.* This again threatens Prozac's image and Lilly's sales. Recently I was called as a medical expert in such a case, and Lilly contacted the prosecution to offer them funds, briefings, background materials, and medical experts. The prosecution was also given a long list of questions specifically formulated by Eli Lilly to ask me on the witness stand. In part, influenced by my written report, the prosecution avoided going to court and the defendant was allowed to plead guilty without receiving any jail time.

Now that Bush and Quayle are gone, perhaps Congress could begin a Psychogate investigation of all the drug companies, starting with Lilly's intervention in the justice system. But it must be kept in mind that many drug companies vie with Lilly for influence in the psycho-pharmaceutical complex.[36]

---

*There is a great deal of evidence that Prozac can produce bizarre impulsive behavior (See Breggin and Breggin, 1994).

The Latest on Upjohn

The issue of the psycho-pharmaceutical complex came up again in 1992 when it was revealed that President George Bush had been taking the minor tranquilizer Halcion on a trip to Japan. The question was raised, "Why was the president taking a sedative drug that had been outlawed in England?" Among other things, Halcion can cause memory loss, psychosis, paranoia, and violence—risky side effects in the president of the United States.*

To explain why Halcion had not been banned in the United States, I wrote a letter published in the February 11, 1992, *New York Times.* My letter points out that Upjohn, the maker of the drug, has recently given an unrestricted cash gift of $1.5 million to the American Psychiatric Association.

Instead of denying its dependence upon the pharmaceutical industry, the medical director of the American Psychiatric Association, Melvin Sabshin, wrote a rebuttal to my letter in which he boasted of the association's "partnership" with the drug companies. He called it a "responsible, ethical partnership that uses the no-strings resources of one partner and the expertise of the other. . . ." How or why an industry would give away huge sums of money with no thought of corporate gain went unexplained.

Upjohn, like APA, is proud of its "partnership" with the psychiatric association. When neurologist Fred A. Baughman, Jr., wrote a letter to *Clinical Psychiatry News* criticizing Upjohn's power over psychiatry, Upjohn official Jeffrey M. Jonas replied by quoting Melvin Sabshin about the "partnership" between Upjohn and APA.[37]

Upjohn spends money lavishly to influence psychiatry. Recently we discovered another connection, this time with Steven Paul. In 1990, Upjohn published a flashy, colorful twenty-page booklet entitled *The Psychophysiology of Anxiety.* Directly under the title on the cover is "Prepared in cooperation with Steven M. Paul, M.D." Inside the cover, Paul is identified as acting director, Intramural Research Program, and chief, Section of Molecular Pharmacology, Clinical Neuroscience Branch, NIMH. Below the impressive titles is a disclaimer saying that his views do not reflect the policies of NIMH.

The booklet is very supportive of drug interventions. Upjohn makes Xanax, the most widely sold minor tranquilizer for anxiety, as well as Halcion. Both are very addictive.

Big-name psychiatrists are usually well paid for lending themselves to these kinds of projects. We do know through the FOIA that Paul also received a grant from Upjohn through FAES while at NIMH, but we have not yet been able to ascertain the amount.

---

*Recently the British minister of health announced that Upjohn's latest bid to gain approval for Halcion in the United Kingdom was being turned down (Melillo, 1993).

Meanwhile, Upjohn has been in considerable trouble in the United States and England over allegations concerning its handling of information about the negative side effects of Halcion. Critics from within the medical profession are claiming that Upjohn committed fraud in regard to its New Drug Application to the FDA and that it concealed data from the FDA over a period of two decades. Upjohn admitted to some errors in reporting, but denied any intent to mislead.[38]

Racism and Sexism at NIH

Given that researchers are bound to be influenced by drug companies, are they also influenced by racism, sexism, and other societal prejudices? Is science without bias too much to hope for from NIMH and other agencies?

The violence initiative reflects not only racism within the nation but within the government. NIH, for example, has a long history of racist and sexist policies.

The Montgomery County NAACP and Blacks in Government (BIG) have been sponsoring monthly demonstrations against racial and sexual discrimination at NIH. On May 17, 1993, despite thunderstorms, more than 150 people gathered during their lunch hours in Building One, which housed NIH director Bernadine Healy's offices. The NAACP and BIG have been joined by organizations of professional women who have experienced sexual discrimination while employed at NIH. More than 130 new discrimination complaints were filed against NIH in the month after the NAACP began its demonstrations. These are in addition to 242 discrimination and harassment complaints filed in 1992 against NIH.

We attended this demonstration, which was part rally, part information update, and part show of solidarity for those who have come forward. NIH deputy director Jay Moskowitz boasted about the institutes' successes in fighting disease, and then explained that it was forming a task force to forcefully and quickly resolve complaints, including charges of nepotism, favoritism, and rampant sex- and race-based discrimination. Senior Policy Advisor and Counselor to the Director Sandy Chamblee, a black woman, then spoke reassuringly about the task force's intentions.

In the back of the hall another black woman stood with a hand to her face, wiping away tears of frustration. The expressions on the faces of the overwhelmingly black audience were often filled with fear and skepticism, not hope. Ruby Fields, one of the founders of BIG, stood and addressed the group, asking, "What has been done in Dr. Moskowitz's twenty-five years at NIH to eradicate the disease of racism?"

Since those demonstrations, recent testimony before Congress has confirmed that "the nation's premier facility is plagued by pervasive, long-standing racial discrimination that has clustered black employees in low-paying jobs with little chance of advancement." According to *Washington Post* reporter Veronica Jennings, witnesses drew a portrait of twenty years of a "deeply entrenched culture of bias" during which, NIH admitted, not one person had ever been disciplined for racial bias. The recently deposed head of NIH, Bernadine Healy, did not deny the charges, but claimed she had tried to reverse the trend during her tenure.

Charges of sex bias also came up at the hearings, and it was noted that NIH had "imposed sanctions" in eleven cases of sexual harassment by supervisors. Another 1993 *Washington Post* report, this one by S. S. Greenberger, detailed the story of psychiatrist Margaret Jensvold, who (as mentioned in Chapter 1) has been instrumental in publicizing sexual harassment at NIMH.* Jensvold ran afoul of the old boys' club while studying premenstrual syndrome (PMS) under David Rubinow, clinical director of NIH. According to Jensvold, Rubinow deprived her of a variety of routine professional opportunities that were available to men. Rubinow, meanwhile, has denied any discrimination.†

Although head of a section devoted to research on women, clinical director Rubinow kept on his office wall an obscene postcard from a fellow researcher who has an NIH grant. The greeting card shows a nurse with her skirt hiked up, seemingly performing fellatio on a man fully clothed in battle fatigues who is holding a syringe as tall as himself.[39] Inside the card, the researcher wrote:

> Got to change with the times. No more of that wimpy touchy-feely warmth and understanding stuff. We biological psychiatrists got to be real men . . .

When Jensvold protested sexist attitudes at NIMH, her boss, Rubinow, referred her to a psychiatrist for treatment. The psychiatrist, according to Jensvold, turned out to be an employee of NIH who would not guarantee her confidentiality. It was another example of psychiatry for social control, in this instance, the suppression of an outstanding professional woman who would not "stay in her place."

Is it possible that science, even in the best of circumstances, let alone the currently charged climate at NIMH and NIH, can function apart from its social and institutional context?

---

*It may be helpful to recall that NIMH is now an institute within the umbrella organization NIH.
†Jensvold recently won her suit in a jury trial in Baltimore.

The Justice Department's Version of the Violence Initiative

While our initial focus was on the health agencies, we gradually put together information showing that another part of the government was already sponsoring a large-scale version of Goodwin's plans. Entitled the "Program on Human Development and Criminal Behavior," it is funded by the DOJ and the MacArthur Foundation, probably with money from NIH as well. In the words of the DOJ, "It represents an unprecedented partnership between federal government and a private foundation."[40]

The director of the project, Felton Earls, as well as co-director Albert J. Reiss, Jr., were key figures in developing the NRC's blueprint for the violence initiative.[41] Earls is a professor of child psychiatry at Harvard Medical School and a professor of human behavior and development at the Harvard School of Public Health. Reiss is a professor of sociology at Yale's Institute for Social and Police Studies, and lectures at the law school.

Earls's vision, like Goodwin's, is based on "disease prevention"[42] and aims at screening and identifying individual children as potential offenders in need of preventive treatment or control. Nine groups of subjects, "starting prenatally and at ages 3, 6, 9, 12, 15, 18, 21, and 24, will be followed for 8 years." A total of eleven thousand people will be studied. It will "link key biological, psychological, and social factors that may play a role in the development of criminal behavior" and search for "biological" and "biomedical" markers for predicting criminality.

Again according to the DOJ, the first of the project's "Questions to be answered" is:

> Individual differences. What biological, biomedical, and psychological characteristics, some of them present from the beginning of life, put children at risk for delinquency and criminal behavior?

This is entirely consistent with Goodwin's plan.

While Earls also believes in the importance of the environment, he focuses his project on the role of biological and genetic factors in predisposing the individual and perhaps in driving him toward violence and crime. In a 1991 publication, "A Developmental Approach to Understanding and Controlling Violence," he writes "advances in the fields of behavior genetics, neurobiology, and molecular biology are renewing the hope that the biological determinants of delinquent and criminal behavior may yet be discovered."

In discussing "key developmental questions" that he wishes to answer, Earls emphasizes genetic and biological factors. In a chart, he lists "neurotransmitters" and genetic abnormalities ("especially XYY") as "plausible risk factors" for violence.* Earls declares there is evidence for a genetic factor "in violent behavior among individuals." But the only study that he cites as evidence comes to the opposite conclusion, stating definitively that it could "find no evidence of hereditary transmission of violent criminal behavior" and that "a genetic predisposition to violence was not supported by this review of our data."[43] Earls believes that spinal taps are intrusive and unwarranted by our current state of knowledge, but wants to measure serotonergic activity through blood samples and testosterone levels through saliva.[†]

Reiss recently told reporter Gilbert Charles of *L'Express* (Paris, France) that the project is receiving $12 million per year for the eight years from all sources, including some previously unidentified money from NIH.[44] Playing on President Bush's "New World Order," Charles's lengthy analysis is entitled "Etats-Unis: Le nouvel ordre biologique." The combining of Harvard and Yale, the DOJ, NIH, and a prestigious private foundation does raise the specter of a political "New Biological Order." This multimillion-dollar effort can be considered a major violence initiative in itself.

The project is truly Big Brother in scope, but because of private sector involvement, it will be very difficult to monitor.[‡] The existence of this program—as well as Goodwin's plans and the NRC report—suggests the need for a congressional investigation to ferret out all aspects of these disturbing efforts.

We originally heard a rumor that the violence initiative controversy was making it difficult for Earls to get communities to accept his project. On November 9, 1993, Ginger Ross Breggin spoke by telephone with Christy Visher, the project contact at the DOJ, and was told that all project work to the present time was preparatory. Only a few pilot projects had come to completion, including one on testosterone in boys. Visher explained that full implementation of the study is scheduled to begin shortly, with all eleven thousand subjects located in the Chicago area.

As we are writing the final copy for this book, *Chicago Tribune* staff writer Ronald Kotulak has published a front-page four-part series on December 12–15, 1993, enthusiastically quoting government researchers in support of genetic and biological theories of aggression, as well as the biomedical social control of violence. Seemingly timed to support the Earls's project as it is unveiled in the city, the *Chicago Tribune* series far exceeds any-

---

*This is surprising, since genetic researchers no longer consider the XYY syndrome to be a cause of violence (see Chapters 3 and 8).
†Testosterone level differences among individual men are not correlated with violence, but NIMH has funded the development of the testosterone saliva test (see Chapter 5).
‡The MacArthur Foundation, Earls, and NIMH are also collaborating on violence initiative projects (Chapter 4).

thing yet written in promotion of violence initiative theory and practice, and confirms our worst fears and predictions.

Is the Threat of Biomedical Social Control Over?

The NIH panel on violence brought to light hitherto hidden details of federal research and resulted in criticism of its bias toward individual vulnerability and biomedical causes. Fred Goodwin has avoided talking to the press or making public statements that touch on the subject, and in October 1993 was forced to withdraw from a Los Angeles conference after protests from African-American activists.[45] Goodwin's 1994 NIMH budget proposal contains no plans for funding an umbrella violence initiative. The massive NRC report, seemingly designed as a blueprint for Goodwin's plans, itself became a subject of controversy, and further embarrassed the government. Louis Sullivan's $400 million government-wide public health approach to inner-city violence was, in the words of the *Boston Globe,* "shelved."[46] Instead of wooing Congress with new approaches to violence in the 1994 budget, NIMH seemed for a while in danger of suffering its largest setback ever, as President Clinton recommended a cut in its budget.[47] Finally, as noted in the "Authors' Update" at the beginning of the book, Frederick Goodwin has announced his intention to leave NIMH and the government.

Is there no longer any threat from organized psychiatry's programs for biomedical social control? Has NIMH stopped funding research based on individual vulnerability? Is the debate resolved regarding genetic vulnerabilities and biochemical imbalances as a cause of social problems? Have biological and behavioral scientists given up their efforts to direct the nation's limited research resources toward genetic and chemical solutions for the nation's most pressing problems? Do most Americans reject racially tinged genetic explanations for social conflict? Can we stop worrying about yet another biomedical violence initiative?

In reality, none of the programs and none of the issues have been laid to rest. While the latest incarnation of the violence initiative has endured a great deal of negative publicity, the underlying scientific and political thrust remains intact, and all of the ongoing research has weathered the storm. Previously funded research, requests for proposals, and lobbying by the biomedical research community continue unabated. Backed by one of the strongest lobbies on Capitol Hill, Congress reversed the administration's proposed NIMH budget cut and instead gave it a 5 percent increase over the previous year.[48] As documented by Ronald Kotulak in the *Chicago Tribune,* NIH researchers continue to promote biomedical social control. The city of Chicago, meanwhile, is the site of a giant federally funded violence initiative project.

Children's disorders and disruptive or violent behavior in particular remain growth markets. Powerful vested interests, including giant pharmaceutical firms, stand to profit mightily from proposed applications of biological research. Biomedical researchers and their labs and institutes will not readily fold or retrain and retool for a wholly different kind of research.

Health Care Reform and Biomedical Control

In response to a request from the U.S. Senate, the National Advisory Mental Health Council completed a report in June 1993 with recommendations on the future of health care reform in regard to "severe mental disorders."[49] While stating that its views do not necessarily reflect those of the federal health agencies, it is very close to an official set of recommendations for the future. The National Advisory Mental Health Council is appointed by the government, and Frederick Goodwin, the director of NIMH, is its chairperson. The report was published as the lead article in the October 1993 issue of the official journal of the American Psychiatric Association.

The council estimates that 3.2 percent of children age nine to seventeen years of age have severe mental disorders, from schizophrenia and depression to obsessive-compulsive disorder. The most common childhood diagnosis, attention deficit–hyperactivity disorder, is not included in the analysis, probably because it usually does not meet the standard of extreme severity.

The council offers an assessment of treatment efficacy that takes an extreme biopsychiatric position.[50] Under the rubric of "established treatment efficacy" for children and adolescents, it recommends several classes of adult psychiatric drugs, from lithium and the neuroleptics to Prozac. Yet these uses are not FDA-approved for children or supported by a convincing body of literature.* In its brief statement under "New Developments," still more drugs are mentioned, including the old-fashioned but extremely dangerous monoamine oxidase inhibitors.

Finally, the National Advisory Mental Health Council lends support to chairperson Goodwin's violence initiative: "For the most severe forms of aggression and conduct disorder, there are encouraging studies evaluating early psychosocial interventions as well as the use of medications for some individuals." This statement contradicts a consensus within psychiatry that there are no effective medications for the treatment of children diagnosed with conduct disorder (see Chapter 5).

These recommendations for psychiatry under the planned health care system make clear the direction being pushed by federal psychiatry toward

---

*The most commonly used drug for children, Ritalin, is not discussed. The report does not deal with the less-disabling behavioral disorders for which Ritalin is typically prescribed.

the biomedical social control of children, including preventive interventions with drugs for the control of crime and aggression. Meanwhile, biomedical social control remains a political shape-changer, able to disguise itself first as one thing and then another. Its latest expression is "health care reform."*

Under the new reforms, there will be a general emphasis upon efficiency and cost effectiveness. Biomedical control gives the illusion of both, despite the fact that it does more harm than good. Regardless of the hazards and injustice involved, the diagnosis and drugging of children is likely to receive strong impetus.

Similarly, "prevention" will gain in importance under the Clinton plan. *The Journal of NIH Research* declares, "The hot word this month, among those in the Clinton administration who are planning NIH's future, is 'prevention'—and biomedical researchers will probably like what administration officials mean when they say it." The journal predicts increased attention to this principle in mental health through early childhood interventions, including the arena of violence.[51] While prevention is an excellent approach within medicine itself, it paves the way for rampant abuses within psychiatry, especially when it is biomedically oriented.

The equation between cost-cutting and pushing psychiatric drugs is already being implemented, as insurance companies increasingly refuse to fund psychotherapy and other psychosocial interventions while paying for "medication management." Often they will cancel insurance coverage if the patient or treating doctor refuses to prescribe medication.† There is scant evidence that medication in fact reduces the need for other interventions, but the idea is promoted by contemporary psychiatry and appeals to medically oriented insurers.

Meanwhile, there has been no effort to cut back on any of the government's ongoing biomedical research into violence, some of it involving the inner city. As we shall see in Chapter 5, federal health agencies are developing new programs for drugging children who come into conflict with their families, schools, and society. Tragically, the biomedical approach in general continues to jeopardize and damage untold millions of children. Many of the ongoing violence research and treatment projects continue to be hidden from the public and are presented under the guise of studying or treating mental disorders in children.

The mental health establishment continues to throw its weight behind

---

*David Oaks, a psychiatric survivor and publisher of *Dendron* (see Appendix), first pointed out to us the implications of the council report for health care reform. He and other survivors are planning to publicize the dangers before the new health care system is put in place.
†While the Clinton health care proposal at present includes thirty days of psychotherapy per year, insurers will have the right to refuse or withdraw coverage if the patient or the doctor rejects the insurer's demand to prescribe medication. Situations like this are already common.

biological causation and medication. Both the American Psychiatric Association and the American Psychological Association made the integration of biology and behavior the themes of their recent annual conventions—the psychiatric association in 1992 and the psychological association in 1993. Both associations failed to criticize the violence initiative; their lifeblood research funding depends on federal agencies and congressionally funded research. Even the American Psychological Association is now encouraging drug company participation and pro-drug seminars at its annual conventions.

Understanding and Preventing Violence, the National Research Council's blueprint for a psychiatric violence initiative, will continue to influence the direction of research funding in both the government and the private sector. The scientists and researchers who make their living in biomedical research will not be denied because of a few temporary setbacks. Their critics are largely part-time volunteers like ourselves who receive no funding. By contrast, the biomedical researchers and scientists are devoted full-time to these issues, and their livelihood depends upon justifying their research in terms of public policy. They are backed by large national organizations and supported by powerful interest groups. They have massive federal and private funding to support their promotional activities. And finally, the Department of Justice version of the violence initiative is set to go full steam ahead in Chicago.

3

Born to Be "Violent"?
Genes and the New Eugenics

Science uses money. People earn their living by science, and as a consequence the dominant social and economic forces in society determine to a large extent what science does and how it does it.

—R. C. Lewontin, *Biology as Ideology* (1991)

The myth of the all-powerful gene is based on flawed science that discounts the environmental context in which we and our genes exist. It has many dangers, as it can lead to genetic discrimination and hazardous medical manipulations.

—Ruth Hubbard and Elijah Wald,
Exploding the Gene Myth (1993)

WE WERE SITTING IN A SMALL PIZZA PARLOR—NEARLY ALL THE TABLES LINED up along one long wall—when we overheard words stage-whispered seemingly in jest from the table directly behind us:

"Shhh . . . We're in Bethesda, where Breggin lives. He could be in the restaurant."

This was followed by anxious laughter and then a somewhat louder but muffled taunt, "Is Peter Breggin in the restaurant?"

Clearly an answer was not expected.

Ginger responded with dismay, "Yes, he's sitting right behind you." My chair was touching back-to-back with one of theirs.

We turned to find David Wasserman, his wife, and a member of his staff at the University of Maryland's Institute for Philosophy and Public Policy. Spread in front of them were our publications urging the cancellation of federal funding for Wasserman's conference on "Genetic Factors in Crime," scheduled for October 9, 1992, at the university. We assumed they were in Bethesda to discuss the crisis with officials of the National Institutes of Health (NIH), the agency sponsoring the conference.

It took Wasserman considerable time to believe we really were Peter and Ginger Breggin. Everyone tried to handle the situation as diplomatically as possible, and then we talked. It turned out that the Wassermans had been honeymooning in Europe when the conference came under attack, and they had been forced to return home.

We tried with no success to convince Wasserman that the mere existence of a conference entitled "Genetic Factors in Crime" suggested that there was significant evidence for making such a connection, and that the American public's fear of black crime would tend to link the presumed genetic factors to African-Americans.

We explained that questions like "Do genes influence the development of violent crime?" might seem innocent enough to some researchers, but that many African-Americans took them very personally. To them, the researchers were really asking, "Are black babies born to be bad?"

When our observations did not convince Wasserman, I tried to make my comments more personally relevant.

"David, you're Jewish, right?"*

Cautiously, "Yes . . ."

"Well, so am I. Now imagine if someone were planning a conference on 'Genetic Factors in Junk Bond Dealing' while the public was especially concerned about so many of the perpetrators, like Milken and Boesky, being Jewish. Don't you think the Jewish community would protest the conference? And how would you feel, if the sponsors of the conference dismissed their fears the way you are doing? As a Jew, wouldn't you remain suspicious about the conference's intentions? Wouldn't you be fearful about the impression it would give about Jews? Wouldn't you be afraid it would fan anti-Semitism? Wouldn't you want the conference called off?"

A comparison was made between the situation of Jews in Nazi Germany and that of blacks in America. Wasserman dismissed the comparison. He did not think discussing the genetics of crime would encourage biomedical social control, and, anyway, ideas should not be rejected because of potential political implications.

Wasserman, a professor at the University of Maryland, believed that his conference would generate objective scientific debate. He felt that public discussion, not the suppression of an academic conference, was the democratic approach.

I tried another tack. "David," I said, "before Hitler took power, the greatest German geneticists were openly discussing the supposed genetic dif-

---

*This is a reconstruction without notes and can only be considered a personal impression of what took place.

ferences between Jews and 'Aryans.' And the comparisons weren't all negative. They agreed that Jews were better at some things, like making money and composing music. Jewish leaders wanted these scientists to stop making the comparisons, fearing that no good could come of the exercise. But the academics couldn't understand why the Jews wanted to stifle scientific inquiry."

Toward the end of the conversation, Wasserman repeated that he still could not imagine why African-Americans, or anyone else, should feel threatened by his proposed conference. As for himself, he said, he was not personally advocating genetic research into violence or the use of pharmacological agents, and he believed the debate should be left up to the experts.

We suggested that Wasserman demonstrate his good faith by renaming the conference "Myths of Genetic Factors in Crime." He refused, and a few weeks later, reaffirmed his position in an interview:

> Although Wasserman says that the conference may be given a new title, the original concept will not change. "We don't want people to think that we ever assumed the existence of genetic factors," he says. "But we also have no intention of renaming the conference 'The Myth of Genetic Factors in Crime.' "[1]

The Conference Brochure and the Violence Initiative

We based our initial opposition to the conference on its brochure, which promoted research on the "genetic regulation of violent and impulsive behavior."[2] The supposed discovery of genetic factors in psychiatric conditions was put forth as an encouraging precedent. The alleged failure of psychosocial approaches was also cited:

> But genetic research also gains impetus from the apparent failure of environmental approaches to crime—deterrence, diversion, and rehabilitation—to affect the dramatic increases in crime, especially violent crime, that this country has experienced in the past 30 years.

The conference brochure anticipated the possibility of treating genetically "predisposed" individuals by means of "drugs," as well as unnamed, less-intrusive therapies.

To obtain federal funding for his proposed conference, Wasserman had applied to NIH. The lengthy application read like an elaboration of Goodwin's plans:

> Genetic and neurobiological research holds out the prospect of identifying individuals who may be predisposed to certain kinds of criminal conduct . . . and of treating some predispositions with drugs and unintrusive therapies. . . . Such research will enhance our ability to treat genetic predispositions pharmacologically. . . .

The Human Genome Project

The "Genetic Factors in Crime" conference was funded by NIH's controversial, highly publicized Human Genome Project.* The Human Genome Project is a large federal program aimed at mobilizing international science to map the complete set of human hereditary factors. As if anticipating the "Genetic Factors in Crime" conference, George J. Annas and Sherman Elias warned in *Gene Mapping* about suggestions that "the fruits of the Human Genome Project may help solve society's homelessness and crime problem."[3]

The idea of a conference linking crime and genetics caught the media and the public's attention. That critics were trying to stop the conference from taking place heightened the drama.[†] Concern spread to England and Germany, countries in which the eugenics[‡] movement had thrived prior to Hitler taking power. Comparisons were made between the theme of the conference and similiar discussions in Nazi Germany. Heated debate was generated in major newspapers and magazines and in scientific and academic journals. It resulted in panels at political and scientific meetings, dozens of radio interviews, and TV coverage as well.[4]

---

*NIH's National Center for Human Genome Research—the Human Genome Project—funded the project through its Ethical, Legal, and Social Issues Program (ELSI).
†Stopping the conference was never our top priority. We did not know about the conference when we began our national campaign against the violence initiative in early April 1992. The decision to oppose the conference was made after we discovered its existence in June and brought it up at a strategy session immediately before speaking at a meeting at Howard University. Those involved in the decision to oppose the conference were Ron Walters, department director and professor of political science at Howard; Sam Yette, former professor of journalism at Howard and author of *The Choice*; and Lorne Cress Love, a radio talk show host at WPFW-FM, Washington, D.C.
‡Eugenics, the use of coercive government policies to improve the genetic stock of a society, is discussed further in Chapter 7.

The Cowering Inferno

A month before the conference, NIH withdrew its grant and the University of Maryland canceled the conference for lack of funds. But the university did not reject or abandon the idea: it set in motion a formal protest over NIH's withdrawal of support and continued to seek funding.

Some defenders of biomedical research into violence accused NIH of backing down out of cowardice. In November 1992, Nancy Touchette of *The Journal of NIH Research* called NIH the "cowering inferno":

> Curiously, however, NIH, NIMH, and HHS cowered from Breggin's criticism and only recently have begun to respond to his accusations.* In addition to NIH's halting the genetics and crime meeting, NIMH in early September abruptly canceled a workshop on "Clinical Factors in Aggression" slated for Sept. 21–22. Goodwin . . . was ordered by HHS officials to cancel [media] interviews.

Academic Freedom or Political Irresponsibility?

The Human Genome Project has enormous prestige. We feared that its support for the genetics conference lent the appearance of legitimacy to a debate with no substance, making it seem as if there must be *something* worth discussing. After all, why would the Human Genome Project hold a conference with no scientific merit? Why would it hold a conference that moved America one step closer to biomedical social control?

Experience convinced us that whatever might actually be debated at the conference, the press would play up the biological and genetic arguments. Biopsychiatric claims regularly make newspaper headlines, and psychosocial ones almost never do. While conference advocates claimed it would stir up "healthy public controversy," we felt it would encourage the false conclusion that violent criminals are genetically flawed. Opposition to the conference, as it turned out, created a much larger and more searching public discussion than the unopposed conference could possibly have done.

---

*Did NIH and its giant parent agency, the Department of Health and Human Services (DHHS), cave in before one person's—really one couple's—criticism? While we started the ball rolling and worked hard to educate the public and the professions, many organizations and individuals—especially from the African-American community—joined the avalanche of criticism against both the violence initiative and the conference. That opposition remains active today.

A Dangerous Precedent?

Was the government setting a dangerous precedent by withdrawing under pressure from a conference? Some expressed the concern, "Never before had a federal health agency bowed to pressure in such an unholy way."

Ironically, we had previously been involved in the earlier cancellation of a conference, this time from the other side of the fence. In the spring of 1989 I was invited to Kentucky as a speaker at a conference sponsored by a statewide organization of past and current psychiatric patients, many of them seriously disabled and taking the strongest psychiatric drugs, such as Thorazine, Mellaril, Haldol, and Prolixin. They wanted more complete information on the dangers of the medications.

Under federal legislation mandating support for consumer groups and their programs, NIMH gave money to the state of Kentucky for use at the conference. It was to provide transportation and housing scholarships for psychiatric consumers who could not otherwise afford to attend. But when former NIMH psychiatrist E. Fuller Torrey got wind of the conference, he wrote to the director of NIMH, demanding that the agency withdraw funding from it because of my participation.

It wasn't as if the consumers were overexposed to views critical of medication. To the contrary, they were deluged with biopsychiatric propaganda from their doctors and the media. Torrey himself had given a talk to the very same group that he was trying to prohibit from hearing me.

Those at NIMH who were immediately in charge of the funding were appalled at being pressured to withdraw the money; but higher-ups took over, contacted the state, and withdrew the funding. The conference folded.[5]

More Cowering?

The Kentucky conference was not the first one the government canceled to protect establishment interests. NIH itself had previously retreated before a truly powerful adversary, the international pharmaceutical industries, and canceled support for a European conference on worldwide antibiotic use that it was co-sponsoring with the World Health Organization (WHO). Because industry critics had been invited, several drug companies objected, and NIH withdrew its funding. The story was covered by Jill Turner in *Lancet* in 1986, but received little or no attention in the United States. We were informed about it by M. N. G. Dukes, now the editor of the *International Journal of Risk and Safety in Medicine,* who was, at the time, with WHO.

In one sense, however, the cancellation of the "Genetic Factors in Crime" conference was precedent-setting. It was probably the first time groups *opposed* to powerful vested interests were able to pressure NIH to withdraw conference funding.

A Scientific Basis for the Crime Gene?

In his speeches touching on the violence initiative, Frederick Goodwin had emphasized genetic factors in crime as a justification for psychiatric interventions in the lives of children and their families. In February 1992, he told the National Advisory Mental Health Council[6] that there are *strong* genetic factors driving violent crime. Despite being criticized for these remarks, Goodwin amplified them in May 1992 before the American Pyschiatric Association (APA). He stated flatly that there is a genetic factor in antisocial behavior and crime, and elaborated:

> Whereas in the absence of genetic vulnerability, there's no environmental effect at all. So what this means is that the environment does not cause one to be violent or to develop a criminal record if there isn't a vulnerability already there, but if it's already there, then certainly a bad environment can amplify it.[7]

These remarks to the APA were similar in thrust to ADAMHA's written plan for the 1994 violence initiative that emphasized individual vulnerability and mentioned genetic factors as if their existence were a proven fact.[8]

Is there any scientific basis for Goodwin's statements? To support his genetic claims in his address to the APA, Goodwin cited a well-known study of adopted Danish children by Sarnoff Mednick, William Gabrielli, Jr., and Barry Hutchings, published in *Science* in 1984. In his statement, Goodwin completely misrepresented the conclusions of the Mednick study. While the study did find a genetic connection for property crime, it specifically showed no genetic connection in regard to *violent* crime. Thus Goodwin's only "evidence" is a study that actually disproves his point.*

The National Research Council (NRC) report *Understanding and Preventing Violence* tries to review the best available data in support of biomedical causes. On genetics, it finds that the crucial data from three

---

*There seemed little possibility that Goodwin merely misinterpreted the Mednick data, because the study's conclusions are clearly stated and very well known. In defending Goodwin against our criticism, the Department of Health and Human Services, 1992 (p. 6), nonetheless admits that "Dr. Goodwin did err in lumping violence and criminality in his reference to Mednick's data . . ."

Scandinavian studies "suggest at most a weak role for genetic processes in influencing potentials for violent behavior."[9] The NRC conclusion is misleading, since none of the cited studies, again including Mednick, supports a genetic factor in violent crime.

One of the papers was actually a review by C. R. Cloninger and I. I. Gottesman. Although these researchers are professionally committed to the genetic viewpoint, they nonetheless conclude with a warning that the NRC should have heeded:

> All attempts at intervention with high-risk families must be tempered by our limited ability to predict who will actually develop antisocial behavior and the imperative to protect individual civil rights. Therefore, we must improve general social circumstances and provide help as early as possible to those who request it.

The NRC commissioned a paper on "Genetics and Violence" from Gregory Carey at the Department of Psychology and Institute for Behavioral Genetics at the University of Colorado. As yet unpublished, the paper is much more definitive than the waffling NRC report. Carey declares, "At the very least, there is no positive evidence to suggest that heritability plays an important role in group differences in violence within the United States." In fact, genetics is not known to play a role in violent behavior in any group anywhere in the world.

Testosterone Poisoning

While there are no apparent innate racial differences in the potential for violence, males in general do seem more prone to physical aggression than females. Whether this is cultural or inborn continues to be the subject of considerable debate, but it has thus far proven impossible to attribute this difference to genetic or biological factors, such as excesses of testosterone or biochemical imbalances. There are clinical reports that overdoses of male hormones, such as the use of anabolic steroids by athletes, can sometimes increase irritability and aggressiveness. But a large body of research indicates that the level of natural testosterone in individual men has nothing to do with their varying degrees of aggression.[10]

Although very supportive of biopsychiatry in general, Kenneth Tardiff (1988) concludes that male violence is best understood in terms of social role and societal expectations: "Recent studies have not found a relationship between androgens [testosterone] and violent behavior. This leaves us with the probable conclusion that increased rates of violence by men in society arc accounted for by other factors such as role expectations in society."[11] It's hard to translate "role expectations" into genetics and biochemistry, and equally hard to treat it with drugs.

NIH and Louis Sullivan Take a Stand

In April 1993, NIH officially notified the University of Maryland that it was canceling support for the genetics conference. NIH claimed that Wasserman's brochure deviated from the approved application and, futhermore, that the brochure gave "the distinct impression that there is a genetic basis for criminal behavior, a theory that has never been scientifically validated."[12]

Despite DHHS secretary Louis Sullivan's allegiance to the Republican administration, as an African-American he was not likely to look favorably upon the more racist implications of the violence initiative,* and eventually he publicly endorsed NIH's decision on the conference. In an address to the American Academy of Child and Adolescent Psychiatry on October 22, he explained:

> There is, of course, no credible evidence, no body of research data, no scientifically valid studies that bear out the statements made in the [conference] brochure. The very idea of a "crime gene" is simplistic and misleading. Genes do not code for those kinds of things. In fact, there has been no human behavior for which any single gene has been found to be the cause.[†] The determinants of human behavior are many and complex.
>
> Consequently, my department does not support, and I do not support, the implication of a genetic basis for crime. For this reason, NIH felt compelled to embargo the funds originally granted for this conference, and the conference was eventually cancelled.

Sullivan thus ultimately confirms what common sense tells us—that genetic factors play little or no role in individual propensities for physical aggression. Environmental factors account for the relatively recent escalation of violence in the inner city. After all, black children in other environments

---

*During a televised interview with Del Walters on WJLA-TV in Washington, D.C., for example, he admitted under prodding that he was angered by Goodwin's remarks comparing rhesus monkeys and inner-city children.
†There are no *groups* of genes, either, that have been found to determine human behavior.

as diverse as Canada and Africa don't develop attitudes and behaviors like those of children in America's urban ghettos. As we shall find in describing the history of racism in medicine (Chapter 8), African-Americans were originally characterized as excessively docile to justify their enslavement.

Genetic Factors in Monkey Research

Animal research has also been cited as providing evidence for genetic factors in violent crimes. The current dean of rhesus monkey research is Stephen Suomi of the National Institute of Child Health and Human Development, a part of NIH.* His lab is a habitat in Beltsville, Maryland. His research separating monkeys from their parents has confirmed a large body of earlier studies showing how this profound *environmental* stress can produce emotional disturbances, including violent behavior. As quoted by Nancy Touchette in a 1992 article in *The Journal of NIH Research,* Suomi confirms the environmental viewpoint. "For monkeys living in benign circumstances, there is rarely a problem with violent behavior," he says. "It is only under stress that these problems come out."

This is a remarkable commentary from a man whose research is cited by Goodwin and by *The Journal of NIH Research* as supporting the biological and genetic origins of violence. Suomi's research not only demonstrates the primary role of stress, especially family and social disruption, it reaffirms the efficacy of psychosocial interventions. And human beings are far more environmentally influenced than monkeys.

Suomi observes that the serotonin levels drop in the spinal fluid *after* the animals have been forcibly removed from their families. Obviously, these reactive serotonin changes didn't occur because of genetic makeup. If the findings of biochemical changes turn out to be valid, the alterations are probably in response to forced removal from family or to subsequent traumatic events, such as violent conflict.

In human behavior, environmental factors carry far more weight than in monkeys or apes. In the inner city, where the stresses are excessive, the lesson seems obvious: look beyond individual differences and instead reduce the community-wide stress that produces violence in so many individuals.

Very recent studies continue to demonstrate that primates and humans experience physical and emotional breakdown during stress and frustration, and can react with hostility and aggression. The research demonstrates that

---

*Also see discussion of rhesus monkey and human studies of aggression and serotonin in Chapter 5.

"affiliation protects animals from the potentially pathogenic influence of chronic stress."[13] Even monkeys don't need drugs; they need strong social bonds.

Learning from the Chimps

Our nearest relatives are the chimpanzees, who possess many psychosocial methods of controlling conflict within their family and tribal groups.[14] Among chimpanzees, battles for dominance by the large, silver-backed males—called alpha males—rarely lead to injury. After the struggles, the adult males, females, and children go through a variety of healing or pacifying activities. To resolve conflict, chimps show deference to each other through subservient body positioning and, more positively, through hugging, kissing, mutual grooming, food sharing, and playing. Grudges rarely last, and after conflicts, individuals often end up bonding more closely. Chimps not involved in the dispute may act as conflict resolvers, soothing and calming the protagonists.

As human beings, we have a lot more to learn from chimpanzees than from rhesus monkeys. We have a lot more to learn from chimpanzees, for that matter, than from behaviorists and biopsychiatrists who plan programs that defy the basic principles of human life.*

There is more about love and altruism in Jane Goodall's books on chimps than in any standard psychiatric textbook. There is more about family upbringing and personal loss as a cause of suffering and depression in her descriptions of chimpanzee life than in those textbooks. Psychiatry has literally been expunging the humanity from human beings, while Goodall, Frans de Waal, and other sophisticated animal observers have been seeing "humanity" at work within chimpanzees.

Is Goodwin's "Jungle" a Reality?

Goodwin offended the black community when he seemingly compared the inner city to a jungle and inner-city youth to monkeys. Had he been reading chimpanzee research, he might have sought a different metaphor. As de Waal observed in *Peacemaking Among Primates* (1989), "The law of the jungle does not apply to chimpanzees."[15]

In reality, the "law of the jungle" does not apply to the jungle either.[16] Violence does occur between different species of animals, such as carnivores

---

*Violence initiative research, when it is not biochemical, is behaviorist. Yet behaviorism as a viewpoint has undergone a rapid decline in modern psychology and, as described by C. Boneau (1992), has largely disappeared in recent years from the academic community.

killing and eating other animals. But physically damaging aggression within species is uncommon, usually limited to mating rituals between males that rarely inflict serious harm. Most higher animals live either in relative isolation or in highly cooperative societies of individuals who often sacrifice themselves for the protection and preservation of the group.

The Shallow End of the Gene Pool?

There is a growing movement of young black men who have rejected their previous gang membership. On the anniversary of the Watts riots, they held conferences in Los Angeles and Kansas City.[17] They are working for peace among the gangs and encouraging the autonomy and creative self-development of African-Americans. These young men are not genetically determined toward destructive behavior, or they would not have transformed themselves with growing insight and maturity, and with exposure to new educational experiences.

We don't condone the past criminal actions of these former "gangbangers." But the miracle—and the lesson—is that they are transforming themselves and their lives.

Sports writers appreciate the qualities of young men. So it may not be surprising that the sentiments we've been trying to communicate are eloquently expressed by *Washington Post* sports writer Thomas Boswell:

> As we watch our 100th TV documentary on the L.A. riots or the war on drugs, don't we ever notice that the teenagers who are at the center of the disaster—carrying the problem forward even as it crushes them—are, by and large, the strong kids? They may be angry, alienated, uneducated, unemployed and a hundred other things. But they don't look like the shallow end of the gene pool to me. They look like healthy, high-spirited kids who have gone wrong, or been driven wrong. Maybe they've gone over the line from tough and proud to mean and arrogant. It's not a long distance.

Some of our friends and colleagues in the African-American community believe that the purpose of government interventions like the violence initiative is to search out and silence the community's potential leaders—people who might otherwise model themselves after Harriet Tubman, Frederick Douglass, Malcolm X, or Martin Luther King, Jr.

Is There a Biology of "Mental Illness"?

Because of all the psychiatric promotion about biological causes of mental illness, people are prepared to believe in similar causes for violent crimes. There are, however, no known biochemical abnormalities in the brains of people routinely seen by psychiatrists, including those with the most severe labels, such as schizophrenia, major depression, or manic-depressive (bipolar) disorder. That none of the psychiatric claims is true is so hard to believe that I devote many pages of *Toxic Psychiatry* to examining the data. Nor are we alone in concluding that there is no substance to the science of biopsychiatry.[18]

Psychiatry bases its argument for biological causes of mental disorder on the grounds that drugs "work." But there is no necessary connection between the relief a drug provides and the underlying cause of the distress. People use alcohol, marijuana, and a variety of other substances, including food, to reduce emotional suffering. This says almost nothing about the source of that suffering. It is no different with psychiatric medications.

In *Toxic Psychiatry* I document that the apparent symptom relief from psychiatric drugs is a result of drug-induced brain dysfunction. Depending on the drug, the dysfunction produces emotional indifference or shallowness, dulled awareness or reduced self-insight, memory impairment, sedation, and in some cases an artificial energizing or high. These effects are mistaken for improvement by doctor and patient alike.

There are some real diseases that produce brain damage and mental dysfunction. The defects can be genetic, as in a limited number of cases of Alzheimer's disease, in some forms of developmental retardation, such as Down's syndrome, and in dementing disorders such as Huntington's chorea. In each case there is a generalized impairment of the brain, resulting in measurable losses of mental function, such as short-term memory, calculating, and abstract reasoning. These losses can be detected in a clinical interview and often they can be roughly quantified on neuropsychological testing. But even in severe psychiatric disorders, such as "schizophrenia" or "manic-depressive disorder," brain function is not impaired, and no biological cause has been discovered.[19] Often the individual is functioning at a superior level of intelligence and mental ability.

When psychiatrists do find physical impairments in the brains of mental patients, they are almost invariably the result of treatment with drugs and electroshock. It is shameful that treatment-induced brain disorders are blamed on the patient's so-called mental illness.[20]

Is There a Gene for "Mental Illness"?

As skeptical as I've become over the years, I was nonetheless startled when I was first informed about the enormity of the fraud being perpetrated by genetic advocates and researchers in psychiatry. I was sitting at lunch with psychiatrist Loren Mosher, interviewing him in preparation for writing *Toxic Psychiatry*. Mosher had been the director of the center devoted to research on schizophrenia at NIMH when the institute was funding the well-known Danish genetic studies of schizophrenia.

I asked Mosher what the genetic studies really showed about "schizophrenia," and he answered tersely, "They proved that it's environmental and not genetic." I was shocked, but my own reading of the actual publications would confirm what he told me. Later, on a trip to Copenhagen, I had the opportunity to publicly debate the Danish psychiatrist in charge of the studies, Fini Schulsinger. When I analyzed the data—which literally favors an environmental cause—he could not deny what I was saying. His only response was, "We have better studies now."

Occasionally leaders in biopsychiatry admit that they haven't proven any psychiatric disorder to be genetic. When the latest claim fell through for the genetics of manic-depressive disorder, a nationally known researcher admitted that genetics remains an unproven article of faith: "Fundamentally, we still believe strongly that mental illness has a very, very strong genetic component," NIMH's Steven M. Paul said in 1989. "We just haven't found the genes yet."[21]

In another rare admission, in 1989 the *Psychiatric Times* sported a headline "Confidence Wanes in Search for Genetic Origins of Mental Illness." The news report states, "But so far the evidence is so equivocal that some competent observers deny that there is any convincing evidence for the genetic basis of any major psychiatric illness."[22]

One of psychiatry's most active gene researchers is Kenneth S. Kendler. The December 1992 *Psychiatric Times*[23] quoted him:

> There is no area of psychiatry where the ratio of heat to light is greater than in the area of how genes and environment interact. Everybody speculates about this and waves their hands about that, but the amount of actual, rigorous data that we have is really very modest and is limited mostly to a couple of adoption studies.

These quotes will seem astonishing to readers who have been inundated by books, articles, and TV specials making genetic claims during the same period in which the experts were privately recording that they had little of substance to show for decades of research.

Over the years, *Scientific American* has generally supported biopsychiatry, but a recent review by its senior writer John Horgan sheds doubt on genetic claims across the board. Pointing out that "eugenics is back in fashion," he offers a summary box entitled "Behavioral Genetics: A Lack-of-Progress Report" that lists various failures in regard to the genetics of crime, manic depression, schizophrenia, alcoholism, intelligence, and homosexuality.

The latest claims about a gay gene brought a remarkable observation from columnist and psychiatrist Charles Krauthammer:

> For years we have been treated to breathless reports announcing the discovery of genetic markers for alcoholism, manic-depression and schizophrenia. All these claims were subsequently retracted or refuted. The retractions, unlike the discoveries, tend not to make the front page.

In reporting on the recent Dutch study of genetics and violence, Natalie Angier of *The New York Times* correctly noted that the field of behavioral genetics "has lately been in disarray as previous announcements of genes for manic-depression, schizophrenia and alcoholism have either been disproved or come under withering criticism." The long list of discouraging failures should lead biopsychiatrists to greet these latest claims with skepticism. But because these failures endanger the prestige, media image, and economic power of biopsychiatry, the profession instead tends to inflate the importance of every new claim.

A Genetics of Alcoholism?

The hottest genetic item in recent times has been alcoholism. The National Institute on Alcohol Abuse and Alcoholism (NIAAA) actually put out a brochure entitled "Alcoholism: An Inherited Disease."[24] Claims have been made not only for a biochemical and a genetic link to alcoholism, but for a link between the two. That is, researchers have claimed to have found the gene for the presumed biochemical defect.

Eventually the latest genetic house of cards collapsed. The debris can be found buried inside the January 1993 issue of *Clinical Psychiatry News*.[25] A review presented at the annual meeting of the American Society of Human Genetics found that the original studies were in error and that newer ones were failing to confirm them:

> Although the finding should help put an end to the "lively controversy" surrounding this theory, it also means that psychiatrists and geneticists will have to go "back to the drawing

board" in their search for genetic mechanisms behind alcoholism and its severity . . .

Still more recently, in April 1993, Joel Gelernter and a team from the Yale University School of Medicine reviewed the literature on alcoholism and the dopamine gene. They reported in the *Journal of the American Medical Association* that existing studies do not support the dopamine gene hypothesis.

Daniel J. Kevles and Leroy Hood (1992) point out that it was front-page news in *The New York Times* in 1990 when researchers used autopsies to demonstrate a gene for alcoholism; but it was page-ten news when NIH researchers failed to confirm these findings. The public cannot avoid getting the wrong impression.

The surprising truth is this: no so-called psychiatric disorder has ever been proven to be genetic. The failed genetic studies tend to reconfirm that environmental factors are almost certainly at work.

Claiming that there are biochemical and genetic mental disorders is a very old strategy, going back several hundred years to the origins of psychiatry. The identity, authority, income, and social role of psychiatry as a *medical* profession depends on these assertions. The vigor behind the claims has waxed and waned over the years, depending on political considerations, and not at all on scientific evidence, which has failed to materialize.

Aren't Murderers Sick?

Even within psychiatry, the urge to commit violence is not considered an illness, but a reaction that springs from many sources.[26] Except to extend the authority of medical doctors and health officials, there is little or no reason to call violent behavior a disease.

But what about murderers? Aren't some of them "sick"? That depends upon what is meant by the word. Murderers may be viewed as morally reprehensible, hateful, and very bad. The word *sick* can be used as a metaphor to express our revulsion over them. But it is another thing to take the metaphor so seriously that "sick" is given a physical meaning. However revolting their acts, being a murderer is not in reality equivalent to being physically ill.

Labeling a mental state as "sick" does little to enhance our understanding of it and, if anything, suggests that it cannot be empathically grasped or otherwise understood as an expression of the human condition and human experience.

Whether murderous thoughts and actions are motivated by dispassionate self-interest or by passionate rage, whether they are sanctioned by military orders or by seemingly private preoccupations—no insight is added by attributing them to "mental illness." Biological psychiatrists, in fact, have generally come to the same conclusion. They now tend to discard the ill-defined, unscientific concept of "mental illness." Instead, they believe that at least some murderous thoughts and behavior are caused by an actual genetic and biological disease This *is* a scientific proposition, albeit one that remains unconfirmed. But are there better ways to understand seemingly irrational acts of violence?

The Lives of the Murderers with "Sick" Minds

Lonnie Athens, who has a doctorate in criminology from the University of California at Berkeley, is a researcher who believes in direct contact with his subjects. His brief, little-known book, *The Creation of Dangerous Violent Criminals,* is based on hours of interviews with thirty-eight incarcerated perpetrators of heinous crimes, men who became violently enraged and wantonly killed or maimed their victims. Instead of standing outside their world and analyzing it, Athens developed rapport with them, listened to the detailed stories of their lives, and drew common threads from them.

Athens found a remarkably consistent pattern of childhood subjugation to violence and humiliation, and later self-empowerment through violent perpetration and retaliation. He divides creation of these extremely violent personalities into four stages (1) brutalization, (2) belligerency, (3) violent performances, and (4) virulency.

In stage one, *brutalization,* these future criminals invariably suffered humiliating, violent subjugation during childhood. Often this included "personal horrification" through witnessing violence being perpetrated against others, especially family members. As helpless witnesses, these youngsters falsely concluded that their own "impotence" allowed the injustice to occur. This fueled their determination to react violently when threatened in the future. As still another aspect of brutalization, the future criminals underwent "violent coaching," repeated lessons from older role models in how to react violently to conflict.

> My father told me that I had to grow up and be a man like him and stop being a boy and taking shit from people. He said, "If you're going to be a man, you have to stand up to people. I don't take any shit off anybody and neither are you." He would say, "Son, at ten years old I was whipping all the little pussies' asses in my neighborhood. . . ." After he kept on threatening to beat my ass and calling me a pussy for not

fighting and telling me how tough and mean he was all the time, it got driven into my head. [p. 55]

In the second stage, *belligerency,* these young victims of brutality learned to ask themselves, in effect, "What can I do to stop undergoing any further violent subjugation and personal horrification at the hands of other people?" It is an "agonizing" problem that the victim/perpetrator resolves by "taking violent action himself against other people who unduly provoke him."

> I still get upset when I think about all the things that happened. I can never forget the beatings my father gave me, the beating that I saw my mother and older sister take from him and all his loud bragging about what he had done to people. The things my father did to us made me feel ashamed and mad. It built my anger up and up until I got mean and crazy. . . . I was ready to kill people who fooled and fooled around with me and wouldn't stop. [p. 60]

Eventually, the victim and future criminal enters stages three and four, *violent performances* and *virulency.* During virulency, he initially learns to his dismay that his violent reactions to humiliation get him labeled as "mentally unbalanced," "a violent lunatic," or "insane killer." To him, his reactions make perfect sense.

The new labels end up having redeeming features for the perpetrator. He becomes fear-inspiring and gains respect among his peers. No one wants to "mess" with him. For the first time in his life, he experiences increasing personal power. "He only too gladly accepts his violent notoriety and the social trepidation that comes with it."

The victim becomes a victimizer, transformed "from hapless victim of brutalization to a ruthless aggressor—the same kind of brutalizer he had earlier despised." He has also become a menace to society—an emotional bomb waiting to go off at the slightest psychological jostle. A minor altercation can result in his creating mayhem.

As much as anyone, Athens has furthered our understanding of how the supposedly "sick" mind works. Instead of a person incomprehensibly deranged, we find an individual whose attitudes and actions flow from his personal experiences.[27]

Meanwhile, it is important to realize that inner-city crime relatively rarely attains the violent extremes studied by Athens. Few of the African-Americans who run into trouble with the law have committed violent crimes. Most have been convicted of non-violent drug-related offenses (see Chapter 8).

Furthermore, it has not been proven that everyone subjected to extreme childhood brutalization will necessarily develop into a perpetrator of violence. Brutalized children undoubtedly suffer as adults from their earlier victimization; but clinical experience suggests that many, if not most, choose to handle their emotional pain without inflicting it on others. Even children and youths can exercise judgment, responsibility, and ethical restraint in defiance of horrendous provocation. But Athens does show us the compelling conditions that push people toward committing brutal acts.

Predicting Violence

A few decades ago, psychiatrists commonly made believe that they could predict who would perpetrate dangerously aggressive acts, and frequently voiced that opinion in the criminal justice system. Then in the famous *Tarasoff* decision (1976) in California, psychiatrists were held responsible for taking actions to protect other people who might be endangered by their patients. If, for example, a psychiatrist knowingly failed to warn a potential victim or to take other preventive measures, the psychiatrist could be held liable for damages.

Threatened by *Tarasoff*, organized psychiatry did an abrupt about-face, and tried to argue that psychiatrists have no such predictive powers, and therefore should not be held responsible.[28] In a brief submitted in the *Tarasoff* case, the American Psychiatric Association declared, "Study after study has shown that this fond hope of the capability accurately to predict violence in advance is simply not fulfilled." The APA went so far as to deny that "mental health professionals are in some way more qualified than the general public to predict future violent behavior."[29]

In 1976, the California Supreme Court upheld the *Tarasoff* decision, ruling that therapists do have an obligation "to use reasonable care to protect the intended victim" of one of their patients. Psychiatry has been so snakebitten by its earlier claims for predicting violence that textbooks now tend to ignore the issue, as if hoping it will go away.*

---

*As concern over violence has increased, however, the MacArthur Foundation has stepped into the void to fund and direct a seven-year "Research Network on Mental Health and the Law" to study "the risk of violence posed by the mentally disordered."

Whose Violence Are We Talking About?

When the government and a state university host a conference on "Genetic Factors in Crime," they will not focus on the police beating up Rodney King, the mob violence of police hurling racial insults at former Mayor David Dinkins of New York City, the white racists who seem such an inextricable part of the American social fabric, or the psychiatrists who perpetrate shock treatment and lobotomy on their patients. They won't focus on the violence of organized mobsters or the more subtle but devastating results of white-collar and corporate crime. They won't focus on those politicians who compulsively lie to the public or who commit the country to endless, unofficial wars against nations that have no capacity to strike back.

Those who represent the nation's vested interests will not have their genes put under the microscope. And that, as much as anything, is the inherent danger of biomedical research into violence—it will be directed by people in power against people who have little or none. If the victims belong to a feared and hated minority, all the greater the threat.

When the dominant group in society wants to investigate another, less-powerful group to see if it is genetically and biochemically defective, the conscience of the country ought to shake with a resounding alarm.

The Eugenic Impulse Lives

The violence initiative and the "Genetic Factors in Crime" conference surfaced during a time of growing emphasis on eugenics in the United States. In the mid 1980s, a series of books revived the debate on the origins of crime and violence.[30]

Ferris State University professor Barry Mehler has documented the increased attention that American academia is giving to eugenics theories. He cited a presentation at the January 1989 conference of the American Association for the Advancement of Science (AAAS) that claimed that data shows whites and Asians are superior to blacks who are "smaller brained, slower to mature, less sexually restrained and more aggressive." The speaker used "measurements of sixty difference characteristics to put forward his case for blacks being less advanced in evolution."

A recent article in *Time*,[31] "Seeking the Roots of Violence," supports the genetic theories behind the government's plans:

> No one believes there is a "crime gene" that programs people to maim or murder. Rather, a person's genetic makeup may give a subtle nudge toward violent actions. For one thing,

genes help control production of behavior-regulating chemicals. One suspect substance is the neurotransmitter serotonin.

Time resurrects the ideas of Richard Herrnstein, a Harvard psychologist
who once claimed that unemployment is genetic.[32] Herrnstein explains that
an inborn "restless impulsivity, an inability to delay gratification," may inspire crime. This is one of the core concepts behind the diagnosis antisocial
or sociopathic personality.

Prisoners tend as a group to have a lower than average IQ, probably because convicted criminals tend to come from poverty backgrounds and are
relatively lacking in academic skills. The "IQ Question" is examined in
Daniel Seligman's recent book *Question of Intelligence: The IQ Debate in
America*. Seligman, a journalist and former *Time* editor, buys the basic genetic and biological model. A laudatory review of Seligman's book in *Forbes*
also fails to raise any significant questions, instead praising Seligman for dar-
ing to write about a "taboo" subject.[33] Meanwhile, current research confirms
the obvious: it is better to be rich than poor. Poverty, not race, is responsible
for lower performances on intelligence tests.[34]

The Future of Genetic Profiles

At present the issue of gene mapping and violence may remain an abstract or
theoretical problem for many people. In reality, millions of Americans are already having their genetic profiles stored on record. The armed forces have
begun this process for the purpose of identifying the bodies of future war casualties. The FBI is doing it for the purpose of identifying criminals. In July
1992, reporter Vince Bielski observed:

> Whether the biological research will lead authorities to even-
> tually classify people as being at risk for violence and thus dis-
> criminate against them is a topic of great concern. The FBI,
> for instance, is creating a huge genetic data bank of profiles of
> repeat offenders. Who will be on this list, and who won't, and
> how will the FBI use this information, particularly when the
> genetic basis of crime is only a theory?

With increasing numbers of Americans being profiled in genetic banks,
the potential for abuse of this information seems infinite.

Understanding Violence

A person's tendency to respond violently or non-violently depends upon many factors: past experiences, often going back to early childhood; ideals taught within the family and other institutions; the presence or absence of restraining or aggravating influences among family, friends, and social organizations; the nature and degree of current provocations; the hope for a just world and a fair resolution of conflict; and innumerable other intangibles that are often hard to define, especially personal responsibility and ethics.

In our society, many factors contribute to violence—patriarchal values of domination and control; competitiveness; racist humiliation; poverty. Understanding how these and other social forces come together to impinge on the individual is no easy task; but it seems apparent that they fall heaviest on minority children.

We can increase our understanding, as Lonnie Athens and others have done, by examining the life histories of people who murder or abuse others.[35] But there can be no simplistic "scientific model" for such subtle, complex human conduct.

Modern conflict-resolution views violent conflict as reaction to the frustration of basic human needs, such as esteem, love, security, justice, and autonomy.[36] Violence erupts in response to frustration of these deeply felt human needs, in the absence of more rational, loving methods of conflict resolution, and usually in the presence of forces that encourage violent responses. As Athens so dramatically describes, the underlying emotion is humiliation.[37] Through violence, the individual seeks to overcome that dreadful sense of personal worthlessness and impotence.

Overcoming Humiliation

Overwhelming shame and humiliation—including underlying feelings of worthlessness and impotence—drive most seemingly irrational aggression.[38] To ward off these feelings, young men can kill each other over trivial insults or hints of disrespect. Following the murder of a high school football star in the inner city of Washington, D.C., one of his teammates explained:

> The biggest thing everybody is looking for is respect in the streets. It isn't money. They are just trying to make sure you respect them. People are just pushing each other to the maximum to get respect. And the maximum is death.[39]

No one is born with such a compulsive drive to compensate for feelings of worthlessness. Such needs arise from living under degrading conditions and especially from growing up in a racist society.

While lifetime incarceration might be necessary for some criminals, the added humiliations of imprisonment won't make them better, less violent men. Prison will more likely confirm their worst impressions of life. Fear of consequences will mean comparatively little to those of them who would rather die than submit to what they perceive as further degradations. Biomedical control and other forms of coercion are at best stopgap methods with limited effectiveness; and because they cause humiliation, they are likely to inflame further violence.

People become less violent when they feel less reason to be violent, when they feel more in control of their lives, and when they learn to value their own life and the lives of others. Usually this requires learning new ways to view themselves, others, and life. In the past few years, for example, we've met many men who have turned their lives around by joining the Nation of Islam and other self-empowering, African-oriented groups. Some have left the gangs to join self-help organizations, aimed at bringing peace to the inner city.

These young men learn to replace feelings of shame with feelings of pride in themselves, and they transform violent impulses into a determination to work for the good of themselves, family, and community. Instead of being labeled and "put down" by psychiatric or criminal justice interventions, they accept personal responsibility and become empowered through new values, ideals, and relationships.

No one person or group can supply all the solutions to the plight of America's children. But we can be certain that the answers won't be found in humiliating diagnoses, coercion, and biomedical control. Hope surely lies in the opposite direction—toward the encouragement of self-respect, personal responsibility, liberty, and community.

The Controversy That Won't Go Away

While there is no sound evidence that individual levels of destructive aggression can be attributed to a genetic factor, any study that hints at the possibility is vigorously promoted by organized psychiatry. A recent Dutch project, for example, received enormous media attention when it claimed to prove that a specific genetic defect had caused a wide range of antisocial behavior in one family.[40] While the particular genetic aberration was so rare that it could make no contribution to the overall problem of violence, it might establish the principle that faulty genes can sometimes cause violent behavior.

One flaw in the Dutch study is reminiscent of earlier research that attempted to link the XYY chromosome anomaly to aggression and crime in individual men.* It was ultimately found that XYY males are not violence-prone, but some may suffer from lower than average intelligence, which is known to be associated with increased rates of criminal conviction and incarceration.[41]

Mental retardation can place emotional burdens and social handicaps on people who live in complex and often insensitive societies, even though it cannot specifically cause aggressive or antisocial behavior. The genetic defect found in the Dutch study also causes borderline mental retardation, and as in the XYY syndrome, this could account for any increased rate of psychological and social problems among the men.

Meanwhile, the Dutch study's basic finding of a correlation between the genetic disorder and violent behavior is itself questionable. The genetic defect is described as the cause of a broad spectrum of misconduct in this particular family—from erratic, irritable, and verbally abusive behavior to arson and rape. There is no known behavioral disorder or clinical syndrome that encompasses such a range of misconduct, and so the presumed genetic defect is being connected to something that, in reality, does not exist. The attempt to link the gene to such a hodgepodge of misbehavior reflects the project's failure to link it to any specific problem. Nor is it likely that the supposed biochemical defect, a widespread one in the brain, could selectively increase aggressivity.[42]

Jonathan Beckwith of Harvard Medical School faulted the researchers for providing too little detail about the family's behavior. According to Sheryl Stolberg of *The Los Angeles Times,* Beckwith was "stunned" that there was plenty of statistics about the gene mapping, but "basically no information about whether the people were truly aggressive." Despite the media stir it caused, the study lacks merit.

Meanwhile, as we complete this book, the Maryland conference on "Genetic Factors in Crime" is being revived. The Grant Appeals Board of NIH has decided that the health agency canceled the funding inappropriately and that the government must renegotiate the grant with Wasserman and the University of Maryland.[43] It seems unlikely that the conference can or will be shorn of its menacing aspects, and so the controversy is likely to break out once again. The conference has been rescheduled for October 1995 at the University of Maryland.

---

*Federally funded XYY research at Johns Hopkins on African-American boys drew criticism in 1970 (Chapter 8).

4

Born to Be "Disruptive"?
Diagnosing and Drugging America's Children and Youth

> The past 25 years has led to a phenomenon almost unique in history. Methodologically rigorous research . . . indicates that ADD [attention deficit disorder] and hyperactivity as "syndromes" simply do not exist. We have invented a disease, given it medical sanction, and now must disown it. The major question is how we go about destroying the monster we have created. It is not easy to do this and still save face. . . .
>
> —Diane McGuinness, "Attention Deficit Disorder: The Emperor's New Clothes, Animal 'Pharm,' and Other Fiction" (1989)

> Diagnosis is too often antithetical to the interests of a particular youngster.
>
> —Jerome G. Miller, *Last One Over the Wall* (1991)

ZAC IS A SMALL, BLOND-HAIRED BOY WITH BLUE EYES THAT SHINE WITH MIS-chief and intelligence. At nine years old, his teachers and community have already decided his future for him. He fits all the profiles—restless, easily distracted, smart but doing just average in school, and too often into trouble. Chances are he'll be one of those boys who picks up "tagging"* in the neighborhood by the time he is twelve. At fifteen he'll be known by the police, and if drugs don't get him, alcohol will.

How can they be so sure about his future? Because they've read about attention deficit–hyperactivity disorder (ADHD) in newspapers and magazines, and seen reports about it on TV.

Zac's school counselor and the teacher will have a chat about Zac and then invite his mother to a meeting to inform her that he has ADHD. His

---

*Graffiti.

mother, who has already heard about the "disorder," will feel some relief even before she gets her son to the psychiatrist.

No one seems equipped or willing to deal with Zac's real problems—an absent father, a distracted and overwhelmed mother, an impatient teacher with an overcrowded classroom, and Zac himself with a wondrous abundance of energy that doesn't fit well into his world. So the psychiatrist prescribes Ritalin for Zac, and within an hour of taking the first dose, the boy is sitting much more quietly in class. His teacher is happy because her classroom is more peaceful. His principal is happy because the school can receive extra money for a special education class for Zac. His mother—who didn't know what to do about her son—now feels she is doing everything she can for him. And it *is* much more peaceful at home. She makes sure he takes his medicine every morning before leaving for school. The nurse at school has a bottle with Zac's name on it for the noontime dose.

Zac's story is being repeated around the United States. Every day during the school year, a million kids, mostly boys, take their Ritalin. Hundreds of thousands more are taking other drugs, such as lithium and Prozac. Usually labeled ADHD, these children have their destinies laid out for them.

Recently *Newsweek* asked, "Where do the great minds come from? And why are there no Einsteins, Freuds or Picassos today?"[1] There is a tragic possibility: they are being psychiatrically diagnosed and drugged. Any biography of Einstein, Freud, or Picasso will demonstrate enough childhood "pathology" to warrant diagnosis and drugging with the inevitable suppression of his unique contribution to life.

How Could They Get Away with It?

The government's plans for an inner-city violence initiative shocked many Americans. How could NIMH have thought it would get away with plans aimed at drugging tens of thousands of inner-city children? In reality, the government had no reason to anticipate taking flak. NIMH has been pushing drugs for children for many years all across America, and there has been no public outrage. The media seem uncritically accepting of the diagnosing and the drugging of children, as psychologists and psychiatrists join hands with parent groups devoted to managing children medically.

Throwing "The Book" at Children

Periodically, committees of the American Psychiatric Association update the association's *Diagnostic and Statistical Manual of Mental Disorders* (*DSM*). The current version is the third edition, revised, published in 1987 and called *DSM-III-R*.

In psychiatry, diagnoses tend to be used very loosely, with considerable reliance on subjective impressions. Hardly any psychiatrists can recite the association's more or less official requirements for the diagnoses they routinely use, and rarely do they turn to the manual itself to make sure a patient meets all the standards. The standards themselves are controversial even within the profession. But they are important in setting clinical and research trends, and they tell us a great deal about official psychiatric dogma. Their very existence creates a strong, if misleading, impression of validity for diagnosing in general.

The diagnosing and drugging of America's children is rationalized on the basis of the *DSM*. Frederick Goodwin's plans for the inner city and most of NIMH's research funding were based on its diagnoses.

The same diagnoses influence how millions of parents and teachers view the children in their care. Anyone who deals with kids has heard of "hyperactivity," or ADHD, and many non-professionals are sure they can diagnose it.

The DBDs

The children we're concerned with are usually diagnosed as suffering from one or another of the disruptive behavior disorders—the DBDs. The DBDs are divided into attention deficit–hyperactivity disorder (ADHD), or sometimes just attention deficit disorder (ADD); oppositional defiant disorder; and conduct disorder. These diagnoses often overlap each other, and NIMH often refers to them as one group, the DBDs.[2]

The *DSM-III-R* states that DBD children are "characterized by behavior that is socially disruptive and is often more distressing to others than to the people with the disorders." The "illness" consists of being disruptive to the lives of adults—a definition that seems tailored for social control.

Oppositional Defiant Disorder

To be diagnosed as having oppositional defiant disorder a child must meet five of the following nine criteria:

1. often loses temper
2. often argues with adults
3. often actively defies or refuses adult requests or rules, e.g., refuses to do chores at home
4. often deliberately does things that annoy people, e.g., grabs other children's hats
5. often blames others for his or her own mistakes

6. is often touchy or easily annoyed by others
7. is often angry and resentful
8. is often spiteful and vindictive
9. often swears or uses obscene language.

What child with any spunk would not qualify—at least at some time in his or her life? And once diagnosed, the label sticks. And while some children might fit only two or three of the criteria, that would not prevent them from being diagnosed. After the *DSM-III-R* committee designs the official criteria, individual mental health professionals freely indulge in their own subjective impressions.

It doesn't matter that the child has good reasons for being angry or upset. The diagnostic manual specifically states that these children feel justified about being angry or resentful toward the adults around them. To make matters worse, the displays of anger and resentment may exist in only one situation, such as home or school.

Any child in serious conflict with adults would surely end up fitting the diagnosis. Children—especially little ones—aren't equipped to handle conflict with adults by staying cool and acting mature. They aren't equipped to handle their painful emotions without showing them. Since the diagnosis can include "mild" cases that cause "only minimal or no impairment in school and social functioning," it encompasses every kid in the world who's got any gumption.

It's as if the committee members added up all the things their own kids ever did to aggravate them and then took revenge. At best these so-called disease criteria are a hodgepodge of things that boys (as discussed below, most DBD kids *are* boys) do that particularly annoy adults.

Who's Got the Problem?

If the list of criteria for oppositional defiant disorder has any use, it identifies children who have lost respect and trust for the adults around them. This shouldn't red flag the children. It should red flag the adults.

When a small child, perhaps five or six years old, is persistently disrespectful or angry, there is always something wrong in that child's life—something over which the child has little or no control. Typically, the child is not being respected, because children learn more by example than by anything else. When treated with respect, they tend to respond respectfully. When loved, they tend to be loving. While the source of the child's upset may end up being more complicated than that—perhaps the parent is too afraid or distracted to apply rational discipline and lets the child run wild—the source always lies in the larger world. Children do not, on their own, create severe emotional conflicts within themselves and with the adults around them.

Diagnosing a child as suffering from oppositional defiant disorder is a means of denying adult responsibility and shifting blame to the wounded child.

Children aren't "spoiled" or "unruly" by nature; but this stigmatizing label implies they are. These children are usually more energetic, more spirited, and more wonderful than their parents and teachers can handle. Yet they are being called "mentally ill"—a label that can follow them into adulthood to ruin their future lives.

Conduct Disorder

For Goodwin and other biopsychiatrists, conduct disorder is a genetic and biological precursor to adult antisocial personality disorder, criminality, and physical aggression. The goal of the violence initiative—and a raft of related research being carried on at NIMH—is to identify and treat these children before they become a menace to society.

The *DSM-III-R* states, "In *Conduct Disorder* all of the features of Oppositional Defiant Disorder are likely to be present. . . ." It is a continuum from labeling the child "pretty bad" to labeling him "very bad."

In the old authoritarian system, supposedly bad kids were yelled at and spanked. In the new authoritarian psychiatry, "mentally ill" children are given drugs and hospitalized. While we do not advocate yelling at kids or spanking them, these methods can be less damaging and demoralizing than a psychiatric label, drugs, and a mental hospital. Nowadays it is safer to be labeled bad than mentally ill.

To be labeled "conduct disorder," a child must meet a mere three of thirteen criteria. It's not worth repeating the criteria word for word, but we can catch the flavor of the first five: (1) stealing on the sly ("without confrontation of a victim") at least twice, (2) running away from home "overnight at least twice," (3) "often lies," (4) fire setting, and (5) "often truant."

The APA diagnostic manual remarks that the first three items are the most "discriminating"—the most consistently effective in making the diagnosis. Yet these three criteria simply reflect a child in conflict with adults.

Why Do Children Lie?

In order for lying to qualify as a criteria for conduct disorder, the child must lie "other than to avoid physical or sexual abuse." Yet it is impossible for any psychiatrist to know why a child is lying, and whether the child is being threatened with physical or sexual abuse. And why focus on physical and sexual abuse? Children can react at least as fearfully to purely emotional threats, such as abandonment or loss of love. Probably the single most common reasons children lie is that they don't trust their parents or authorities to be fair, empathic, helpful, or benign.

The *DSM-III-R* must make believe that psychiatrists can discern whether or not children have good reasons for lying. If children do have good reasons to lie, then it looks absurd and unjust to label them mentally ill.

Children who lie are almost always afraid and distrustful; they believe they are lying in self-defense. Instead of reflexively resorting to punishment or psychiatric diagnosis, it is better for their parents to focus on earning their children's trust.

Attention Deficit–Hyperactivity Disorder

The official standard for ADHD requires any eight of fourteen items. The first five items are described as the most useful or discriminating, in descending order, and include:

1. often fidgets with hands or feet or squirms in seat (in adolescence, may be limited to subjective feelings of restlessness)
2. has difficulty remaining seated when required to do so
3. is easily distracted by extraneous stimuli
4. has difficulty awaiting turn in games or group situations
5. often blurts out answers to questions before they have been completed.

The remaining nine in abbreviated form are: (6) difficulty following instructions, (7) attention problems, (8) jumping from one thing to another, (9) "has difficulty playing quietly," (10) "often talks excessively," (11) interrupts others, (12) "often does not seem to listen," and (13) "often loses things."

The public has been taught to think of ADHD as a specific "mental illness" with a genetic and biochemical cause. But as the list of criteria demonstrates, it's just one more DBD—another way a child gets labeled disruptive. As observed by Gerald Golden, a professor of pediatrics and neurology in Memphis and an advocate of the diagnosis, "The behavior is seen as being disruptive and unacceptable by parents and teachers. . . ."

A dean of ADHD ideology, psychologist Russell Barkley, says, "Although inattention, overactivity, and poor impulse control are the most common symptoms cited by others as primary in hyperactive children, my own work with these children suggests that noncompliance is also a primary problem."[3] But who can blame children for being noncompliant with Barkley? Not only does he want to drug them, but he blames nothing on the parent and everything on the child. As he puts it, "there is, in fact, something 'wrong' with these children" (p. 4). As for the parents, he continually makes clear there's nothing wrong with them. That's how he has become so popular with so many parents.

The forthcoming *DSM-IV* will provide diagnostic "fine-tuning." One change involves separating ADHD from the DBDs. The committee found that while disruptive behavior and attention problems "often occur together," "some" ADHD children are not hyperactive and disruptive.[4] The drugs, however, will continue to be used for behavioral control.

Diagnoses Tailored to Social Caste

ADHD tends to be a middle-class diagnosis. Most ADHD kids could as easily be called oppositional defiant disorder or conduct disorder. But because they come from "good families" in a "good neighborhood," they get called ADHD. In the inner city, the same behavior in an ethnic minority child is more likely to earn a label of mental retardation (MR) or severely emotionally disturbed (SED).

Instead of the relatively interesting high-tech teaching programs offered to some children labeled ADHD, inner-city children are likely to be shunted into special education.[5] Many will be lied to and told that passing the general-equivalency-diploma (GED) exam is as good as getting a real diploma, and they'll drop out of school.

Cruel Diagnoses

A variety of ADHD scales are given to parents and teachers to rate their children and pupils. One of the most popular, the Revised Conner's Questionnaire, was recently brought to me by a parent who was being urged to drug her child. The forty-eight items include "sassy," wanting to "run things," "daydreams," "shy," pouting, "feelings easily hurt," "childish . . . clings, needs constant reassurance," not getting along with siblings, bragging, and getting pushed around—or pushing around—other kids.

One of the items of the Conner's scale simply states "cruel." Two of its items are "Basically an unhappy child" and "Feels cheated in the family circle." We think it's cruel and unjust to label such a child mentally ill instead of examining the problem in the family.

The Conner's Abbreviated *Teacher* Questionnaire, with only ten items, is even more simplistic and potentially abusive. The criteria include restlessness, overactivity, failing to finish things, fidgeting, and so on. It's an inventory of the ways children can annoy and frustrate their teachers.

A Disease That Goes Away When Kids Get Attention

The symptoms or manifestations of ADHD often disappear when the children have something interesting to do or when they are given a minimal amount of adult attention. This is agreed upon by all observers and even indirectly finds its way into the *DSM-III-R.* The manual specifies that the symptoms may not be apparent while the child is playing a videogame or in a "novel setting" or even being examined by the doctor.

Supposedly "impossible" ADHD kids usually do wonderfully during the two hours or so that they are around my home office—playing around the back yard, visiting with my wife in the house, or talking seriously in a family session about how to get more attention from their parents. Most advocates of ADHD as a diagnosis also note that it tends to go away during summer vacation.

Whose Disease Is This, Anyway?

Most so-called ADHD children aren't getting enough attention from their fathers, who are separated from the family, too preoccupied with other things, or otherwise impaired in their ability to parent. This is so typical that in *Toxic Psychiatry* I proposed calling the diagnosis DADD—dad attention deficit disorder.

The "cure" for these kids is more rational and loving attention from their dads. Young people are nowadays so hungry for the attention of a father that it doesn't even have to be their own. A whole bunch of seemingly impulsive, hostile children will calm down when a caring, relaxed, and firm adult male is around.

Arlington High School in Indianapolis was canceling many of its after-school events because of student unruliness, when a father happened to attend one of them:[6]

> That evening there was an odd quietness on [the father's] side of the auditorium. It turned out that when he would tell his group to settle down, some students would second him. One said: "That's Lena's father. You heard him. Be quiet; act right."

Since then the school has begun to enlist volunteer dads for its after-school events.

At other times, the so-called disorder should be called TADD: teacher attention deficit disorder. The problem is almost always rooted in parents and teachers who feel overburdened, unable to reach out, or frustrated in trying to impose discipline.

Whose disease is ADHD?

Whose disease is oppositional defiant disorder?

Whose disease is conduct disorder?

These are not our children's problems, they are ours.

Every Therapist Needs a Magic Wand

Recently an eight-year-old girl showed astonishment after sitting for only a few minutes with her parents and me in my office. She practically yelled, "Wow, is this different."

"How?" I asked her.

"Have you ever tried to talk to a wall with ears and a pad." She pointed at the wall behind me. Humor, anger, and pain came together as she repeated her impression of her previous psychiatrist, "Like that wall, only with ears and a pad."

If possible, I try to meet new clients—children and their families—in my back yard by the fish pond. I want the youngster to know right away that this is going to be different—an experience aimed at making them comfortable and providing for their basic needs. I want the parents to realize the same thing.

Often it's obvious in a few minutes that there are serious family conflicts. As the little boy eagerly leans over the pond, Dad may be standing back as if he has no idea how to play or to enjoy himself. Mom may be dragging on her son's arm to "keep him from falling in." Dire warnings may be issued concerned the child's malicious tendencies. Meanwhile, I'm standing by thinking to myself, "This looks like a really nice kid. How can he stand this?"

Recently a ten-year-old boy, Tommy, came to me with his parents. At the pond, Mom seemed relaxed and in touch with her son, but Dad was so aloof I assumed he was a new stepfather. In the session, when I spoke of him as the stepfather, his wife said, "See, I told you, you don't even act like his real father."

In the office, I asked Tommy if he'd been told why he was here.

"Yeah," he said, "You're the doctor who doesn't believe in drugs for my ADHD."

Tommy even knew the acronym for attention deficit–hyperactivity disorder.

"It's worse than that," I kidded him. "I'm the doctor who doesn't even believe in ADHD."

I then explained to Tommy that there was nothing at all wrong with him and that I wouldn't make any diagnosis. Instead, I would help his parents understand how to meet his basic needs and help all of them learn how to resolve their daily and frequently severe conflicts.

Later in the session, I gave Tommy a "magic wand"—a long clear plastic tube filled with colorful sparkles. With his parents' agreement, he could point the wand at them and ask them to change anything about the way they relate to him. The wand, I said, would ensure that they would pay attention to his requests. They might not want to or be able to comply, I added, but they would listen, and we would take seriously whatever he said.

Tommy of course realized there was no magic in the wand. He knew exactly what was going on. We were empowering him to express himself.

Tommy pointed the wand at Dad and said, "I'd like you to spend more time with me. Not going along shopping or stuff like that—fun time."

Tommy's parents told him that we had already come to the same conclusion—that he had DADD, dad attention deficit disorder. Tommy thought that was very funny and right on the mark. We went on to discuss what Tommy meant by fun and arrived at agreements on activities that he and Dad could enjoy sharing. We talked about how Dad seldom played—not even grown-up entertainment like golf or going to the movies—and how it would be beneficial to him to learn to play with his son.

We then talked about the conflicts that were spoiling life in the family—how to deal with them in a non-punitive, empathic fashion. We were able to narrow down disciplinary issues to two or three minimum areas—everyone in the family treating each other with respect, and Tommy learning to take over doing his homework and going to bed at agreed-upon times.

Singing All the Way Home

Later Tommy's parents told me that he was singing in the car on the way home. He hadn't done that since he was a small child. Yet how many children leave a psychiatrist's office singing? None, after a diagnosis and drugs.

Within a few weeks, Dad had transformed his relationship with his son, spending more time with him, more openly expressing affection toward him, and limiting discipline to the most minimal essentials that the entire family had agreed upon. He had given up punishing Tommy and instead relied on a caring relationship to ensure cooperation. Tommy was "one hundred percent better."

Tommy's parents are well-meaning, mature people. They needed help in relating to their son. Other parents may also need help in getting their school to address the basic needs of their children, and sometimes the therapist may have to confer directly with teachers. In my experience, when parents and teachers are well-motivated, the children "get better" within a very short time. When parents and teachers aren't well-motivated, it's unjust and perhaps criminal to drug the child as an alternative.

Do Psychiatrists Have Magic Wands?

Psychiatrists, pediatricians, neurologists, and medical professionals in general do not necessarily have special gifts with children. They have no special capacity to love kids. They have no guaranteed capacities for relating to parents, sizing up family situations, or figuring out what's wrong in school.

What these professionals do have is the talent for getting accepted into highly competitive, scientific training programs, and then for graduating from them. They have had to distinguish themselves as bookworms and lab moles, and if they are well suited to being with children, it is a quality they have preserved despite their training.

Becoming a medical specialist is so long and arduous that it often discourages people who delight in human relations, children, and family life. Now that psychiatry is obviously dominated by biology and behaviorism, young doctors who choose to enter the field are likely to be especially aloof and insensitive.

The medical training experience itself flattens the child within every adult by suppressing the imaginative, playful, intuitive side of the future professional. Psychiatrists must learn to categorize people as if they are defective devices, and to lock them up and drug them against their will. They must also agree to give shock treatment or end up getting fired from their training programs. The experience pushes them toward becoming power-oriented and authoritarian, and hardens them to the suffering they cause. It makes them comfortable in suits and lab coats, and uncomfortable getting down on the floor with a child.

Many psychiatric residency programs no longer provide extensive training in talk therapy. Despite the public's misconceptions, they do not require the future psychiatrist to undergo psychotherapy or even to attend an occasional workshop in human relations. What do they learn? The *DSM* diagnoses, genetic and biochemical theories, and drugs. Parents who have read a few self-help or parenting books, and have perhaps attended a few human relationships seminars, probably know more about modern psychology than most psychiatrists, pediatricians, or neurologists. And by natural bent, the average parent is likely to be more intuitive and empathic as well. The selection and training of psychiatrists especially tends to discourage the development of those all-important qualities.

By selection and training, a psychiatrist is among the least likely persons to help a child or a family with its problems. Now that the profession is so thoroughly dominated by the medical approach, a psychiatrist is likely to do more harm than good.

Professionally Discredited

We are not alone in believing that ADHD and other childhood "disorders" do not exist as genuine medical or psychiatric syndromes.[7] In 1993 Fred Baughman, Jr., a neurologist in La Mesa, California, noted that studies have failed to confirm any definite improvement from the drug treatment of these children. He concluded his critique with these neglected questions:

> What is the danger of having these children believe they have something wrong with their brains that makes it impossible for them to control themselves without a pill? What is the danger of having the most important adults in their lives, their parents and teachers, believe this as well?

Baughman cites estimates of the frequency of ADHD that vary from one in three to one in one thousand. He therefore asks, "Is attention deficit–hyperactivity disorder, after all, in the eye of the beholder?"

The eye-of-the-beholder theme echoes the thoughts of Diane McGuinness, who has systematically debunked ADHD as the "emperor's new clothes." But psychiatry in general shows no inclination to admit that it's parading around naked when it comes to diagnosing children.

A Physical Basis to ADHD?

A 1990 study led by NIMH's Alan Zametkin received a great deal of publicity for finding increased brain metabolism in positron emission tomography (PET) scans of adults with a history of ADHD in childhood. However, when the sexes were compared separately, there was no statistically significant difference between the controls and ADHD adults. To achieve significance, the data was lumped together to include a disproportionate number of women in the controls. In addition, when individual areas of the brains of ADHD adults were compared to the same areas of the controls' brains, no differences were found. It is usually possible to massage data to produce a particular result, and Zametkin's study is a classic example of such massaging.

Since ADHD is not a disorder but a manifestation of conflict, we doubt that a biological cause will ever be found. In 1991, Gerald Golden put it simply:

Attempts to define a biological basis for ADHD have been consistently unsuccessful. The neuroanatomy of the brain, as demonstrated by neuroimaging studies, is normal. No neuropathologic substrate has been demonstrated. . . .

No Specific Drug Treatment

Contemporary experts agree that Ritalin affects all children in the same way—not just "hyperactive ones."[8] Within an hour after taking a single dose, any child will tend to become more obedient, more narrow in his or her focus, more willing to concentrate on humdrum tasks and instructions. Parents in conflict with a little boy can hand him a pill, knowing he'll soon be more docile.

It is commonly held that stimulants have a paradoxical effect on children compared to that on adults. In the past, I've accepted that view; but I've now begun to believe it isn't true. The drug probably affects children and adults in the same way. At the doses usually prescribed by physicians, children and adults alike are "spaced out," rendered less in touch with their real feelings, and hence more willing to concentrate on boring, repetitive tasks.

The British are much more cautious about using stimulants for children. The 1992 *Oxford Textbook of Clinical Psychopharmacology and Drug Therapy* suggests that stimulants may work in children the same way they impact on rats, by "inducing stereotyped behavior in animals, i.e. in reducing the number of behavioural responses. . . ." Stereotyped behavior is simple, repetitive, seemingly meaningless activity, and is often seen in brain-damaged individuals. The textbook states somewhat suggestively, "It is beyond our scope to discuss whether or not such behavioural control is desirable."[9]

At higher doses, both children and adults become more obviously stimulated into excitability or hyperactivity. It's a matter of relative dose, but people vary in their drug responsiveness, and a number of children and adults will become "hyper" and more inattentive at the lower doses as well.[10]

Toxic Psychiatry

One way to understand the routine effect of any psychiatric drug is to look at its more extreme or toxic effects. The clinical or "therapeutic" effect is likely to be a less intense expression of the toxic effect. In discussing Ritalin's "cognitive toxicity," James M. Swanson and his coauthors summarized the literature:

> In some disruptive children, drug-induced compliant behavior
> may be accompanied by isolated, withdrawn, and overfocused
> behavior. Some medicated children may seem "zombie-like"
> and high doses which make ADHD children more "somber,"
> "quiet," and "still" may produce social isolation by increasing
> "time spent alone" and decreasing "time spent in positive in-
> teraction" on the playground.[11]

Meanwhile, as they confirm, there's no evidence that Ritalin improves learning or academic performance.[12]

The Long-Term Effects "Remain in Doubt"

Parents are not told that years of research and clinical use have failed to con-firm any positive long-term effects from Ritalin in behavior or academic per-formance. As NIMH succinctly stated, "The long-term effects of stimulants remain in doubt."[13] The FDA-approved information put out by the drug company CIBA-Geigy admits "Long-term effects of Ritalin in children have not been well established."[14] Yet Ritalin is typically advocated as a long-term treatment.

NIMH further states that studies have demonstrated short-term effects such as reducing "class room disturbance" and improving "compliance and sustained attention." But it recognizes that the drugs seem "less reliable in bringing about associated improvements, at least of an enduring nature, in social-emotional and academic problems, such as antisocial behavior, poor peer and teacher relationships, and school failure."

While estimating that "between 2 and 3 percent of all elementary school children in North America receive some form of pharmacological interven-tion for hyperactivity," NIMH continues to encourage giving Ritalin to in-creasing numbers of children.

Ritalin and Amphetamines

Parents are seldom told that Ritalin is "speed"—that it is pharmacologically classified with amphetamines, has the same effects, side effects, and risks. Yet this is well-known in the profession. For example, the American Psychiatric Association's tome *Treatments of Psychiatric Disorders* (1989) observes that cocaine, amphetamines, and methylphenidate (i.e., Ritalin) are "neurophar-macologically alike." As evidence, the textbook points out that abuse pat-terns are the same for the three drugs; that people cannot tell their clinical effects apart in laboratory tests; and that they can substitute for each other and cause similiar behavior in addicted animals.[15] The *DSM-III-R* confirms these observations by lumping cocaine, amphetamine, and Ritalin abuse and addiction into one category. The Food and Drug Administration (FDA) classifies Ritalin in a high addiction category, Schedule II, which also includes amphetamines, cocaine, morphine, opium, and barbiturates.

Before it was replaced by other stimulants in the 1980s, Ritalin was one of the most commonly used street drugs.[16] In our home town of Bethesda, youngsters nowadays sell their prescribed Ritalin to classmates, who abuse it along with other stimulants. In working with various community groups, I often hear anecdotal reports of individuals who have graduated from using medically prescribed Ritalin to alcohol or street drugs, and I have seen some cases of this in my own practice.

Like any addictive stimulant, Ritalin can cause withdrawal symptoms, such as "crashing" with depression, exhaustion, withdrawal, irritability, and suicidal feelings. Parents will not think of a withdrawal reaction when their child gets upset after missing even a single dose. They will mistakenly believe that their child needs to be put back on the medication.

While it is true that doctors don't often report these and many other Ritalin side effects, harmful reactions are probably far more common than the literature suggests. Except when a drug is brand new, doctors almost never report or publish negative side effects. Many physicians do not know there is a mechanism for informing the drug companies and the FDA.[17] In addition, advocates of psychiatric drugs for children have proven themselves especially unwilling to examine or underscore their dangerous effects.*

More Facts Withheld from Parents

Parents are not told that Ritalin, as a stimulant, can cause the very things it is supposed to cure—inattention, hyperactivity, and aggression. When this happens, the child is likely to be given higher doses of the drug, or an even stronger agent, such as the neuroleptics Mellaril or Haldol, resulting in a vicious circle of inreasing drug toxicity.

Rarely are parents informed that Ritalin can cause permanent disfiguring tics. I've recently seen the case of a young boy in whom routine dosage produced frequent, disfiguring muscle spasms and tics of the head, neck, face, eyes, and mouth.

It is sometimes explained to parents that Ritalin can suppress growth (height and weight), but the explanation is usually given in a manner

---

*For example, in *Psychiatric Drugs* (1983) I became perhaps the first physician to conclude and emphasize that the neuroleptics frequently cause tardive dyskinesia in children, although it has now become a recognized fact. In Chapter 5, we point out that among the dozens of federally funded studies which encourage drug administration to children, none focuses on dangerous side effects or long-term problems.

calculated not to frighten them. Much of the brain's growth takes place during the years in which children are given this drug; but doctors don't tell parents that there are no studies of the effect of this growth inhibition on the brain itself. If the child's body is smaller, including his head, what about the contents of his skull? And if size can be reduced, what about more subtle and perhaps immeasurable brain deformities?

Parents are infrequently informed that like any form of speed, Ritalin can often make children anxious and sometimes cause them to behave in bizarre ways that seem "crazy."

Most surely, parents will not be told about any danger of permanent brain damage from long-term exposure to Ritalin. But how then to account for the following: no consistent brain abnormalities have been found in children labeled ADHD, but one study has found brain shrinkage in adults labeled ADHD who have been taking Ritalin for years.[18] The authors of the study suggested "cortical atrophy may be a long-term adverse effect of this [Ritalin] treatment."

Whenever researchers claim to find a biological defect supposedly caused by mental illness, they rush to the media and garner publicity. But when a researcher finds evidence that psychiatric drugs are producing detectable brain damage, no one is listening, no one cares, no one even bothers to investigate further.*

Finally, parents will not be told by their doctor that there are almost guaranteed non-drug methods of improving the conduct of nearly all so-called DBD children—through more interesting, engaging schools and through more rationally managed, loving family relationships.

Parents frequently contact me because their child's private or public school is insisting upon drug treatment. Sometimes the school has referred the parents to a specific doctor who is inclined to prescribe drugs. Sometimes the school threatens to take punitive measures if the parents don't go along with a prescription of Ritalin. There are instances of public schools refusing to allow children to continue until they have been placed on drugs.

Ritalin for African-American Children

When I travel around the country for speeches and workshops, I frequently hear stories about African-American parents being pushed or coerced into accepting Ritalin for their children, sometimes with very harmful results.

---

* *Toxic Psychiatry* documents this consistent pattern within the profession of minimizing reports of brain damage from drugs. I have published two recent scientific papers dealing with brain damage caused by the neuroleptic or antipsychotic drugs (Breggin, 1990a & 1993b).

Poor, minority parents are especially vulnerable to pressure from the schools. They may be afraid to challenge professional advice, for fear of endangering their resources, such as school programs or welfare payments. They don't have the wherewithal to get second opinions. Many live in single-parent households without an effective male presence and may be thankful for any offer of help. For example, they are aware of how many inner-city boys turn to or fall victim to violence and they will try almost anything to prevent that eventuality.

Is ADHD an American Disease?

ADHD is rarely diagnosed in countries with more evident concern for children, such as Denmark, Norway, and Sweden, where psychiatric drugs of any kind are hardly ever given to children. A doctor working in Britain's National Health Service is not allowed to give Ritalin in routine practice because it is not on the approved drug list of the *British National Formulary.* The doctor could prescribe amphetamines, which have a similar effect, but this is discouraged and rarely done.*

Data from the International Narcotics Control Board for 1991 showed that the United States, closely followed by Canada, uses proportionally much more Ritalin than most other countries.[19] If Ritalin use is a comparative measure of national attitudes toward children, North America is the most pedist region in the world.

Is ADHD a Boy's Disease?

Males are far more frequently given DBD diagnoses than females.[20] Aside from feeling bored or in conflict with adults, why would boys ordinarily tend to act resentfully and rebelliously toward the authority of their mothers and female teachers? A partial answer is that they are trained to be that way toward women in general. In fact, most *grown men* in the world today resent being told what to do by women.

A multiplicity of factors contribute to the conflicts and confusion in little boys: how boys are trained to suppress their tender ("feminine") side and encouraged to be competitive, dominating, and hostile toward women; how these lessons are imprinted through TV and the entertainment media, and

---

*Some doctors in Great Britain would like it to follow in America's footsteps. A recent promotional pamphlet by Christopher Green, head of the Child Development Unit of The Children's Hospital, praises the use of Ritalin and explains the special procedures that will be used to obtain it. It was sent to us by a concerned member of Britain's Hyperactive Children's Support Group (HACSG) of West Sussex.

reinforced in sports and on the playground, as well as in the family and almost everywhere else in society.

It's a wonder that *any* boys learn to restrain themselves in the presence of women or to respect their mothers and female teachers. Add to this the boring, oppressive atmosphere of most schools, and it's a miracle that female teachers are able to manage young boys at all.[21]

Female DBDs?

If DBD is an extreme expression of being socialized as a boy, what's an extreme expression of being socialized as a girl? The female equivalent of DBD would be "compulsive *obedience* disorder." Its most common subcategory would be "compulsive *attention* disorder."

Girls are too often trained to sit still and listen to almost anything an authority says to them. They feel especially compelled to pay attention to everything almost any male says, even while the male is paying no attention whatsoever to them.

Why doesn't the *DSM-III-R* offer any diagnoses for children who are compulsively obedient or attentive? Because it is an instrument of social control and there's no need to suppress already overcontrolled girls and young women—or overcontrolled young men for that matter.

In our modern society, in which girls receive increasingly confusing messages about assertiveness, more and more young girls are being diagnosed with one or another DBD and are being drugged or hospitalized.[22] Often they are girls with potential leadership qualities.

Into the Loony Bin

In the suburbs, psychiatric hospitals have become what jails are for the inner city—alternatives to crumbling society and failing families and schools. In her 1993 book *And They Call It Help,* Louise Armstrong describes the combination of economic and social pressures, and flawed values, that has led escalating numbers of suburban white parents to dump their protesting children in psychiatric hospitals. She cites newspaper headlines aimed at exposing the abuse:

> CAGED KIDS: Behave or Mom and Dad Will Put You in the Nuthouse.

> TREATING TEENS IN TROUBLE: Can the Psychiatric Ward Fill In for the Family?

COMMITTED YOUTH: Why Are So Many Teens Being Locked Up in Private Mental Hospitals?

[pp. 3–4]

Armstrong points out that 270,000 children under eighteen were hospitalized for psychiatric reasons in 1985—double the number from 1971. This is a disaster for our children, since the hospitals are humiliating and stigmatizing, and often do more harm than good. Isolation and physical restraint are common, and drugs are the norm. Visiting privileges and phone calls are heavily restricted, isolating the children from their family and community. Frequently, the children are medicated with agents that can cause permanent brain damage or that have been largely untried on children and youth.

The psychiatric incarceration of children impacts on all children in the community. Among those who frequent our home, a few have been hospitalized, and everyone knows who they are and what they went through. Children who haven't been locked up still know enough to live in fear of it, especially when their parents raise it as a threat during family conflicts.

CH.A.D.D

Founded in 1987, Children with Attention Deficit Disorders (CH.A.D.D.) is an organization of parents who have children labeled with attention deficit disorders. CH.A.D.D.'s official policy views these children as suffering from genetic and biological problems. In the words of CH.A.A.D. president Sandra F. Thomas, "Our kids have a neurological impairment that is pervasive and affects every area of their life, day and night."

CH.A.D.D. leaders claim that their children's emotional upset and anger is in no way caused by family conflicts, poor parenting, or inadequate schools. A recent CH.A.D.D. brochure headline announces: "Dealing with parental guilt. No, it's not all your fault." After stating that ADHD is a neurological disorder, the brochure goes on to explain:

> Frustrated, upset, and anxious parents do not cause their children to have ADD. On the contrary, ADD children usually cause their parents to be frustrated, upset, and anxious.

There could be no better example of pedist child-blaming and mistaken parental exoneration.

CH.A.D.D. has followed the model of its adult counterpart, the

National Alliance for the Mentally Ill (NAMI).[23] NAMI parents usually have grown offspring who are severely emotionally disabled, and they promote biochemical and genetic explanations, drugs, electroshock, psychosurgery, and involuntary treatment. NAMI also tries to suppress dissenting views by harrassing professionals who disagree with them.[24] Now NAMI has developed an affiliate, the National Alliance for the Mentally Ill—Child and Adolescent Network.[25] NAMI-CAN, like CH.A.D.D., believes in BBBD—biologically based brain diseases.

Power Sources

CH.A.D.D. and NAMI parents have developed enormous influence by joining forces with biologically oriented professionals, national mental health organizations, and drug companies. CH.A.D.D.'s National Professional Advisory Board, for example, includes NIMH biopsychiatric stalwarts Alan Zametkin and Judith Barkley, as well as C. Keith Conners and Barbara Ingersoll.

Where is the money coming from to support high-pressure lobbying, media campaigns, and upscale national conventions at hotels like the Chicago Hyatt Regency? CH.A.D.D.'s 1992 convention program, "Pathways to Progress," states:

> CH.A.D.D. appreciates the generous contribution of an educational grant in support of our projects by CIBA-Geigy Corporation.

CIBA-Geigy manufactures Ritalin, the stimulant with the lion's share of the ADHD market.

NAMI has had equal success with its political efforts. It too is closely aligned with biological psychiatry and takes money from the drug companies.[26]

The combination is potent: parents who resort to the biomedical management of their children; professionals who make their living researching, promoting, and practicing it; and the drug companies who profit from selling their products. *There has been no corresponding national organization to* protect *children from psychiatric diagnosis and biomedical control, largely because there is no corresponding power base for more caring, empathic approaches.* In response to the need for an alternative, the Center for the Study of Psychiatry has recently created *Children First!*—a national membership organization that opposes the widespread psychiatric diagnosis and drugging of children and youth (see Appendix).

Stifling All Rebellion

A recent CH.A.D.D. *Educators Manual*[27] was written with the collaboration of professionals, including Russell Barkley. It makes clear the intention to diagnose and drug children who won't conform to strict discipline:

> Attention Deficit Disorder is a hidden disability. No physical marker exists to identify its presence, yet ADD is not very hard to spot. Just look with your eyes and listen with your ears when you walk through places where children are—particularly those places where children are expected to behave in a quiet, orderly, and productive fashion. In such places, children with ADD will identify themselves quite readily. They will be doing or not doing something which frequently results in their receiving a barrage of comments and criticisms such as "Why don't you ever listen?" "Think before you act." "Pay attention."

Children Are Not Adults in Small Bodies

Children, from the time they come into this world as infants, have an infinite number of tasks to learn and developmental goals to attain. Fortunately, nature has built in the impulses needed for the child to grow. For example, as an emerging toddler, a fourteen-month-old baby, newly walking, needs lots of time to practice that activity. Even as the baby is becoming mobile, he or she is also becoming curious about *everything*—from magazines to the dog's tail, from overflowing wastebaskets to the roll of toilet paper, the sooty fireplace to the broken paper clip you dropped a day ago.

This baby has a brain to develop, and is being helped in this task through natural curiosity. Young parents will often feel worn out when their child suddenly starts cruising through the house, looking for new excitement. But the baby's behavior is normal and absolutely essential for proper development and growth.

Instead of lamenting a highly active child, parents need to rejoice in this sign of vitality and intelligence, and to nurture it by providing lots of opportunity for their baby to explore, move about, and grow. But in the face of all the media coverage for ADHD, some parents will wonder if their child is "hyperactive."

Making a Home for Our Children

Children need to have their homes tailored to their needs. Author and educator Thomas Gordon, who developed Parent Effectiveness Training, puts it this way:

> Most parents . . . say they believe [their family home] is exclusively *their* home; the children, therefore, must be trained and conditioned to behave properly and appropriately. This means a child must be molded and scolded until he painfully learns what is expected of him in his parents' home. These parents seldom even consider making any major modifications in the home environment when a child is born into the home. . . .

Gordon goes on to describe how he asks parents what changes they would make in their home if one of their parents was suddenly wheelchair-bound and needed to live with them. A long list of accommodations results from these discussions. Parents who think this through find they are then more willing to make changes in the home environment for their little child.

A home requires many accommodations for a small child—from locking up the poisons to installing baby gates and putting breakables well out of reach. As the child grows older, the changes need to evolve. A ten-year-old isn't going to pull books off a shelf and rip pages, but he may drag a chair around the kitchen and repeatedly climb up on it to reach the peanut butter. We realized at one point that our children were having to hop up on the counter to reach the dishes, so we rearranged the kitchen, placing dishes, snack foods, and other essentials on low shelves.

Parents ought to be thankful for every bit of spunk and spirit their children possess. It demands energy, attention, and involvement on our part as parents, but it will result in bright, creative, spirited, and secure young adults.

Like Shining Stars

Our children relate to us mostly through home and school. In both places we need a new devotion to their basic needs rather than to our old attitudes and ways. Above all else, our children need a more caring connection with us, the adults in their lives. This is now being realized in school systems throughout America as they begin to abandon the large, factory-like facilities of the past in favor of "small is beautiful."

There are many advantages to smaller schools, but the biggest one is this: they allow teachers to get to know their students well enough to better meet their basic educational and emotional needs. At the same time, small schools and classes meet the teachers' basic needs for a satisfying, effective professional identity. Conflict can be resolved more readily as it ideally should be—through mutually satisfying solutions—rather than through suppression.

The result of smaller, more caring schools? *The DBDs are disappearing.* There is no better evidence for how the environment powerfully shapes the behavior that results in children being psychiatrically diagnosed.

In a July 14, 1993, *New York Times* report entitled "Is Small Better? Educators Now Say Yes for High School," Susan Chira reports:

> [S]tudents in schools limited to about 400 students have fewer behavior problems, better attendance and graduation rates, and sometimes higher grades and scores. At a time when more children have less support from their families, students in small schools can form close relationships with teachers.

Teachers in these schools have the opportunity for "building bonds that are particularly vital during the troubled years of adolescence."

Even students from troubled homes respond to smaller, more caring schools. "They are shining stars you thought were dull," said New York City teacher Gregg Staples. "If you're under a lot of pressure and stress, they help you through that," said student Joy Grimage. "They won't put you down or put you on hold."

What a difference from "Behave . . . or else!" It's not that we don't know what our children need. They need more of us—us at our best. The question is, "Are we willing to develop more meaningful relationships with them?"

Environment Molds the Child's Brain and Abilities

Ironically, while there is no convincing evidence that genetic brain disorders cause abnormalities such as disruptive or aggressive behavior, there is increasing evidence that the developing brain has "plasticity" and is permanently influenced by environmental conditions.[28] William Greenough of the University of Illinois at Champaign-Urbana, for example, has found that rats exposed to an enriched environment with toys, food, exercise, and playmates have 25 percent more brain cell connections on autopsy than animals raised in typical drab laboratory cages.

Craig Ramey of the University of Alabama has found similar results in children whose IQs and social skills are permanently raised by early enrichment programs. He also finds that PET scans demonstrated increased efficiency.[29] According to Ramey, "Early intervention appears to have had a particularly powerful preventive effect on children whose mothers had low IQs—while also benefiting other children from economically, socially or educationally disadvantaged backgrounds." Early enrichment programs are costly, but through prevention they end up saving money. Ramey also related his findings to violence prevention: "There's no real mystery about this. When you have high concentrations of people who don't have basic social skills—and being able to succeed in school is a universally required basic social skill—you have chaos."

The implications of brain plasticity are profound. If we don't provide a nurturing, enriched environment for children, they may be permanently disadvantaged by relatively undeveloped brains; while if we do provide the proper surroundings, children show more brain development and better social and academic skills. Under no circumstances should this rule out giving help to older children or adults who have grown up under deprived circumstances; human beings can always benefit from improved opportunities. But it argues strongly for the special importance of early *environmental* interventions, such as Head Start.

"Curing the Child Without Treatment"

Children respond so quickly to improvements in the way adults relate to them that most children can be helped without being seen by a professional person. Instead, the professional can counsel the parents, teachers, and other concerned adults.

Many psychotherapists, for example, routinely practice "child therapy" without actually seeing any children. They help their adult patients become more loving or disciplined parents through the routine work of psychotherapy, indirectly transforming the lives of their children. The children "get better" sight unseen. These therapists, many of whom work only with adults, may not see themselves as child psychiatrists or child therapists. But they are doing more good for children than the professionals who see and diagnose them, and then give drugs.

Children don't have disorders; they live in a disordered world. When adults provide them a better environment, they tend quickly to get their lives together.

Children can eventually become so upset, confused, and self-destructive that they internalize the pain or become compulsively rebellious. They may need the intervention of a therapeutic—unconditionally caring—adult to help them overcome their inner suffering and outrage. Sometimes these children can benefit from learning how to help ease the conflicted situation. But they should *never* be given the idea that they are diseased or defective or are the primary cause of their conflicts with their schools and families.

Children can benefit from guidance in learning to be responsible for their own conduct; but they don't gain from being blamed for the trauma and stress that they are exposed to in the environment around them. They need empowerment, not humiliating diagnoses and mind-disabling drugs. Most of all, they thrive when adults show concern for and give attention to their basic needs as children.

These conclusions are not accepted by the biopsychiatrists who dominate mental health policy and practice throughout the nation. Now we turn to how the federal government is promoting the medical management of children instead of addressing their real needs.

5

Current Federal Programs for the Biomedical Control of Children and Youth

All told, biological psychiatry is often more reductionist than acknowledged, does not come up to current scientific standards, and uncritically cites work which is, or should be, discredited. At the heart of the problem is an implicit ideology within biological psychiatry, with insufficient awareness of its social ramifications: "blaming the victim's body" protects the status quo by holding protoplasm at fault for maladjustment rather than the person, family, or community.

—Alvin Pam, "A Critique of the Scientific Status of Biological Psychiatry" (1990)

What we appeared to be looking at was the increasingly routine use of "treatment" as punishment; the psychiatric policing of children.

—Louise Armstrong, *And They Call It Help* (1993)

ON THE WARDS OF THE NATIONAL INSTITUTE OF MENTAL HEALTH (NIMH), children in conflict with their parents, schools, and society are routinely subjected to biomedical research involving spinal taps, brain scans, and other invasive procedures. Frequently they are subjected to toxic or experimental medications for the control of their behavior. At the same time, NIMH and other federal agencies are spending millions of dollars to fund similar projects carried on throughout the country.

Long before the violence initiative was formally conceived, NIMH was encouraging the widespread diagnosing and drugging of children. The aim was to manage children labeled with disruptive behavior disorders—violent, rebellious, unruly, or merely difficult or "hyperactive" youngsters. Despite the adverse publicity directed at biomedical social control, funding for these projects has been increasing in the past few years. The federal government's sponsorship of these interventions into the lives of children and their families raises many scientific, social, and ethical issues.

Pedist Psychiatry at NIMH

Modern psychiatry goes out of its way to tell parents and teachers alike, "You are not to blame; your kids are." No one is more responsible for this attitude than two influential NIMH child psychiatrists.

When Paul Wender wrote *The Hyperactive Child* in 1973, he was a researcher at NIMH. In that book and its revised 1987 version, he displays a persistent willingness to blame and medicate children. His books abound with suggestions that ADHD children are defective monsters who upset their otherwise perfect families. Here is a sample from a lengthy 1973 description:

> As these infants become toddlers, many of them are bundles of energy. The parents frequently report that after an active and restless infancy, the child stood and walked at an early age, and then, like an infant King Kong, burst the bars of his crib and marched forth to destroy the house.[1]

In recent years, Judith Rapoport has assumed Wender's mantle as NIMH's leading advocate of drugging children. As the chief of the child psychiatry branch, she is a powerful voice. In *The Boy Who Wouldn't Stop Washing,* she declared:

> One great piece of news is already in the literature. *It May Not Be Your Fault That You Or Your Child Has Obsessive-Compulsive Disorder!* Early toilet training, a rigorously disciplined home environment, an unresolved oedipal complex, and endless demands that your child clean up her "disgusting" room may not be and is probably not the cause of this illness.[2] [Italics in original]

Driven to Violence by Sluggish Biochemicals

Timed to come out with the pending announcement of the federal violence initiative, the June 1992 *Archives of General Psychiatry* fielded an entire issue on violence research.[3] It contained the monkey study that most probably inspired Goodwin's comparison to inner-city children. It set out to prove and did find a correlation between sluggish serotonin and aggression, this time in free-ranging rhesus monkeys. Headed by J. Dee Higley, it involved several federal institutes, including NIH and the Food and Drug Administration (FDA).

Because the monkeys were free-ranging, "aggressivity was generally not directly observed; rather, it was largely inferred from the pattern, number and degree of wounds and old scars." Using bite wounds and scars to determine high levels of aggressivity is extremely misleading. The title of the study speaks of "correlates of aggression," but the study actually looks at *victims* of aggression—animals with multiple wounds. Battered wives end up with far more wounds and bruises than their husbands. So do pugilists who lose in the ring, as well as children who get bullied on the playground or beaten by their parents. Most important, the number of wounds, old and new, would reflect stress more than aggressivity.

Why, then, does the NIMH report refer to "correlates of aggression"? Why does the article claim it is studying "associated risk factors involved in excessive aggression"? A more plausible conclusion—that low serotonin levels are the result of being victimized—does not comport with the preconceived notion that violent youth are triggered by biochemical derangements. It is therefore less politically palatable, less newsworthy, less inspiring to congressional funding sources, and ultimately less profitable.[4]

A Biochemical Cause for Delinquency?

The special violence issue of the *Archives* also published a study of twenty-nine children—ages six to nineteen—by a team led by Mark Kruesi on the wards of NIMH. The bias of the authors is made plain: "biological factors may well be more important than environmental factors in a subgroup of conduct disorders that persist into adult life."*

As they had hoped and intended, the study did produce some correlations between presumably sluggish neurotransmission in serotonergic nerves,† and relatively poor outcome for the children, measured by severity of aggression and frequency of institutionalization.

---

*Such an assertion has racist implications, since the nation's concern is so focused on criminal behavior by urban African-Americans. The racial identity of the study subjects is not given, but in response to our criticism for failing to provide the data, the government later claimed that the participants were 76 percent white, 17 percent black, and 7 percent "other" (Department of Health and Human Services, 1992). Kruesi is now at the University of Illinois in Chicago.

†The brain has dozens of kinds of neurotransmitters—chemicals produced by one neuron (nerve cell) in order to activate other neurons, resulting in transmission of the nerve impulse. The release of the neurotransmitter, such as serotonin, may be viewed as the "spark" that fires the adjacent neuron. The theory is that concentrations of serotonin breakdown products or metabolites, specifically 5-Hydroxyindoleacetic acid (5-HIAA), in the spinal fluid reflect the intensity of serotonin neurotransmission in the brain. A low concentration presumably indicates a relatively sluggish serotonin system. Serotonergic nerves are ones that release serotonin into the synapse to stimulate the firing of nerves. The theory itself is fraught with many difficulties, including the leap of faith that correlates gross changes in spinal fluid with fine-tuned activity in the brain. See Breggin and Breggin (1994).

The authors themselves mention many problems in the study. For example, "The follow-up interval is relatively brief; patients are still 'at risk,' and ultimate outcome is still unknown." This points to another kind of "impulsivity"—the compulsive urge that scientists feel to rush data into print when it is politically advantageous. If the ultimate findings prove contrary to the hypothesis, it's unlikely that they will be published with such alacrity.

In addition, there is no description of double-blind procedures that would have prevented the researchers from knowing the results of the spinal taps before evaluating or rating the conduct of the subjects. Consciously or unconsciously, knowledge of the laboratory results could have influenced judgments regarding correlations between spinal fluid findings and behavior, as well as other aspects of the study. Without a double-blind, the study is invalid. For the investigators to proceed without a double-blind casts significant doubt on their credibility.*

In the midst of the violence initiative controversy, Kruesi himself expressed hope that his research might end up supporting early identification for drug interventions. According to a July 6, 1992, report on National Public Radio's *All Things Considered,* "If the serotonin connection pans out, Kruesi hopes these individuals who are at high risk for continuing pathological violence may be identified and helped, perhaps with drugs and therapy early on."[5]

Rapoport Continues Dangerous and Intrusive Studies

An in-house study on the wards of NIMH by Judith Rapoport, "Neurobiology of Disruptive Behavior Disorders," continues the practice of doing spinal taps, as well as magnetic resonance imaging (MRI) of the brain and other biological studies on children and adolescents. It also involves stimulant and antidepressant treatment, as well as administration of experimental drugs. The project has been going on since 1989 and will continue through 1995 or longer. It includes sixteen children and adolescents, and was funded for $424,700 in 1992, making it very high-priced and intensive research.[6]

---

*The ratings of "outcome measures" were made by the two chief investigators, including Kruesi himself, and it would seem extremely unlikely that they could have remained unaware of the overall results of the lab tests. If the evaluation procedures were "blind," it would have been described. For example, the Higley study of monkeys states that the investigators who rated the animals for aggressivity were "blind" to the spinal tap results. The need for a double-blind is even more critical in the Kruesi study because of the greater subjectivity involved in making ratings of aggressivity in human beings. In the absence of the double-blind, investigator bias can even impact on the way the subjects behave, that is, whether they act in conformity to the investigator's hopes and predictions.

It is difficult to ascertain how many children NIMH is studying with intrusive biomedical interventions. For example, a 1990–1991 NIMH "Notice of Intramural Research Project" for the same "Neurobiology of Disruptive Behavior Disorders" seemingly describes the ongoing studies by Kruesi and his colleagues, and then refers to an unidentified "second sample" of "32 hyperactive boys" given spinal taps.[7]

Other DBD Studies

Most children who get psychiatrically diagnosed are in conflict with their families or schools. A study of obsessive-compulsive disorders conducted at NIMH by H. Leonard and others shows that one-half of these fifty-four children also have been diagnosed with disruptive behavior disorders.[8]

The youngsters, age seven to nineteen, were treated with antidepressants, including Prozac. Spinal taps were done to test for serotonin levels, but no correlation with behavior could be made. Despite a generally poor outcome for the children, the report advocates drugs like Prozac.

NIMH's Radiation Experiments on Children

A May 1993 NIMH study led by Alan Zametkin used PET (positron emission tomography) scans to examine ten normal teenagers and ten ADHD teenagers. The PET scan is a brain study that requires the injection of radioactive tracers. It is used to determine the level of ongoing metabolic activity in various parts of the brain over time.

The researchers found no abnormalities in the ADHD children but nonetheless claimed the study was useful because "The feasibility of normal minors participating in research involving radiation was established." They believe that this was the first time normal adolescents (mean age 14.5 years) had been exposed to "radiation for research purposes" in the United States.

Is this something NIMH should be proud of?

We asked an NIH research radiologist—who wishes to remain anonymous—whether it was possible to know if this degree of radiation exposure was likely to harm the youngsters. He felt there was no way to anticipate the future risk of cancer, which would take many years to show up, and that the studies should not have been done.

The NIH radiologist also reminded us that the PET scan itself could be frightening, even to adults: it requires prolonged immobilization in a scary apparatus. It also involves potentially painful injections.

It seems extremely unlikely that the parents were truly informed about the unpredictable risk factors associated with radiation exposure in children or the probable futility of the study itself. We cannot imagine their consenting without first being told that the research would be relatively harmless while significantly contributing to science. The youngsters themselves, of course, were in no position to give consent.

The Impact of Spinal Taps and Other Biomedical Intrusions

Many NIMH projects, conducted at the institutes or funded elsewhere, require spinal taps (lumbar punctures) on children. The NRC report *Understanding and Preventing Violence* calls spinal taps "an uncomfortable procedure that involves some risk."[9] These interventions, especially in children, can be terrifying, as well as dangerous. The child's natural fear of needles is compounded by the procedure. The child must lie extremely still for several minutes on his side with his body flexed, while a local anesthetic and a needle insertion are carried out in his back. Then he must remain immobile with the needle in place while the spinal fluid is slowly removed. It takes little imagination to understand how frightening this could be for some children.

Sometimes sedation is necessary to calm the child. Afterward, it is recommended that the child lie flat with his or her head slightly down for three hours, followed by "at least another 12 hours" flat on the back.

James L. Bernat and Fredrick M. Vincent's 1987 textbook *Neurology: Problems in Primary Care* reports that headaches occur in 10 to 15 percent of routine spinal taps and that these involve both "aching and throbbing" that "usually lasts four to eight days." The pain can extend into the base of the skull, the neck, and the upper thoracic spine.[10] When severe, there may be nausea, vomiting, dizziness, and stiff neck. It can necessitate bed rest for several days or more. Much less frequently, side effects can be life-threatening, including infections of the brain and spinal cord.

Bernat and Vincent warn that spinal taps "should not be performed in a casual or purely routine manner. . . . [The physician] must always ask, 'Does the information to be gained justify the risk of the procedure?'"

An earlier 1990 publication by Kruesi, Rapoport, and their NIMH team hints at the complications and distress being caused by the spinal taps. Among twenty-nine children subjected to spinal taps, at least six developed special problems. One had a "previously undetected coagulation disorder" that could have made the procedure life-threatening.* Two others suffered separately from "obesity" and "muscle spasms" that prevented successful taps, suggesting they were probably subjected to considerable trauma and

---

*While the phrase "previously undetected" suggests that the tap may have inadvertently led to serious medical complications, the authors do not provide any information on the subject.

pain before the doctors gave up trying. And "In a fourth we were unable to obtain CSF [cerebral spinal fluid] despite multiple attempts over a 3-year period." Two others required taps higher up the spinal column than usual because of the failure of initial attempts lower down. Meanwhile, the authors do not tell us about problems in later years or about the more "routine" side effects, such as fear before the procedure and headaches afterward.

Clearly, children are in no position to give consent to such procedures. Given the biological bias of the experimenters, were the parents properly informed before giving consent for their children? Were they told that the studies would contribute absolutely nothing to improving the lives of their offspring and instead might frighten, demoralize, and even injure them?

Is It Ethical to Continue with These Experiments?

The brain is a complex, subtle organ in which hundreds of billions of cells create trillions more connections, and in which an unknown variety of chemical and other neuronal relationships interact. Whole new physical processes are continually being discovered.[11] At this point, science cannot conceptualize how the whole system works together or how its activities result in a single thought or feeling, let alone complex behavior.[12]

It seems highly unlikely that one or another sluggish neurotransmitter will ever be implicated as a contributing factor to widespread psychological problems, social unrest, or crime. This is especially true when we realize that the brain of any child is processing an infinitely complex input from the environment, as well as adding the individual's own unique viewpoint on these life experiences. Furthermore, it's too great a leap of imagination to speculate on brain function from low concentrations of a breakdown product in spinal fluid.

Wishful thinking, rather than science, lies at the root of research projects that attempt to reduce human conduct and social conflict to a grossly sluggish neurotransmission in a particular type of nerve cell. This raises additional doubt about whether these pseudoscientific efforts should be supported by the taxpayer. It raises doubt about subjecting children to these demoralizing and potentially dangerous procedures. Since there is no reason to believe that baseless diagnoses like the disruptive behavior disorders will ever turn out to have a biological cause, these biomedical intrusions become even more questionable.

The DBDs reflect conflict between children and adults, so why assume that the presumed physical defect lies in the children? Performing multiple biomedical tests on these children communicates to them that they are considered physically defective and to blame for their conflicts with adults. After all, why aren't their parents being subjected to the same tests? In reality, it seems highly unlikely that widespread conflict between children and adults will ever be reducible to an abnormal neurotransmitter in either children or adults.

Should such flimsy rationalizations be used to justify biological intrusions in children with so-called DBDs, inflicting upon them spinal taps, brain scans (including PET radiation), and other potentially frightening and dangerous technologies? We believe that this research is in reality a form of child abuse. It is unjustified and should never have been carried out, and ongoing similar projects should be canceled.

The Guns Are More Than Smoking

The studies we have thus far cited attempt to link serotonergic sluggishness to violent or disruptive behavior. From the start, we were concerned about the government's emphasis on serotonin imbalances. The theory implies that these imbalances, and the crimes they supposedly cause, are genetic in origin. It further suggests that NIMH will end up pushing the already big-selling serotonergic drugs—like Prozac, Zoloft, and Paxil—for the suppression of violence.

The government resoundingly denied our conclusions, yet prior to the controversy NIMH researchers had offered enthusiastic predictions that the drugs would cure serotonin imbalances and associated impulsivity and physical aggression. Much later, we located the unsigned speech outline—most likely the work of Fred Goodwin—that specifically connected the violence initiative to the possible use of Prozac and the testosterone suppressant Depo-Provera (see Chapter 1).

With all the denials from NIMH and the DHHS, we ourselves began to think that the government had indeed not yet started funding the genetic and drug studies that we anticipated. Then we obtained the materials recently provided to members of the NIH panel on violence, and our fears were confirmed.

NIMH has awarded a $227,036 grant entitled "Serotonin and Impulsive Aggression: Treatment Correlates" to Emile Coccaro of the Medical College of Pennsylvania in Philadephia. It became effective as of May 1, 1993. Based on the serotonergic theory of impulsive aggression, it will treat aggressive adults with Prozac. The summary says it is "Viewed as a groundbreaking study."

Another grant to Emile Coccaro is entitled "5-HT [serotonin] in aggression." While Prozac is not specifically involved in the study, the ultimate use of the research is defined as "To study the efficacy of fluoxetine [Prozac]." The subjects will be violent men and women over the age of eighteen suffering from "personality disorder" with 20 to 30 percent minority representation.

Yet another such study has surfaced. The National Institute on Alcohol Abuse and Alcoholism (NIAAA) has funded $100,000 in fiscal 1992 for research by David T. George concerning loss of impulse control during "abusive acts." After trials of placebo and a standard tricyclic antidepressant, patients will be tried on Zoloft (sertraline). Zoloft is the second in the series of serotonergic drugs that began with Prozac. The study will be conducted at NIH itself on outpatients.

A several-year research project by Bryan H. King has been recently funded by NIMH with the aim of determining the usefulness of "serotonergic agents" (such as Prozac) in controlling self-destructive behavior. The subjects will include four hundred "developmentally delayed" or "developmentally disabled" individuals, ages eighteen to forty-five, who will be given blood studies and an experimental drug, mCPP,[13] known to frequently cause anxiety and panic. The grant, entitled "Serotonergic Mechanisms and Self-Injurious Behavior," was funded for $145,530 for the first year (fiscal 1992) at the Harbor–UCLA Medical Center in Torrance, California.

Looking for the Crime Gene—Who Can You Believe?

Federal government officials repeatedly said that no agency was conducting research on the genetics of violence. Again, the materials given to the panel confirmed our predictions about the direction of the violence initiative. The NIAAA has awarded $200,000 for fiscal 1992 to David Goldman for "Molecular Genetic Studies of Disturbed Serotonin Function." In the words of Goldman's grant abstract, the research will:

> (a) identify patients with biochemical genetic defects in serotonin dysfunction;
> (b) assess these patients and their family members with respect to neurochemical, behavior, neurophysiological and medical manifestations of genetic serotonin dysfunction;
> (c) characterize genetic transmission of these traits in families; and
> (d) study the DNA obtained from the patients as the source of the isolation of molecular defects in their serotonin genes.

The study summary says that by September 30, 1992, forty-three "violent offenders" and twenty-seven normal volunteers had already been studied. The subjects include an unspecified number of children, whose ages aren't given, with a broad spectrum of diagnoses including disruptive behavior disorder, pervasive developmental disorder, mental retardation, eating disorders, and infantile autism. The project connects all of these disorders to a "serotonergic genetic" cause. On this flimsy and irrational conjecture, the children are being subjected to spinal taps, brain scans, blood work, and other tests.

As soon as the controversy began to slightly cool, government researchers again sought publicity for their claims of a connection between genetics and violence, as well as the promotion of serotonergic drugs. Reporter Jamie Talan recently cited researchers at the NIAAA,[14] who believe their monkey studies support the idea that serotonergic imbalances are genetically determined and induce violence. Talan summarizes:

> These studies come at a time when drug companies are developing drugs for depression that work by increasing the brain's ability to use serotonin. The animal studies show that higher levels of a key serotonin metabolite, called 5-HIAA, make for more playful and gregarious monkeys.

Basing her observations on interviews with federal researchers, Talan goes on to make an extraordinary, scientifically unproven claim:

> On drugs that increase the uptake of serotonin, such as the much-prescribed antidepressant Prozac, both humans and monkeys tend to interact better in social situations and show little aggression.

As we documented in *Talking Back to Prozac,* there is convincing evidence that the drug can *cause* violence and suicide, but there's little evidence that it can cure either one.

Why So Much Focus on Serotonergic Imbalances?

Each of the monkey and human studies we have thus far discussed attempts to correlate serotonergic imbalances with disruptive or violent behavior. They are used to raise hopes that drugs like Prozac, Zoloft, and Paxil will be able to correct serotonergic sluggishness and hence suicide, impulsivity, aggressivity, and disruptive behavior in children and adults.

In Chapter 2 we examined the influence of Eli Lilly, the manufacturer of Prozac, on organized psychiatry and saw how Lilly cash flows into NIMH itself. Both the Kruesi and the Leonard studies involved the Child Psychiatry Branch, headed by Judith Rapoport, and her name is on the published papers. As already noted, Rapoport receives grant money from Eli Lilly, the maker of Prozac; and the research director of NIMH at the time, Steven

Paul, recently went from his government post to a vice presidency at Eli Lilly. Is it surprising that so much of NIMH's research supports presumed biochemical imbalances that might be correctable by a Lilly product?

Years of Promotion for the Biomedical Management of Children

By the time NIMH and Goodwin got ready to announce their violence initiative for major 1994 funding, they had already spent years lavishing federal funds on biologically related violence research and were actively putting fresh programs into place. The studies we have thus far discussed are a tiny sample of the hundreds being carried on at government institutes or funded through outside researchers. NIMH's recent inventory of violence-related projects includes "Testosterone and Antisocial Behavior," "Neuropsychology and Delinquency," "Anabolic Androgenic Steroids and Aggressive Behavior," "Neurological Factors in Marital Aggression," and "Psychophysiology of Violent and Antisocial Behavior."

The testosterone study is one of the more absurd and Orwellian. It is the brainchild of James M. Dabbs of the Department of Psychology at Georgia State in Atlanta. The first phase of the study, funded 1987–1991, studied levels of the male hormone testosterone in saliva. The aim was to find a more efficient, less intrusive test than drawing blood. NIMH is trying to locate a biological marker in spit.

One pales at the image of young men lined up to expectorate into receptacles for the purpose of identifying oversexed, overaggressive, high-testosterone potential perpetrators. It would be more menacing if it had any hope of succeeding. Individual testosterone levels have not been correlated with aggressivity or criminality.

Unbalanced Funding Favors Biological Research

When the NIH panel of thirty researchers met in June 1993 to begin an evaluation of the government's violence research, the first few days of deliberation led many of them to comment that the government's research was unbalanced.[15] On June 11, 1993, Richard Stone of *Science* summarized:

> Much of the NIH violence research is aimed at determining biological factors that may underlie violent behavior. One study is examining how motor neurons control a sure sign of aggression—movements of the gill covers in fighting fish. Other studies explore a possible genetic basis for violent behavior, investigating whether families of suicide victims have higher than average suicide rates.

Actually, the situation is much worse than many of the panel members seemed to realize. Dozens of Ritalin and other drug studies are aimed at biomedical social control.

The Government Funds the Drugging of Children

The federal government is devoting millions of dollars each year to promoting the drugging of unruly, difficult, nonconformist children. While NIMH funds most of the studies, other institutes are involved as well,[16] and while Ritalin and amphetamine are the most frequently involved drugs, others are being tested, including Prozac, lithium, antidepressants, and anticonvulsives.

Rachel Klein from the Long Island Jewish Medical Center in New Hyde Park, as well as the New York State Psychiatric Institute and the Columbia University College of Physicians and Surgeons, is a typical NIMH grant recipient. Her study specifically aims at Ritalin treatment for conduct disorder—"severely aggressive boys and girls (ages 13–16)." Unlike most grantees, she specifically states, "A substantial portion of subjects will be from the minority community."

The number of NIMH projects that include the drugging of children—especially with Ritalin and amphetamine—is staggering. (In an endnote we have put together a partial list.[17]) Keep in mind that these drugs have been used for decades in the United States to treat so-called DBDs; and yet there is no indication that the DBDs are diseases or that drugging is a rational approach.

A Disguised Violence Initiative Project?

While the violence initiative controversy was brewing, NIMH was quietly funding the first year of a multisite national Ritalin study. The recipients have been named,[18] and NIMH will spend $12 million over several years with approximately seven hundred children involved at the start.

Opponents of the study have taken action. Led by J. F. Jackson of the Institute of Human Development in Berkeley, six African-American[19] members of the American Psychological Association sent a letter of concern about the nationwide Ritalin study to the APA's Committee on Standards in Research. They connect the project to the violence initiative and give evidence that NIMH became evasive about the study's existence once the controversy flared up.

Jackson and her colleagues recommend that additional ethical safeguards be required before psychologists participate in research like this where members of "historically exploited and oppressed groups" will be recruited as subjects. They point out that according to NIMH itself, ADHD frequently coincides with conduct disorder, especially among children with low socioeconomic status. They warn that a large proportion of African-American children are likely to receive "invalid, stigmatizing" diagnoses, such as conduct disorder, that would in effect label them violence-prone. The group also challenged the usefulness of Ritalin and suggested that less affluent parents would be hampered in being able to give informed consent.

Screening for Drug Treatment Through the Public Schools

The "Guest Editor's Comments" in a recent issue of *School Psychology Review* makes one of the most vigorous arguments to date for systematically involving public schools in the diagnosis and drugging of children for behavioral control. The author, William E. Pelham, Jr., is professor of psychiatry and psychology at the University of Pittsburgh and the Western Psychiatric Institute and Clinic.

As many of his colleagues have begun to do, Pelham calls for much greater involvement of psychologists in implementing biomedical approaches. He dismisses psychological understanding as unscientific and applauds the shift to biological theories. Pelham believes: "Indeed, it can be argued that the development of pharmacological interventions is on the cutting edge of research in the treatment of childhood disorders."

Since school psychologists are "on the front line of identification and treatment referral for the nation's school-aged children and adolescents," Pelham wants them much more exposed to "biological approaches to treatment." He states that "our goal is to improve treatment of children and adolescents" by increasing the school psychologist's awareness of pharmacological interventions. He wants school psychologists to have "a clearer understanding of the role schools may play in the implementation of pharmacological treatment" and looks forward to "improving the ways that psychopharmacological approaches are implemented in the schools."

In keeping with NIMH's current research policies, Pelham places considerable emphasis not only on the stimulant drugs, but also on those that affect the serotonergic system, including Prozac. As we noted in Chapter 1, when NIMH director Frederick Goodwin discussed the "triage" approach to selecting schoolchildren for psychiatric interventions, he showed no concern about the menacing ethical or political implications. Similarly, Pelham makes no reference to the potential dangers of his controversial proposals.

How closely is Pelham connected to NIMH? As closely as any professional in the nation who doesn't actually work on the premises. He is the current recipient of three NIMH grants for studies of children age eight to fifteen: "Methylphenidate [Ritalin] Effects in ADHD Adolescents";

"Pharmacological and Psychosocial Treatment for ADHD"; and "Pharmacology and Cognitive Motivation in ADHD"—for a grand total of more than $700,000 per year.

Objective Research?

The reader should not take any encouragement from the idea that the use of serotonergic or stimulant drugs in children is being given a scientific airing. The research will not, as some people might imagine, lead to an objective evaluation. The mere fact that NIMH is studying Prozac for violence and impulse control will encourage practitioners to give it a try on their own. As reported in the September 1992 *Clinical Psychiatry News,* a recent NIMH-sponsored conference presented two uncontrolled studies making claims for the management of aggression with Prozac.[20]

NIMH's funding of a Prozac violence study is not the first round in a "scientific evaluation" but the first round in a barrage of Prozac aimed at disruptive children and violent offenders. The public, Congress, the offenders, and their families—everyone will be told that this is a rational treatment based on "known" biochemical imbalances in the brain.

Meanwhile, in the topsy-turvy world of psychiatry, the profession will continue to ignore the reports that have implicated Prozac as a cause of impulsive, unexpected, and often brutal acts of aggression. And it will continue to encourage the use of Ritalin, even though decades of use have failed to demonstrate its effectiveness.

It's Already Happening

In a recent *Clinical Psychiatry News* report from the annual meeting of the Society for Biological Psychiatry in San Francisco, a headline reads, "Limited data suggest fluoxetine [Prozac] safe for children."[21] "Although research data in this age group are sparse," the report says, a Salt Lake City psychiatrist, Elizabeth M. Tully, is pushing it. Led by Tully's Western Institute of Neuropsychiatry, Utah already drugs more of its children than almost any other state.

With unusual candor for a psychiatric newspaper, the article observes, "Despite the paucity of published information, fluoxetine is increasingly being prescribed for children." In fact, the only controlled study available with depressed adolescents showed a "not statistically significant" improvement. The report from the convention goes on to cite the only study of Prozac for ADHD—involving a mere nineteen youngsters—as further confirmation for its value in a wide variety of children's problems.

The Research That Is Really Needed

If NIMH and NIH were genuinely interested in the well-being of children, they would fund the most truly neglected research area: long-term negative effects, including the possibility of permanent brain dysfunction and damage, from the prolonged use of stimulants and serotonergic drugs in children. Not one of the NIMH studies we have found examines the dangers of taking these drugs.

Genuinely worthwhile programs are also ignored in the rush to drug children labeled ADHD. Michael Valentine, a codirector of *Children First!* of the Center for the Study of Psychiatry (see Appendix), has reminded us about the overall failure to research and to promote the most important alternatives of all for children who are restless and inattentive in school—improved instruction and curriculum.

Drugs for Violence Control in Actual Clinical Practice

Are there drugs that are useful in actual practice for the management of violence? Are we putting society at risk by discouraging their use?

Neuroleptic medications—such as Thorazine, Mellaril, Prolixin, Trilafon, or Haldol—can suppress violent episodes by "zonking" the person, crushing all thoughts, feeling, and behavior. But they have no specific effect on anger, rage, or aggression. They flatten normal people and can even be used to tame enraged animals.[22] They are put in the tranquilizer darts so often seen on television wildlife specials. The effect is a "chemical lobotomy" and "chemical straitjacket."[23]

Even the emergency use of psychiatric drugs for violent crises in institutions should not be readily condoned. These outbursts can usually be handled by firm, organized, caring action. In my experience, most violence on mental hospital wards is generated by confusing or humiliating staff practices.

Resorting to drugs is too easy and therefore discourages more humane alternatives. It's as if one party to a dispute had a six-gun readily available to settle the problem. In psychiatric settings, the six-gun is the syringe.

Psychiatrists often write hospital orders for PRN—as needed—medication for troublesome patients. When the ward personnel have conflict with the patient, they can quickly whip out the needle. So there's little motivation to resolve conflicts constructively. If psychiatric professionals were "disarmed," they would find more creative methods of handling severe conflict during emergencies.

Drugs for Violence Prevention

Violence is not prevented by these emergency drug interventions. It is aborted after it has begun. In the area of violence prevention, drugs have no proven effectiveness.

A group of relatively old medications, including lithium and anticonvulsants, have been tried for years for the suppression of aggressive tendencies in adults, and recently other drugs used in general medicine are being tried, with little or no documented success. NIMH is now experimenting with the use of many of these agents in children. Recognizing that there is no known medication for the control of violence, most psychiatrists limit the prescription of the more potent drugs to adults with specific severe psychiatric diagnoses, such as schizophrenia and manic-depression, who also display violence.[24]

As one expert put it, "There is no medication specific to the treatment of violence."[25] Textbooks also agree that there is no medication for treating conduct disorder, the diagnosis for children who demonstrate persistent or pervasive patterns of disruptive, aggressive, or antisocial behavior.[26]

My own clinical impression is that the neuroleptic drugs do sometimes prevent the expression of violent impulses, along with all other feelings and aspirations; but the cost can be prohibitively high in terms of emotional flattening, as well as permanent brain dysfunction and damage. These drugs can also impair judgment, cause anguish (dysphoria), produce an inner distress and hyperactivity (akathisia), and result in emotional suffering during withdrawal—all of which can increase the likelihood of irritability, hostility, and aggression.[27] Once these medications are given to dampen violent impulses, it can become impossible to withdraw the patients, while they can go on to develop permanent drug-induced neurological disorders, such as tardive dyskinesia.

Since psychiatrists have no objective or proven standards for predicting violence, they end up drugging patients in response to their own fears and subjective impressions. They are not equipped to do anything else.*

Meanwhile, the widespread use of these drugs in society has not reduced violence. There's no need to fear that opposition to the use of drugs will rob society of a necessary weapon against violence.

Medications for Inner-City Violence

Despite the false hopes raised by some politically motivated biopsychiatrists, nearly all other pharmacology experts agree that medication has no use in most cases of physical aggression related to inner-city life, such as homicide

---

*As we saw in Chapter 2, the American Psychiatric Association took the position in the *Tarasoff* case that psychiatrists have no specific ability to predict and to prevent violence.

committed during turf disputes, robberies, drug dealing, rape, personal confrontations, or domestic conflicts. Psychiatric drugs are rarely recommended or prescribed for these perpetrators.[28]

Meanwhile, the public's hope that drugs might reduce the danger from "crazed killers" is also unrealistic. Only relatively docile patients will return regularly to clinics to take brain-disabling medications that frequently produce hazardous and disfiguring side effects.[29] Extremely dangerous perpetrators usually require incarceration for the protection of society. Furthermore, serious civil-liberty issues are raised by forcibly substituting brain-disabling drugs for imprisonment.

That drugs have no use in controlling inner-city violence does not mean that psychiatry won't use them in that way. As we have seen with the widespread drugging of children with Ritalin, the psychiatric use of drugs has never been based on science, ethics, or common sense.

Can Private Foundations Be Monitored?

The government's promotion of violence initiative research, including the NRC "blueprint," will continue to encourage private foundations to fund otherwise questionable studies. In addition to Felton Earls's large-scale Chicago project (Chapter 2), which receives funding from both the MacArthur Foundation and the federal government, two other studies illustrate the need to monitor social control research financed by private foundations.

John Mann at the Western Psychiatric Institute in Pittsburgh is receiving nearly $1 million per year from NIMH for suicide studies, including correlations with serotonin metabolites obtained from spinal taps of suicide-prone patients. Meanwhile, under the heading "Biological Markers of Risk," the MacArthur Foundation announced that it is joining in an exchange of information to tap Mann's data for "biological information we can relate to violence toward others."[30] As a part of this, Mann has agreed to include measures the foundation is developing to "assess violence toward others." Because the MacArthur Foundation, rather than the government, is obtaining these data, this violent-perpetrator research will probably not be listed as such in NIMH funding summaries.

Starting in 1991, the Lowenstein Foundation has funded a study by Gail Wasserman, a psychologist in the department of psychiatry at Columbia University. It involves the younger brothers of male offenders in Manhattan and the Bronx, and it aims at identifying "early predictors of anti-social behavior."[31] According to an interview with Wasserman, the group is 50 percent black and 50 percent Hispanic. The study includes

EEGs, blood work, and neurological testing. Spinal taps and brain scans were funded but not performed, according to Wasserman, who decided they might be too intrusive for children.

Many ethical issues seem apparent, including the labeling of innocent children as high risk, the civil liberties and privacy issues raised by the police providing access to the names of younger brothers of offenders for research purposes, informed consent, and the use of frightening and intrusive biomedical studies. According to a New York City Department of Probation memorandum, some of the police officers involved in the Columbia University study were "opposed to identifying ethnicity" as required by the study.

High-Tech Child Abuse

As a result of the efforts of the psycho-pharmaceutical complex, including the drug companies and the federal mental health establishment, many millions of children will be psychiatrically diagnosed and medicated in the future. Prozac, with its stimulant qualities, will probably prove itself able to space out and suppress children in much the same fashion as Ritalin. We fear it will soon rival Ritalin as a widely used agent for the biomedical suppression of children, especially older ones. This is only possible in a pedist society—one that blames its children and ignores the real causes of their upset.

Government studies that promote the biomedical diagnosis and medicating of children for behavior control should be canceled, and parents should refuse to allow their children to participate in them. The government should, instead, fund studies aimed at detecting potential harmful effects in the children already subjected to these interventions. We believe that nothing less than this is ethical.

Most children labeled DBD, including ADHD, are in fact suffering from various kinds of stress inflicted in the settings to which they react so negatively—the home and school. That's why these youngsters often do much better in improved environments, such as a smaller classroom or an overnight summer camp. When mental health professionals subject these children to medical diagnoses and physical interventions in the name of research or treatment, they are victimizing and abusing them. NIMH's medical experiments on children with "behavior disorders" should be considered high-tech child abuse.

Instead of giving psychiatric diagnoses or drugs to our children, let's frankly admit that we are raising a generation of young people who are inadequately cared for, traumatized, or rejected by their families, schools, and society. We should recognize that they are suffering from conflict and stress due largely to the adult world around them. Then their overall situation can be analyzed and approached in terms of child advocacy and conflict resolution. As adults, it is time for us to retake responsibility for all our children throughout society.

6

The First Violence Initiative
Psychosurgery for Social Control

A major difficulty was that psychosurgery, which mutilated irrevocably a part of the brain, was final. Not a dispensable part, such as the appendix, is removed, but an area essential to the human being—to his personality—is forever destroyed.

> —Franz Alexander and Sheldon Selesnick,
> *The History of Psychiatry* (1966)

As a matter of fact, lobotomized patients seldom come into conflict with the law precisely because they lack the imagination to think up new deviltries and the energy to perpetrate them. What the investigator misses most in the highly intelligent individuals is the ability to introspect, to speculate, to philosophize, especially in regard to self. Maybe it was the abnormal development of these intellectual-emotional exercises that got the patient into trouble originally.

> —Walter Freeman (1959)

There is a new [sic] medical procedure which is humane, safe and permanent, one which will eliminate violent criminals from our society, reduce our prison population by 10 to 15 percent and provide for the early release of all individuals. . . . This procedure is lobotomy.

> —Former Colorado Republican State Representative,
> Dale Erickson (1989)

LOBOTOMY AND OTHER FORMS OF PSYCHOSURGERY FOR VIOLENT CRIMINALS? Lobotomy for participants in urban riots and even for African-American leaders of inner-city uprisings? Harvard professors hooking up violent patients to remote-control devices to study and stimulate their brains, and ultimately to coagulate them with hot electrodes? When I first brought these plans and programs to light in the early 1970s, many people were understandably skeptical. Without knowing the facts, the descriptions might sound farfetched and inflammatory. I too found it hard to believe what I was discovering, until I came face-to-face with Thomas R., one of the tragic victims of this first violence initiative.

Discovering the Second Wave of Psychosurgery

In 1971 I discovered that psychiatrists and neurosurgeons were planning and implementing a worldwide revival of lobotomy and other forms of psychosurgery.[1] At the time I was not an activist, but I was aware that no one had publicly opposed the first round of lobotomies in the 1940s and 1950s. I decided to take a stand. That decision led me to form the Center for the Study of Psychiatry and eventually evolved into two decades of psychiatric reform activities.

My medical background convinced me that improving the techniques of psychiatric surgery—for example, by replacing the scalpel with hot electrodes—would not make the interventions any less damaging. Without harming the brain, there could be no "therapeutic" effect. The surgery must destroy enough function to flatten the patient's emotions, and there is no way to accomplish that without creating even more widespread mental devastation, including the relative loss of essential human qualities such as creativity, spontaneity, personal responsibility, self-insight, social sensitivity and awareness, and judgment. Research and my personal experiences would confirm this initial impression.[2]

Psychosurgery, Individual Vulnerability, and Public Health

Shortly after beginning my opposition to psychosurgery, I came under attack in the national media from an unexpected source, three Harvard professors—psychiatrist Frank Ervin and neurosurgeons Vernon Mark and William Sweet. Sweet was director of neurosurgery at perhaps the most respected hospital in the world, Massachusetts General. Mark was the head of the department of neurosurgery at Boston City Hospital.

As the controversy heated up, a physician who asked for anonymity directed me to published remarks made by the three doctors concerning the use of brain surgery to suppress black urban rioters. Soon after, in 1973, I received a brown envelope from an unidentified source in the Department of Justice (DOJ). It contained an in-house memo documenting that Mark and Ervin were receiving funds from the National Institute of Mental Health (NIMH) for experiments in psychosurgery for violence control and that Ervin had a related grant from the DOJ. Sweet was involved as a supporter, co-author, and a member of the private foundation that funneled the government funds to Mark and Ervin.

In a 1967 letter entitled "Role of Brain Disease in Riots and Urban Violence" in the *Journal of the American Medical Association* (*JAMA*), Mark, Sweet, and Ervin, much like current violence initiative advocates, focused on individual vulnerability rather than upon larger social, economic, or political factors. They asked, "If slum conditions alone determined and initiated riots, why are the vast majority of slum dwellers able to resist the temptations of unrestrained violence? Is there something peculiar about the violent slum dweller that differentiates him from his peaceful neighbor?"

Mark, Sweet, and Ervin went on to suggest that this "peculiarity" was "brain dysfunction." They called for large-scale studies of the inner city to "pinpoint, diagnose, and treat those people with low violence thresholds before they contribute to further tragedies." In a supportive *Medical News* report a few weeks later, the *JAMA* lauded Mark and Ervin's psychosurgery as a "public health" measure, a theme that would be repeated by doctors themselves.

In a 1969 book chapter, Sweet, Mark, and Ervin stated:

> In summary, we have presented evidence that we physicians can perhaps make a contribution of as yet indeterminate magnitude to the problem of violence in terms of (1) looking for cerebral disease and (2) conceivably treating it by carrying out appropriate focal cerebral destruction or stimulation. This may prove fruitful even in those criminally assaultive persons who do not have identifiable focal disease.

That is, their psychosurgical approach might work in the absence of any demonstrable physical problem in the brain.[3]

Mark and Ervin must have felt they were on a heroic, Nobel Prize–winning endeavor—providing a solution to worldwide mayhem, and especially to America's urban uprisings. In 1968, a year in which they were aggressively experimenting on patients, they wrote in *Psychiatric Opinion* that "brain dysfunction" was "equally important" to "poverty, unemployment and substandard housing" as a cause of urban violence. They estimated that tens of millions of Americans might be violence-prone as a result of brain damage. They continued to voice these claims in their 1970 book *Violence and the Brain.*

In testimony on civil disorders before a New York State legislative committee in 1968, according to *The New York Times*, William Sweet said that mass "violence might be touched off by leaders suffering from temporal seizures of the brain."[4] Sweet made a pitch for the electrical stimulation of surgically implanted electrodes as a method of calming violent people. In early 1973, he declared, "The proponents of urban disorders seem to be the people who are most likely to suffer from organic brain diseases."[5]

Mark, Ervin, and Sweet had their greatest PR coup when their work made the cover of *Life* on June 21, 1968. Albert Rosenfeld of *Life* observed, "The psychobiology approach, new as it is, is gaining adherents so fast that it might almost be called a movement." *Life* seemed to endorse their efforts toward biomedical social control:

> In a slum neighborhood, everyone may live under the same frustrating set of pressures and tensions, but only a small minority will engage in rioting, and even among the rioters only a handful will actually burn down a building or assault another person. Thus psychobiology proceeds on the premise that violent acts are carried out by violent individuals, even if the individuals are part of a mob.

The article gave a big spread to Mark and Ervin's psychosurgery for violence.

The Fate of Thomas R.

In their book *Violence and the Brain* and elsewhere, Mark and Ervin described Thomas R.[6] as a young white man largely saved from epilepsy and completely saved from violence by psychosurgery. They mention no serious side effects.[7] The patient's mother, Mrs. G., read my criticism of Mark and Ervin in the *Boston Globe* and realized for the first time what had been done to her son. She wrote to me that in reality he had been reduced almost to a "vegetable."

From October 21, 1966, until June 30, 1967, Thomas's brain had been implanted with two dozen electrodes—and been subjected to multiple stimulations, followed by coagulations—the actual melting of brain tissue by means of heating the electrodes. A dozen electrodes were contained in each of two large sheaths. The bundles of electrodes were inserted in the back of Thomas's head, one bundle on each side, and then run the length of his brain to rest in the amygdala, a nerve center in the temporal lobe lying toward the front of the skull. Literally, his brain was skewered from front to back on both sides, and left in this condition for many months. The tips of the electrodes could be used to record electrical activity or to destroy surrounding brain cells.

To add to the Brave New World quality of the experiments, Thomas was outfitted with a remote-control "stimo-receiver" that allowed his doctors to record from his brain and to stimulate it electrically by remote control, without his awareness.[8]

Delgado's Grand Scheme for "Physical Control of the Brain"

The stimo-receiver had been devised by Jose M. R. Delgado, a Spanish neu-rosurgeon who was a visiting professor at Yale. In 1969, the same year he was helping set up the experiments on Thomas, Delgado authored *Physical Control of the Brain—Toward a Psychocivilized Society,* calling for a billion-dollar NASA-like program for education, research, and experimentation in biomedical social control. He advocated propagandizing schoolchildren to accept psychiatric-neurosurgical technology as a panacea for human anguish and conflict.[9]

After Thomas was operated on at Massachusetts General Hospital, the psychosurgery project moved to Boston City Hospital, where Mark contin-ued to operate on patients with Ervin and Delgado's active collaboration, and with Sweet's repeated endorsement and co-authorship of journal articles.

With the Electrodes Hardly Cooled

When the *Medical News* story came out in the *JAMA*[10] of September 25, 1967, readers were told that the "electrolesions" had been placed seven months earlier and that Thomas was subsequently free of violence. Not only had the patient been incapacitated by the surgery, it was too early to evaluate or predict the outcome of the surgery. The brain-damaging effects of psy-chosurgery mature over months and years, potentially leading to dementia later on.

The electrodes, in fact, had been removed on June 30, and Thomas had been discharged from Massachusetts General Hospital on August 21, ap-proximately one month before publication of the *JAMA* report. He had re-turned home to his family in Los Angeles in a confused and frightened state, and was unable to take care of himself. In less than a month after the *JAMA* report, he would be picked up by the police in a confused and helpless state and taken to a psychiatric ward—the beginning of a series of chronic hospi-talizations that continue to this day.[11]

Meeting Thomas and His Mother

When I met Thomas—approximately five years after the surgery—he was a chronic mental patient on a brief home visit for the weekend with his mother, Mrs. G. Thomas. He was lying in bed in a darkened room with his head covered with newspapers. In broken, fragmented sentences, he ex-plained that he had been experimented on by brain surgeons who had raised his IQ to a new high for human beings—"two or three hundred," he said—in order to hook him up with computers to utilize him in international espionage. But while he boasted, he was speaking from beneath the newspapers, explaining, "I've got to cover my head because they're still trying to get me." He said all this in the flat, expressionless manner of psychosurgery victims. He could speak only a few words at a time and they were difficult to follow. He had only enough energy for a few minutes of talk.

Afterward, I sat with Mrs. G. over tea in the back yard of her home. She wept as she explained how her son had lost everything as a result of the surgery: his employment, his wife, his children, his freedom, and his mind.

She had grown concerned when she first heard about the surgery while talking with her son by telephone, and had called Vernon Mark begging for an explanation. She showed me the response—a telegram sent from Mark's project on October 28, 1966, stating her son was "recovering well from minor surgical operation." The minor surgery included the implantation of the two dozen electrodes and the first of a series of lesions in his brain.

After meeting Mrs. G. and her son Thomas, I began obtaining his hospital records and started to reconstruct, in detail, what had happened to him. With his mother's encouragement, I then began publicizing what had really happened to Mark and Ervin's famous cure. I wrote a report through the Center for the Study of Psychiatry[12] and held press conferences, including one that stirred up tumultuous controversy at the annual meeting of the American Psychiatric Association in Hawaii in May 1973.*

In November of the same year, the *JAMA* published a letter by me dealing with their coverage of the psychosurgery issue, including a brief description of Thomas's actual fate. I also began the process of finding an attorney to evaluate Thomas's malpractice claims against Mark and Ervin.

Trying to Tell a Bizarre Story

As dismayed and saddened as I was on discovering Thomas's condition, I was in some ways equally distressed by what I then found in his medical records. On November 20, 1967—before a series of publications by Mark and Ervin boasting about his cure—Thomas had been brought to an emergency room at a V.A. hospital in California after an angry outburst at home.† His mother had called the police because he was uncontrollably violent at

---

*While I was attending a psychosurgery seminar put on by its advocates at the Hawaii meeting, I was verbally attacked and threatened by several of the pro-psychosurgery psychiatrists and neurosurgeons, in front of numerous colleagues. I sued one of the perpetrators, Leo Alexander, for libel and slander, and received a $30,000 out-of-court settlement. In addition to his public remarks, Alexander had written letters and articles attacking me. It was a great deal of money to me at that time, especially since I'd already spent all my resources on the anti-psychosurgery campaign.

†He would be hospitalized at the V.A. for seven months. The publications, with Mark as the senior author, can be found in the bibliography.

home, turning over a bed in a rage. She had never known him to be this way prior to the surgery.

Thomas tried to tell the admitting physicians his incredible story. Perhaps failing to believe him, they labeled him "paranoid schizophrenic." As I read the doctor's write-up, I could not blame the doctor for thinking Thomas was lost in a science fiction delusion:

> chief complaint of paralysis from the waist down. Patient stated that the origin of the paralysis was because [doctors from] Massachusetts General Hospital were controlling him by creating lesions in his brain by microwave and that they had placed electrodes in his brain tissue some time before. Stated that they can control him, control his moods, and control his actions, they can turn him up or turn him down.

Was Thomas inherently "crazy," or had the doctors driven him insane by stimulating and melting his brain, including remote-control experiments? We don't have to speculate. In a paper delivered at a Bar Harbor, Maine, conference in 1971, Mark, Ervin, and Sweet described Thomas's response after the second psychosurgical lesion was made in his brain. Thomas required antipsychotic medication because he developed "delusions (of remote brain stimulation)." Given the stimo-receiver experiments, the use of the word "delusions" in this context is deeply misleading.

On the first V.A. admission, as noted, Thomas was talking about being "paralyzed" when he was seemingly normal physically. Where would such a bizarre idea come from? In a 1969 article by Ervin, Mark, and Oregon neurologist Janice Stevens, Thomas's reactions to various points of stimulation are listed on a diagram, including one area that made him feel "everything leaving, paralyzed." During another stimulation he said, "Somebody else is controlling me and moving my arms and legs (no movement visible)."

The hospital records confirm that Thomas's "delusions" developed in reaction to the placement of the lesions in his brain. In April 1967, for example, there are notes "demanded that we turn off the machine in his head" and "belief [*sic*] he is regularly stimulated and lesioned." In June, another note states he has feelings in his head "as if being lesioned."

Stevens, Mark, and Ervin describe Thomas's "psychotic" reaction to the surgery in another 1969 article subtitled "Long Latency, Long Lasting Psychological Changes." Very long-lasting! As I talked with Thomas's mother, Mrs. G., over the years, she has spontaneously reported on several occasions that "Thomas is still waiting for them to take out the electrodes."

"Murder!"

During the first few months and years after his surgery, Thomas continued telling doctors on the West Coast what had happened to him. One V.A. hospital record observes "his affect was flat"* and "he feels they control him by microwaves, put electrodes in his brain and are gradually killing his brain." While on the wards of another V.A. hospital, he wrote notes that he was being murdered by electrodes. He also got in trouble for scrawling "murder" on the day room wall. I found the handwritten notes lying loose in Thomas's records in the hospital record room and photocopied them before anyone knew his case was being investigated.[†]

In December 1972, a V.A. doctor wrote:

> Patient is delusional and violent. . . . Attacked his father physically today. Very assaultive to PCT [psychiatric aide] and decided we were trying to destroy him with microwaves.

The chart includes a heartbreaking handwritten appeal from Thomas to his ward physician:

> Doctor: The Mass General and Labs who have frequencies to my brain are taking my life by transmitting to me and killing all the useful cells in my brain to take my life.

During a severe emotional disturbance some years after surgery, Thomas was committed to a V.A. hospital. The commitment papers say:

> Claims he is a guinea pig of the government and goes wherever he is ordered by the 'Group.' He feels he is some sort of robot.

Thomas seemed to realize that he had been an experimental subject in a program funded by the government.

"Consenting" Under Brain Stimulation

Why would anyone consent to such bizarre experimental surgery? In *Psychiatric Opinion,* Mark and Ervin described how Thomas, under electrical stimulation of his brain, showed "bland acquiescence to the suggestion that the medial portion of his temporal lobe was to be destroyed. This sug-

---

Affect is emotion. Flattened emotions are typical of psychosurgical patients. It is the sought-after clinical effect.
[†]His mother, as his legal guardian, had authorized me to obtain his records.

gestion, under ordinary circumstances, would provoke wild, disordered thinking." Eight to ten hours after stimulation, "coincident with the disappearance of the detached hyper-relaxed feeling, he became wild and unmanageable and protested vigorously against any destructive lesions in his amygdala."

The scenario is confirmed in several articles: a frightened, helpless man is pushed into psychosurgery during stimulation of his brain. In *Violence and the Brain*, Mark and Ervin once again explain how and why Thomas went along with the making of "a destructive lesion" in his brain: "He agreed to this suggestion while he was relaxed from lateral stimulation of the amygdala." But when the stimulation wore off, "The idea of anyone's making a destructive lesion in his brain enraged him. He absolutely refused any further therapy, and it took many weeks of patient explanation before he accepted the idea."

It seems that Thomas had become addicted to the brain stimulation prior to the coagulations. One note in his medical record states, "On daily stimulation he is maintained in a euphoric state." Later on, he is temporarily discharged in a euphoric state. It is common for brain dysfunction and damage to produce euphoria—an unrealistic sense of well-being—as seen, for example, in an amphetamine or alcoholic "high."

Mixing Up Before and After

Eventually, Mark was forced by Thomas's mother to release his pre-surgery records to me. Despite references to outbursts of violent temper in Mark, Ervin, and Sweet's publications about him, the only known violent episodes involved marital disputes in which he allegedly threw objects at his wife without hitting or harming her. There was no other documented physical aggression, or any indication that he ever injured anyone. He had no police record and no prior psychiatric hospitalizations, until shortly before the planned surgery, when he panicked. He had been employed as an engineer, had made several patented inventions, and was considered very creative and inventive. Then a car accident and ongoing family problems upset him shortly before being sent to Mark and Ervin. The marital conflicts led to his wife suing him for divorce while he was hospitalized for the psychosurgery.

The surgery transformed a temporarily unemployed, brilliant young engineer with marital problems into a chronically unemployable, mentally incompetent, demented, and sporadically violent psychiatric inmate. It was as if the doctors had reversed their story, mixing up the before and the after.

Mark Defends Himself

In 1974 the *JAMA* gave the surgeon the opportunity for a lengthy letter of rebuttal to my charges. Without dealing with whether Thomas was violent after surgery—something that cannot be denied—Mark instead claimed ignorance, explaining that he was told Thomas was "free of rage attacks" by an unidentified physician who followed Thomas during 1971 and "most of 1972." But the V.A. hospital records document Thomas's anguish, anger, and violent outbursts beginning as early as the latter part of 1967. Furthermore, neurologist Ernst Rodin was told about Thomas's post-surgery psychosis and dilapidation when he visited Mark's Boston project. In an August 9, 1972, memo on the visit, Rodin wrote that Mark and Ervin also knew that they "figure prominently in [Thomas's] delusional system."[13]

"Terminal Man" Revisited

Prior to the anti-psychosurgery campaign, Mark and Ervin's work received much notice, none more dramatic than a fictionalized starring role in Michael Crichton's best-selling novel *Terminal Man*.* Crichton was a medical student at Harvard when he learned firsthand about Mark and Ervin's research, and the main character in his book, Harry Benson, bears a striking resemblance to Mark and Ervin's description of Thomas.

After the start of the anti-psychosurgery campaign, the Epilepsy Foundation of America and others appealed to Crichton to make a statement renouncing Mark and Ervin's theory that epilepsy can cause physical aggression. In December 1972, Crichton wrote a postscript to that effect for the Avon paperback edition, saying "I am persuaded that the understanding of the relationship between organic brain damage and violent behavior is not so clear as I thought at the time I wrote the book." Unhappily, the postscript is gone from recent reprintings.

Law-and-Order Psychiatry at NIMH

During a several-year period of investigation, I was able to unearth some of the political maneuvering that had led to Mark and Ervin's federal funding. In the 1970s, researchers almost always pursued funding through the competitive process of applying to one of the health institutes. Mark, Ervin, and Sweet used a political approach. After aggressive lobbying, Congress allocated $500,000 per year to NIMH specifically for Mark and Ervin's psychosurgery project.

---

*Crichton is also the author of the recent novel *Jurassic Park*.

The director of NIMH, Bert Brown, did not resist this end run around the established grant approval process. In support of the project, Brown told a congressional committee:

> I just want to add that this is another aspect or dimension of how important it is for us to work with the Department of Justice. We are dealing here with people who may someday blow and may attempt to kill you, the really aggressive person who is very dangerous.

Although identified as a political liberal, Brown had met in Colorado Springs with President Richard Nixon and Attorney General John Mitchell, as well as Nixon's assistants, H. R. Haldeman and John Ehrlichman. Their aim was to integrate NIMH with the newly developed Law Enforcement Assistance Administration (LEAA) of the Department of Justice. This led to the two grants that were coordinated between NIMH and LEAA. The NIMH grant, as already mentioned, went to Mark and Ervin for psychosurgery, while the LEAA award for $108,000 went to Ervin for genetic investigations of violence. The monies were dispersed through the Neuro-Research Foundation, a private nonprofit organization run by Sweet, Mark, and Ervin that used Sweet's home address.[14]

Mark and Ervin Lose Their Funding

As a result of the anti-psychosurgery campaign, all of Mark and Ervin's federal funding for psychosurgical experimentation was cut off. The LEAA ended the smaller $108,000 grant to Ervin and rejected another for more than $1 million that was pending.

As a long-delayed satisfaction to us, we learned this year that the Center's campaign had brought about a dramatic reversal in official government policy. A guideline entitled "Use of LEAA Funds for Psychosurgery and Medical Research" was signed by the LEAA administrator, Donald E. Santarelli, on June 19, 1974. The guideline declared that any future grant applications for psychosurgery would be denied. It further stipulated that all "medical research," unless risk-free, would be denied and referred instead to the Department of Health, Education, and Welfare (DHEW, now DHHS). It forbade states to use LEAA block grants to do psychosurgery or medical experimentation.

Thomas's Day in Court

On behalf of her mentally incompetent son, Mrs. G. brought a malpractice suit against Mark and Ervin that came to court in 1978; but the protracted trial was lost.[15] Mark and Ervin's colleagues testified on their behalf, some claiming that the surgery wasn't experimental! Because of my role in originating the legal action against Mark and Ervin, I did not appear as an expert witness and had no role in the trial.

Despite their victory in court, the publicity was too much for Mark and Ervin. Mark stopped doing the psychosurgical procedures and in 1980 told *JAMA* reporter E. R. Gonzalez that he didn't wish to resume them.

Meanwhile, Thomas never recovered from the surgery. He has been continuously medicated on Haldol, a powerful neuroleptic drug, and chronically hospitalized the majority of the time over the years. He leaves the hospital only to visit his mother. When he has headaches, according to his mother, he still says "the beam is aiming at my head." Most of the time he is quiet, and typical of many psychosurgery patients, "He does not volunteer any conversation whatsoever. He only responds to questions." Mrs. G. still has difficulty convincing doctors what was done to her son.

Thomas now suffers from tardive dyskinesia—a permanent, untreatable neurological disorder that involves abnormal movements of the body. It is caused by the neuroleptic drugs that Thomas has been taking since his psychosurgery. His official Veterans Administration medical chart describes him as also suffering from headaches. His primary diagnosis is "organic delusional disorder"—delusional thoughts caused by brain damage.[16]

More from Vernon Mark

A headline in the November 21, 1985, *Boston Globe* declared "Mass. Neurosurgeon Suggests Quarantine for AIDS Carriers." The story, written by Judy Foreman, explained how Vernon Mark advocated the use of a former leper colony on an island in Buzzard's Bay to quarantine AIDS carriers who behave "irresponsibly." He made his remarks at a conference he helped to organize along with a conservative organization called Morality in the Media. In 1986 Mark was chairman of the World Congress of Biological Psychiatry, and advocated another quarantine proposal—this time for criminals with brain dysfunction.[17]

As recently as 1989, the BBC did a story entitled "The Violent Mind" as a part of its series *The Mind*. It presented Mark's two-decade-old psychosurgery for violence in a positive light, as if it were a breakthrough.

Embarrassed by vocal opposition to him at Yale, Delgado returned to Spain in the early 1970s. William Sweet withdrew from the controversy. Frank Ervin's career became more complicated.

Violence Centers Throughout Urban America

In his 1973 State of the State message, California governor Ronald Reagan announced plans for the establishment of a biomedical facility, the Center for the Study of the Reduction of Violence.[18] Supported by state and federal funds, the first center was planned for the psychiatry department at UCLA, headed by Louis Jolyn "Jolly" West, a flamboyant psychiatrist known for his ability to hitch himself to hot topics.[19] An early draft of West's proposed UCLA center described using schools in Chicano and African-American neighborhoods to screen for possible genetic defects. It also mentioned the possibility of psychosurgery. The suggestion of psychosurgery for violence was especially menacing in California because Santa Monica neurosurgeon M. Hunter Brown was strongly advocating it.*

Meanwhile, Frank Ervin had left the collapsing Boston project and came to join West at UCLA. Ervin's arrival at this critical juncture alerted people to the center's potential dangers. Despite denials from psychiatrists West and Ervin, the discovery of references to genetics and psychosurgery in the original proposal proved politically fatal. Opposed by a coalition of West Coast reformers,[20] the planned string of federal violence centers never got off the ground.

Ervin continued to make headline-grabbing biopsychiatric claims. A 1977 article by Lois Timnick in *The Los Angeles Times,* "Chemical Found in Schizophrenics' Blood," credited Ervin and another UCLA researcher for locating an abnormal, toxic protein that might cause schizophrenia.[21] Ervin described himself as "high" on the controversial discovery, which of course failed to pan out. Drawing criticism on the East and then the West coasts of America, Ervin eventually left for McGill University in Canada, where he remains to this day doing research on monkeys.

Inspired by the current controversy, Ervin once again is speaking out as a proponent of biomedical screening for organic causes of violence. On a July 5, 1993, national television show, *Day One,* he advocated medical workups for anyone who appears in court more than twice for violent crimes.

Operating on Young Black Children

As far as we know, Mark and Ervin did not perform their psychosurgery experiments on any African-Americans. With more limited political aims, perhaps, another surgeon was operating on numerous black children.

---

*In an interview with Peter Schrag, 1978, Brown declared, "It is either this [psychosurgery] or a further escalation of violence and chaos in society that does not serve the best interests of the United States."

When I began researching the return of psychosurgery in the early 1970s, I quickly came upon the work of O. J. Andy, director of neurosurgery at the University of Mississippi—Ole Miss—in Jackson. He was publishing reports on multiple surgical interventions into the brains of children, age five to twelve, who were diagnosed as aggressive and hyperactive. Of his thirty to forty patients, he wrote me, most were children.[22]

Before the controversy hit the press, I phoned Andy, who told me he could not recall the race of *any* of his psychosurgery patients. Later I contacted a civil rights attorney in Mississippi who was able to determine that most of the children were housed in a segregated black institution for the developmentally disabled. The attorney got onto the wards, where the nurses told him with frustration that Andy had a completely free hand in picking children for psychosurgery.

In 1966 Andy described J.M., age nine, who was "hyperactive, aggressive, combative, explosive, destructive, sadistic." Over a three-year period Andy performed four separate mutilating operations involving at least six lesions with implanted electrodes. The youngster was at first said to be doing well. In a subsequent 1970 article, Andy again claims that J.M. was no longer so combative and negative. Then he adds, "Intellectually, however, the patient is deteriorating."

While Andy did not take an activist political position like Mark, Ervin, and Sweet, he did tell B. J. Mason, a reporter for *Ebony*, that black urban rioters "could have abnormal pathologic brains" and "should undergo tests with whatever capacity we have now." Following worldwide publicity about his operations during the anti-psychosurgery campaign, in 1973 a committee of his peers at the university declared his research experimental, and when Andy did not establish appropriate experimental protocols, he was prohibited from operating. Andy himself declared in 1980 that he had been forced to stop operating due to "sociological pressures" in his home community.[23]

The Kaimowitz Trial

In 1972 the state of Michigan and the Lafayette Clinic of Wayne State University were planning to begin an experimental psychosurgery program for the control of violence using "voluntary" inmates of the state hospital system. Gabe Kaimowitz,* at the time a Michigan Legal Services lawyer, heard about the upcoming medical event, and intervened in the court on be-

---

*Kaimowitz, who now practices in Florida, is one of those special attorneys with a deep devotion to human rights.

half of "John Doe" and two dozen other state psychiatric inmates scheduled for eventual enrollment in the experimental program.[24]

The three-judge panel convened for the Kaimowitz case quickly decided that the proposed patient was being held unconstitutionally and further that he was no longer a danger to himself or others. They released him from the hospital with his brain intact.

Although the patient had been discharged and no longer wished surgery, the judges decided to hear the case in principle. They were concerned that the state and the university might carry out similar projects in the future.

Comparing Blacks to Bulls

Ernst Rodin was the chief neurologist and the moving force behind the Lafayette Clinic's psychosurgery project. In 1973, Rodin wrote a lengthy speech describing psychosurgery and castration as a fitting treatment for some of the violent behavior displayed in the riots that had raged in his city of Detroit. Rodin voiced doubts about doing psychosurgery without sterilization, because with surgery alone "the now hopefully more placid dullard can inseminate other equally dull young females to produce further dull and aggressive offspring."

Rodin argued that children of limited intelligence tend to become violent when they are treated as equals. He wanted them brought up in an "authoritarian life style," and declared that many of them, like aggressive bulls, should be turned into docile oxen by means of castration. In the neurologist's own words, it was time to "get down to cold-blooded medical research dealing with individuals rather than masses."

The Verdict

Kaimowitz invited me to testify as his medical expert, and during two days on the stand, I gave a history of state mental hospitals and psychosurgery. I wanted the three judges to understand that state mental hospitals are similar to Nazi concentration camps in how they suppress and humiliate their involuntary inmates; and I wanted to suggest the applicability of the Nuremberg Code.

The Nuremberg Code was written into the final opinion of the judges at the first War Crimes Tribunals in postwar Germany. It consists of ten principles for "permissible medical experiments." The first principle states in part that the human subject "should be so situated as to be able to exercise free power of choice, without the intervention of any element of force, fraud, deceit, duress, over-reaching, or other ulterior form of constraint or coercion."[25]

The Nuremberg Code meant that Jewish inmates of concentration camps were not actually voluntary when they seemingly agreed to participate in medical experiments, such as being frozen in ice water. If they did acquiesce to these experiments, their consent was coerced by fear of other worse alternatives, such as torture or death in the gas chambers.

After hearing witnesses representing a broad spectrum of views, the three judges agreed with the substance of my testimony, including the devastating effects of the most modern psychosurgery.* Their official opinion cited the Nuremberg Code and used it as one reason for prohibiting consent to psychosurgery in the state mental hospitals of Michigan. The judges found that "involuntarily confined patients cannot reason as equals with doctors and administrators over whether they should undergo psychosurgery." They declared that under First Amendment freedoms the "government has no power or right to control men's minds, thoughts, and expressions. If the First Amendment protects the freedom to express ideas, it necessarily follows that it must protect the freedom to generate ideas."

The opinion was never appealed and stands to this day. It continues to inhibit the performance of psychosurgery throughout the country, especially in state mental hospitals and prisons.

The Psychosurgery Commission

Beginning with the writing of a bill that was introduced into Congress by Louis Stokes in March 1973, I worked on legislation with the Congressional Black Caucus to prohibit all federal funding of psychosurgery, including at NIMH and in V.A. hospitals where it was also being performed. When passage of the bill proved impossible, I cooperated with Senator J. Glenn Beall, Jr., a Maryland Republican, on an amendment calling for a special committee to investigate psychosurgery under the National Commission for the Protection of Human Subjects of Biomedical and Behavioral Research. When the amendment became law, the special committee became known as "the psychosurgery commission."

In retrospect, I was politically naive to hope for much from the psychosurgery commission. I had little understanding of how the regulatory process routinely becomes co-opted by the regulated.[26] Yet a kind of miracle unfolded. In 1976 the commission gave tentative approval to the surgery, but called it "experimental" and therefore unsuitable for routine clinical use. Psychosurgery advocates wanted to avoid the label "experimental," with its special requirements for institutional oversight and informed consent. The

---

*The technique of psychosurgery has not changed since the Kaimowitz case.

commission suggested that no further psychosurgery should take place until a national system of review boards was established. As a part of that process, the committee planned to hold a series of public meetings around the country.

The conditional approval given to psychosurgery drew an avalanche of criticism from patient rights advocates and psychiatric survivors. Carrying signs like "Lobotomy Is a Crime Against Humanity," the survivors—including Jenny Miller, Wade Hudson, and Leonard Frank—picketed the psychosurgery committee's attempt to hold a public meeting in San Francisco in 1976. With additional criticism from organizations such as the American Civil Liberties Union and the National Organization for Women, the psychosurgery commission never finished its work.[27]

The psychosurgeons were left facing a federal recommendation for a moratorium until adequate safeguards could be set up, but the official safeguards never materialized. While the recommendations had no legal force, they created a moral and political limbo for psychosurgery, a limbo in which it remains to this very day.

One Indomitable Psychosurgeon

With one notable exception, the big-name psychosurgeons gave up performing psychosurgery—or at least said they did. The exception was H. T. Ballantine, who remained active at the Massachusetts General Hospital. The federal psychosurgery commission set up a research project at the Massachusetts Institute of Technology (MIT) to study Ballantine's patients.[28] At first the project was very cozy with Ballantine and seemed bent on doing everything it could to make him look good; but then there was a falling out and Ballantine refused to send them any more patients. Despite optimistic conclusions by the authors of the MIT study, their clinical descriptions of the patients show that many suffered from lobotomy effects.[29]

In subsequent years, MIT made progress reports to NIMH which we obtained through the Freedom of Information Act. The reports show that a large percentage of Ballantine's post-surgery patients and their families—50 out of 164—refused to have anything further to do with the research project. They would not even answer telephone calls or letters from the researchers. Since the patients and their families had originally agreed to the follow-ups, their utter rejection of all entreaties from the researchers sounds suspiciously like fear and resentment, or worse, incapacity. An additional fifteen more patients disappeared without leaving any forwarding address. Another 12 percent of the patients, about whom information was available, had committed suicide.

I have independently reviewed the records and conducted interviews of five of Ballantine's patients, four of them women, and all were mentally disabled by the treatment. One suffered from gross dementia that rendered her unable to communicate or to care for herself. These dreadful outcomes are not mentioned in positive reviews of the entire patient group published by Ballantine and his colleagues.

One of the women was sent to Ballantine by a psychiatrist at Duke University in North Carolina who was prescribing her an extreme amount of addictive drugs and having sex with her. He seemingly wanted to shut her up when she threatened to blow the whistle on him. I have no reason to believe that Ballantine knew anything about the motives of the referring physician or the fact that the physician was sexually abusing the patient; but the story highlights the potential abuse of such devastating interventions.

After my deposition, the Duke University psychiatrist who referred the patient to Ballantine settled the woman's malpractice case against him for a large sum of money. The case involved many abuses, of which the referral to Ballantine for psychosurgery was but one example.

In the meantime, Ballantine has retired, leaving psychosurgery without a vocal American leader. In 1985 Ballantine himself summed up the impact of the anti-psychosurgery campaign:

> So great was the political pressure that most psychiatrists and neurosurgeons were reluctant to become involved. Investigators and clinicians all over the world were exposed to ridicule, scorn, and harassment. [p. 2535]

Some States Begin Regulating Psychosurgery

As a result of lobbying efforts by the Network Against Psychiatric Assault (NAPA) and other reform groups, including many psychiatric survivors, the state of California passed legislation in 1974 requiring informed consent and independent medical opinions before psychosurgery could be performed. It also required the reporting of all psychosurgery to the Department of Mental Hygiene. The requirements proved too stringent for the surgeons, and no psychosurgery has been reported in the state since that time.

However, one of the country's most active psychosurgeons, M. Hunter Brown, was charged in 1978 with performing psychosurgery without complying with the California statute. Although he had performed his standard series of multiple psychosurgical coagulations in varied parts of a patient's brain, Brown defended himself by claiming that he was operating for epilepsy. Brown was found innocent of the charges but then stopped performing the operations.[30]

With the support of neurologist Robert Grimm in Portland, even tighter legislation was passed in Oregon, and again the surgeons stopped operating. Nonetheless psychosurgery is still being done in the United States, and although the numbers are probably small, no exact figures are available.

At This Moment—Yet Another Comeback for Psychosurgery

The psychosurgeons are once again testing the waters to revive their flagging image and their relatively infrequent operations. In their 1990 book *Madness in the Streets,* Rael Jean Isaac and Virginia C. Armat devote three consecutive chapters to what they describe as Breggin's domino approach to toppling biopsychiatry, starting with psychosurgery and then proceeding to electroshock and finally to psychiatric drugs.* In a chapter favorable to a return of psychosurgery, they make clear how little stands between the psychosurgeons and the full-scale resumption of their operations:

> Breggin's Luddite boast to us was clearly not an idle one. With Ballantine's retirement, said Breggin: "I think there is no really active psychosurgeon in the United States. I'm sure there are some people doing it but they won't publish because they don't want me to see their publications. They don't want Peter Breggin finding out they're doing it." And indeed one neurosurgeon refused to discuss the operations he had performed with us on the grounds that "it is not professionally safe."

The Resurrection of Psychosurgery for the Treatment of Violence

Joann Ellison Rodgers is the director of media relations for the Johns Hopkins Medical Institutions in Baltimore and is the author of another book, geared to lay audiences, that attempts to refurbish the public image of psychosurgery—*Psychosurgery: Damaging the Brain to Save the Mind* (1992). The public views Johns Hopkins as one of the outstanding medical centers in the country, but its department of psychiatry is among the most rigidly biological.[31]

Rodgers begins a chapter entitled "The Law-and-Order Lobby" by quoting former Colorado state representative Dale Erickson's 1989 remarks in favor of lobotomizing criminals. While cautious about Erickson's extremism, she observes that "some surgeons and psychiatrists, however, believe

---

*It is true that historically my active opposition to biological psychiatry has focused in order on psychosurgery, electroshock, and drugs, although I remain concerned with all of them.

psychosurgery for violent behavior benefits patients at least as much as society, and possibly more." Rodgers quotes California surgeon Oscar Sugar as favoring psychosurgery for violent, incurable "sociopaths."

Somewhat surprisingly, Rodgers praises some successes of the antipsychosurgery campaign. She believes that it

> stopped practices that mutilated the brains of an estimated forty to fifty thousand Americans. It limited the potentially abusive power of psychiatrists and surgeons to experiment on hospital and prison inmates, and helped to create a strong medical consumer movement and protection for mental patients.

But Rodgers laments that the "backlash drove rational debate and research on psychosurgery underground." In the tradition of Mark, Ervin, and Sweet, she describes the case of a patient whose epilepsy allegedly caused him to be violent.

According to Rodgers, leaders in psychiatry and neurosurgery at Johns Hopkins want to revive psychiatric brain surgery. The chief of neurosurgery, Donlin Long, and the chief of psychiatry, Paul McHugh, both "support preliminary plans to convene and host a small, international symposium" on psychosurgery. Long, she says, recognizes the political liability of developing a psychosurgery program, but he is nonetheless working on a "blueprint" for it at Hopkins.

More Psychosurgery at Harvard

Psychiatrists at Harvard Medical School and the Massachusetts General Hospital are more openly promoting psychosurgery, as for example in a 1991 article written by Michael Jenike that also includes Ballantine among the authors.[32] In the article, the review of Ballantine's patients is based on questionnaires filled out and sent in by mail from the surgically brain-damaged patients themselves who were not clinically evaluated by anyone, let alone by objective outside parties. Out of thirty-three patients, four had died by suicide, two had died from other causes, and nine would not participate in the follow-up or were missing. Fifteen, or nearly 50 percent, of the group could be suffering from bad outcomes directly related to the surgery.

Overall, psychosurgery is again making a comeback from North America to northern Europe and Australia.[33] The summer 1990 issue of the APA's *Journal of Neuropsychiatry and Clinical Neurosciences* focused on psychosurgery in America and Great Britain, with a supporting editorial by psychiatrists Stuart Yudofsky and Fred Ovsiew. The editorial concludes that if "the public can overcome outdated attitudinal barriers, we believe this realm may, in the future, offer a treasure trove of therapeutic opportunities for our patients."

The American Psychiatric Association Supports Lobotomy

While discussing plans for reviving psychosurgery at Johns Hopkins, Rodgers quotes supportive advice from the medical director of the American Psychiatric Association, Melvin Sabshin:

> "From a political standpoint," Sabshin says of Long's interest and concerns, "it's true that if you stick your head up out of the trench, you may get shot down. But as anyone familiar with trench warfare knows, you can use mirrors to see out of the trench, defend yourself, and take proper aim at a target. . . . It's time to have that meeting [at Hopkins on psychosurgery] and to think through related policies.

Psychosurgery at NIMH?

As chief of the Child Psychiatry Branch at NIMH, Judith Rapoport is one of the most powerful psychiatrists in the country. In her mass-market book *The Boy Who Wouldn't Stop Washing* (1989), Rapoport speaks of the "success" of earlier lobotomy operations. She describes a young man "cured" of mental illness by a self-inflicted gunshot to the head that destroyed a portion of his frontal lobes. This is a cure the National Rifle Association would love.

Appealing directly to the public in an interview in the March 13, 1989, issue of *People* magazine, Rapoport commented on another lobotomy case in a patient with obsessive-compulsive disorder (OCD):

> It cured his OCD, but unfortunately, because the surgery was not as sophisticated 20 years ago as it is now, he suffered personality changes and began pinching young women and urinating in the street.

It's no safer to mutilate brain tissue today than twenty years ago. Nor is it reassuring to hear Rapoport claim that the surgery would be considered only after "every other possible treatment had failed." With so many failures in psychiatry, there is no limit to the potential number of candidates.

Why is such a high-ranking NIMH official going out of her way to support psychosurgery?* We fear that Rapoport is testing the waters for a resurgence of psychosurgery.

What keeps advocates of psychosurgery from moving ahead full throttle? Is it their own scientific caution? Is it ethical concerns? In *Psychosurgery,* Rodgers quotes Donlin Long, the Johns Hopkins director of neurosurgery:

> "You'd also need an institutional commitment to absolutely pristine science and the guts to tell the Peter Breggins of the world to stuff it," he added, referring to psychiatrist Peter Breggin's lifelong battle to ban psychiatric surgery.

---

*As reported in the July 1989 *Clinical Psychiatry News,* Rapoport also discussed psychosurgery at an annual meeting of the American Psychiatric Association.

7

Condemned by Science
The Role of Psychiatry in the Holocaust

The path to grave horror begins with minor transgressions.

—Daniel Goleman (1993)

Criticism should not be focused on Nazi Germany alone but extend beyond to include physicians in democratic countries, as well. Physicians outside Germany before the war, in the United States in particular, were well aware of the evolving racist thrust of the health care system. They chose to remain silent.

—William E. Seidelman (1992)

Since the Third Reich, paranoia levels have run high when the state enters to screen a population for a genetic problem, especially when the population at risk coincides with racial and ethnic designations.

—Troy Duster, *Backdoor to Eugenics* (1990)

WHEN I FIRST BEGAN CRITICIZING BIOMEDICAL SOCIAL CONTROL IN THE early 1970s, the comparison to Nazi Germany frequently came up. I was aware that genetic and biological psychiatry had contributed to the Holocaust, but had no idea to what extent.

Over a period of twenty years, I gathered research and lectured on the subject, but until recently ran into enormous resistance when trying to publish anything about it.*[1]

---

*We recently visited the U.S. Holocaust Memorial Museum in Washington, D.C., with author Jeffrey Masson, an expert on psychiatry's role in the Third Reich, and we found that its exhibit did scant justice to the topic. We were informed by the director of the museum archive that it contained only one publication on the subject. As it turned out, it was my own article (1993b), which is the basis of this chapter. It was originally presented at a historical conference in Germany on medicine under the Nazis (Breggin, 1992h) and in that process was reviewed by historians of the period. I especially wish to thank Benno Müller-Hill, director of the Institute for Genetics in Cologne, Germany, for editing the various manifestations of this material.

A Jewish Soldier Discovers the Psychiatric Holocaust

I had limited knowledge of what had happened in Germany, when Robert Abrams heard me talking on the radio more than two decades ago and got in touch with me. For the first time since the end of the war he shared his story and displayed his photographs.

Abrams was a young officer in a U.S. Army public relations office in occupied Bavaria in July 1945, when he was approached by a German army physician who had recently returned from the front. The medical doctor was outraged to find that psychiatrists were killing mental patients in the state hospital near his home town of Kaufbeuren.

Abrams and a fellow soldier grabbed a Tommy gun and headed for Kaufbeuren. When they arrived and asked the children in the street for directions, they were told, "Oh, that's where they kill people."

The inmates, as Abrams's photographs showed, looked skeletal, with sunken faces like concentration camp victims. Most of the records of the mass murders at the hospital had been destroyed; but what remained showed a death rate of 25 percent during the past year. The patients were killed by means of medication poisoning and gradual starvation on "scientific diets." The victims included one hundred children.

The crematorium ovens had been burning right up to the moment that Abrams and his comrade arrived. The doctors and nurses admitted to burning 350 to 400 bodies during the first six months of 1945; but unlike the Holocaust extermination camps, which shut down as the American soldiers drew near, the hospital continued killing its inmates until forced to stop. Abrams showed me a picture of the gloomy staff forced to stand before the ovens for their grisly portrait.

None of the psychiatrists showed remorse. The doctor who led Abrams around the hospital was not a Nazi party member, the nurses belonged to a religious order, and they all believed that they had acted benevolently. The psychiatric director of the institution, however, may have anticipated feeling humiliated at the liberation of his hospital; he hanged himself on Abrams's arrival. That too was memorialized with a photograph.

Evidence for a Master Murder Plan

Records uncovered by Abrams brought to light some the earliest information on the systematic murder of mental patients that formally began before the Holocaust with the distribution of euthanasia forms in October 1939.[2] At no time was the program made legal, yet it was completely organized in a bureaucratic, efficient manner under the leadership of psychiatrist Werner Heyde.

Euthanasia forms were filled out on thousands of patients by hospital doctors throughout Germany and then sent to Berlin for the final life-and-death determination by a team of fifty psychiatrists, including ten professors of psychiatry. A total of 283,000 cases had been reviewed from all over Germany, with approximately 75,000 patients rated for "euthanasia" and exterminated. The deadly criteria were twofold: failing to respond to treatment and inability to work. Typically, the patients were given electroshock treatment and, if that failed, they were readied for the next, worst step.

The condemned patients were shipped to holding facilities and then to one of the six psychiatric extermination centers—Hartheim, Hadamar, Sonnenstein, Grafeneck, Brandenburg, and Bernburg.* In these facilities, some freestanding and some attached to mental hospitals, the first seventy thousand or more patients were killed, until public protests ended the organized euthanasia efforts.[3]

Unlike the subsequent mass enslavement and murder of the Jews, the killing of the mental patients drew heated criticism from the public and some religious leaders, and in August 1941 Hitler withdrew his approval. Acting without official sanction, doctors continued the killings on their own in local mental hospitals, destroying another 70,000 to 100,000 inmates.[4]

New patients continued to be admitted, sometimes specifically for extermination. By the end of the war, some of Germany's large psychiatric facilities had been emptied. Müller-Hill (1991b) estimates that about 80 percent of those who survived the formal euthanasia program ended up dying of "hunger, infections, or mistreatment in the psychiatric institutions."[†] The murder rate actually peaked in the last year of the war.

Private and religious institutions were even more zealously murderous than public ones. In occupied France, without an official order, psychiatrists killed an estimated 40,000 of their patients.

The Extermination of Children

Children are even more vulnerable than adults to any form of coerced intervention and that concern motivates and informs much of this book. Biomedical abuses like the violence initiative are likely to make children their first targets. In Nazi Germany, the children's "euthanasia" program preceded the one for adults and was more officially recognized. It officially

---

*The suppression of information has been so complete that these names, deserving of notoriety, are almost unknown to the general public.

†Eventually, 250,000 to 300,000 patients were murdered throughout Europe by a variety of means, including shooting (*Trials of War Criminals*, 1949, p. 66). There is no record of Hitler's views on the unofficial continuation of the euthanasia program within German hospitals and throughout Europe.

began on August 19, 1939, with an ordinance of the Ministry of the Interior requiring physicians and midwives to report newborn babies with deformities. The death sentence was then passed by a panel of three experts, including two pediatricians and the psychiatrist Hans Heinze.[5]

The slaughter of children proceeded with special ruthlessness under this separate euthanasia program—motivated by public health policy—called the Federal Board for the Scientific Registration of Hereditary or Other Severe Congenital Disorders. The torturous method of killing was a combination of gradual poisoning with toxic drugs and slow starvation. The murders were conducted in this controlled manner in order to justify them as medical procedures.

Testimony at Nuremberg provided a particularly heartrending description of psychiatrist H. Pfannmüller, the director of Eglfing-Haar Mental Institution, holding up a skin-and-bones starving child "like a dead rabbit" for display.[6]

Pediatrician Werner Catel headed the "action" against the children, which began in 1939. Unlike the adult euthanasia program, the killing of children continued to receive official sanction throughout the war. The maximum age of eligibility was extended from three to seventeen by war's end. According to J.-E. Meyer, after the war, while Catel headed the department of pediatrics in Kiel, he continued to advocate the destruction of so-called monsters.

There were more than twenty or thirty facilities where children were killed, including the asylums at Eichberg, Idstein, Gorden, Kalmenhof, Kentenhof, Lubliniec, and Eglfing-Haar.

The Cover-ups Persist

The medical murder program recently became the focus of international attention when Hans-Joachim Sewering was elected president of the World Medical Association.[7] In 1942, as a young physician, Sewering had sent a fourteen-year-old to her death at Eglfing-Haar.[8] Sewering claimed that the murder program was over by 1942; but it was generally known that individual facilities continued their operations unabated, and the form Sewering signed had the unmistakable tone of a "euthanasia" authorization. Records show that 1,432 patients died at Eglfing-Haar in 1942.

Werner Heyde, the psychiatrist who headed the adult euthanasia program, escaped from the Americans after the war. Under an assumed name, but known to his colleagues, he continued to work as a successful, highly visible administrative physician and psychiatrist. When arrested in 1959, he hanged himself before trial.[9] Of the fourteen physicians known to have worked in the killing hospitals in the euthanasia program, only one was brought to justice.[10]

An Answer to "How Could They Do It?"

Many people have wondered how ordinary Germans could have became inured to working in Holocaust murder camps. One key lies in the medicalization of murder in the euthanasia centers, where, in Müller-Hill's words, the victims were "gassed by killer teams headed by psychiatrists." The psychiatrists did not merely supervise: "It was the duty of a psychiatrist to open the valve of the cylinder containing the carbon monoxide."[11]

If *doctors* legitimized and carried out the murders, others could more easily rationalize their own participation in the "special treatment." The presence of physicians and other health professionals also disguised the lethal purpose from the victims. These medical murder centers pioneered the use of fake wooden soap and other details to disguise the carbon monoxide gas chambers as showers, and the mass cremation of bodies to hide the fate of the victims.[12] In *The Murderers Among Us,* famed Nazi-hunter Simon Wiesenthal reports that the psychiatric euthanasia centers were structured like medical schools.

The psychiatrists were not ashamed of what they did, and they repeatedly sought but failed to gain legalization of the murder program. Meticulous records were kept for each of the six institutions, permitting a relatively accurate accounting after the war. In his 1988 book *Racial Hygiene: Medicine Under the Nazis,* Robert Proctor underscores "the banality of the operation," including a staff celebration with beer at Hadamar when it cremated its ten thousandth patient.

From Euthanasia Centers to Extermination Camps

Psychiatry's contribution to the larger Holocaust reached beyond the euthanasia program. Christian Wirth, who supervised the center at Hartheim, was designated supervising inspector in the early stages of the extermination camps, including Belzec, Sobibor, and Treblinka.[13]

Wirth's successor at Hartheim, Franz Stangl, later became commandant of Treblinka. Asked how he became inured to killing people, Stangl explained that he had been trained by doctors in the euthanasia program in 1940. A euthanasia program psychiatrist was, for a short time, one of the first commandants in one of the large eastern extermination camps.

The equipment used in the euthanasia centers was dismantled and used to construct the Holocaust extermination camps.[14] Consultants from the euthanasia centers helped set up the extermination camps, and personnel from the centers provided most of the initial manpower for the Final Solution.[15] In Müller-Hill's words, "the experienced killers moved to Poland and the U.S.S.R. in 1942 to set up the first death camps for the mass murder there of Jews and Romanies."[16]

Historian Henry Friedlander, from the Department of Judaic Studies at Brooklyn College, recently paralleled the psychiatric murder centers and the later extermination camps. He concludes: "As the SS was searching for a better means to implement the killings in the East, they chose to use the methods tried and tested in the euthanasia program." From stonemasons to executioners, men from the euthanasia program "composed almost the entire personnel of the extermination camps."

Friedlander quotes a German who worked first at Hartheim killing mental patients and then at Belzec and Sobibor killing Jews: "The method employed in the camps was the same as the one utilized at the castle in Hartheim, except that those killed [in the camps] were all Jews." Friedlander explains:

> In both places the victims were told that they had to take showers for hygienic reasons, and the gas chambers were disguised as shower rooms, while the belongings of the victims were carefully collected and registered to maintain the illusion of normality. . . . The system of stealing gold teeth and gold bridge-work from the corpses of the murdered victims was first introduced into the euthanasia killing centers and then copied in the extermination camps. . . .

In as direct continuity as possible, the first extermination camp, Chelmno, "was originally planned as a euthanasia institute," but went directly into operation as a Holocaust extermination center.[17]

Proctor (1988) confirms the origins of the extermination camps in the psychiatric murder centers:

> [G]as chambers at psychiatric institutions in southern and eastern Germany were dismantled and shipped east, where they were reinstalled at Belzec, Majdanek, Auschwitz, Treblinka, and Sobibor. The same doctors and technicians and nurses followed the equipment. Germany's psychiatric hospitals forged the most important practical link between the destruction of the mentally ill and handicapped and the murder of Germany's ethnic and social minorities. [p. 212]

Psychiatry Enters the Concentration Camps

Before the Final Solution was fully implemented, psychiatrists went into the camps and conducted the first official, systematic murders of Jews.[18] Werner Heyde from the euthanasia program led teams of psychiatrists into the concentration camps to select Jews for extermination. These teams "diagnosed" and selected victims using the euthanasia forms, then had the inmates sent to their deaths at the psychiatric extermination centers. Another psychiatrist, Friedrich Mennecke, sent at least 2,500 concentration camp prisoners to the psychiatric murder facilities.[19] Meyer estimates that 10,000 people were killed by psychiatry in this early stage of the Holocaust.

Did Psychiatrists Act of Their Own Free Will?

In *A Sign for Cain,* psychiatrist Fredric Wertham lays the blame for psychiatry's actions at the feet of the profession:

> The tragedy is that the psychiatrists did not have to have an order. They acted on their own. They were not carrying out a death sentence pronounced by someone else. . . . [T]hey supervised and often watched the slow deaths.

Historians agree that the psychiatrists were in no way coerced. Proctor (1988) put it bluntly:

> Doctors were never *ordered* to murder psychiatric patients and handicapped children. They were *empowered* to do so, and fulfilled their task without protest, often on their own initiative. [p. 193]

Reviewing books and interviewing historians in Germany, I was able to find only one gesture against the program in the entire profession, a psychiatrist who walked out of a meeting.*[20]

Psychiatrists Make "Good Use" of the Murder Victims

Psychiatrists did not hesitate to "take advantage" of the "research material" made available by the euthanasia centers and from the individual mental hospitals that had become death factories. Carl Schneider, professor of psychiatry at the University of Heidelberg, "ordered" the corpses of murdered children with "interesting" deformities from the facility for mentally ill children at Eichberg Hospital.[21]

---

*I don't know of any American psychiatrists who took an active role in protesting Germany's psychiatric holocaust. To this day, the tendency is not to think about it.

Julius Hallervorden, an internationally respected professor of neuropathology at the famed Kaiser Wilhelm Institute for Brain Research ordered the brains of hundreds of patients from Brandenburg. Hallervorden described the best methods of removing and preserving the brains, and provided the containers.

Leo Alexander, an American psychiatrist, was the investigator for medical crimes at Nuremberg. He deferentially refers to his colleague "Dr. Hallervorden" throughout his 1949 G-2 intelligence report, and found no cause to seek charges against him. Speaking of the brains of these murdered patients, Alexander says, "Still there were interesting cases in this material," and he proceeds to describe them with medical enthusiasm. Hallervorden's amicable conversation with Alexander concealed his yet deeper involvement in the murder program, including the performance of postmortems on the spot immediately following the murders.

Alexander's report also shows that the internationally praised genetic researcher Ernst Rudin had fled the Kaiser Wilhelm Institute before Alexander's arrival, "presumably because of the part he had played in the program of killing the insane."

Psychiatry as the Gateway to the Holocaust

The physicians who were most intimately involved as observers and witnesses at the Nuremberg trials *all* agreed that psychiatry was indispensable to the Final Solution. Alexander Mitscherlich headed the German Medical Commission assigned to monitor the first War Crimes Trial. With co-author and physician Fred Mielke, he wrote *Doctors of Infamy* (1949). Mitscherlich and Mielke observed that the eugenics and euthanasia programs "inexorably" led to the Holocaust.

As the only full-time medical investigator at Nuremberg, and as a psychiatrist, the American Leo Alexander was ideally positioned to evaluate the psychiatric crimes. Although he was very protective of psychiatry at the trials and thereafter, he too concluded that the euthanasia program was a stepping-stone to the larger Holocaust. He called it "the entering wedge for exterminations of far greater scope in the political program for genocide of conquered nations and the racially unwanted."

The American Medical Association sent physician Andrew Ivy as its representative to the Nuremberg trials.* Ivy wrote, "Had the profession taken a

---

*Alexander claimed that he had "authored the Nuremberg Code." I have corresponded with those directly involved with the Nuremberg trials—including Telford Taylor, the chief counsel for the war crimes tribunal under whom Alexander served—and all confirmed that Alexander played no role whatsoever in the development of the code. It was Andrew Ivy who testified before the tribunal about the AMA code of ethics on medical experimentation, from which the judges developed the Nuremberg Code.

strong stand against the mass killing of sick Germans before the war, it is conceivable that the entire idea and technique of death factories for genocide would not have materialized."[22]

Historians like Richard Rubenstein have pointed out that the scientific bureaucratization of murder was unique to the Holocaust, but apparently without realizing the source. Bureaucratic, scientific killing was conceived and first implemented by organized psychiatry.

The German citizen was taught that the people (*Volk*) must be cleansed of genetically defective individuals and groups—first, the medically and psychiatrically impaired, and later the racially inferior. This cleansing would prevent further contamination of society. The participation of medical doctors—lead by psychiatry—justified the process.

Life Unworthy of Living

Karl Binding was one of Germany's most outstanding jurists and Alfred Hoche one of its most esteemed psychiatrists. In 1920, before Hitler came to power, they co-authored the first book justifying large-scale medical exterminations. It was entitled *The Sanctioning of the Destruction of Life Unworthy of Living.* Hoche, like many of today's biopsychiatrists, was openly critical of psychologically oriented psychiatrists, considering them unscientific.

Hoche refers to the "mentally deceased," "human burdens," and "defective persons." He calls for destroying between twenty thousand and thirty thousand German mental patients on the basis of "lack of productive output," a "state of complete helplessness," and "needing the care of others."[23]

While visiting Germany in 1988, I spoke with historians and looked in archives, confirming that Binding and Hoche's treatise led to a lively debate within German medical, legal, and theological circles during the 1920s. Students wrote their dissertations on the euthanasia debate. This prepared the way for later acceptance of the murder program when Hitler took power. Despite some protests against the euthanasia program,[24] psychiatry demonstrated that Germans would not rise up against the extermination of their own people.

Eugenics and the Holocaust

Along with the rest of organized medicine, psychiatry helped establish the principle of treating the *Volk* as a body from whom individuals, like cancer cells, could be removed in the name of public health.

Eugenics is science in the service of justifying programs that supposedly improve the stock of one group of people, usually at the obvious expense of another.[25] Almost all observers agree that international eugenics was one of the earliest and most important stepping-stones toward the murder of mental patients and the Final Solution.[26] Until Hitler took power, the main preoccupation of the eugenics movement, even in Germany, was not "the Jewish question." It was the declining birthrate and the "growing number of mentally ill in state institutions."[27]

While eugenics did not originate in psychiatry, psychiatry became its chief champion throughout Europe and America. On July 14, 1933, the "Law for the Prevention of Progeny of Hereditary Disease" was passed as the first official legislation under the Nazis. It called for the *compulsory* sterilization of patients with schizophrenia, manic-depressive (bipolar) disorder, feeblemindedness, severe alcoholism, and other presumed hereditary diseases. Most of the estimated 350,000 to 400,000 people sterilized against their will between 1934 and 1939 in Nazi Germany were labeled mentally ill.

Hitler's Psychiatrist

Ernst Rudin embodies the direct link between psychiatry and Hitler. Rudin was one of the four founders of the Society for Racial Hygiene in 1905 and became its head under the Nazi regime in 1933. He was director of the Department of Heredity at the Kaiser Wilhelm Institute of Psychiatry, which itself was supported by the Rockefeller Foundation during Germany's desperate financial period immediately prior to World War II. During that time, Rudin was sponsored by the Carnegie Foundation to lecture at academic and research institutions in America. He was probably the most widely published and internationally respected psychiatrist in genetic research.

Rudin was among the most powerful forces behind Hitler's 1933 sterilization law. He was made Nazi party leader for the merged specialties of psychiatry and neurology. On his seventieth birthday in 1944, he was given the Goethe medal for art and science by Hitler, who declared, "To the indefatigable champion of race hygiene and meritorious pioneer of the racial-hygienic measures of the Third Reich I send . . . my heartiest congratulations."*[28]

---

*As a eugenicist, Rudin was in the company of the world's leading psychiatrists of the first third of the twentieth century, including Emil Kraepelin (1856–1926) and Eugen Bleuler (1857–1939). In the current biopsychiatric ascendancy, some textbooks (e.g., Talbott et al., 1988, p. 46) have begun once again to cite favorably "the Berlin school," including Rudin, as well as Franz Kallmann, who tried to outdo Rudin with the scope of his recommendations for eugenical sterilization.

Hitler Learns from the German Scientists and Psychiatrists

While writing *Mein Kampf* in prison, Hitler reportedly read the leading German eugenic textbook by Baur, Fischer, and Lenz (1923).[29] German researchers Christian Pross and Götz Aly agree that "Hitler bases his racist and eugenic theories in 'Mein Kampf' on large parts of this book." J. Lauter and J.-E. Meyer report that Hitler used Binding and Hoche's 1920 euthanasia textbook "in justification of the extermination of mental patients."

Hitler did not inspire the psychiatrists and other medical professionals; rather, they came first and inspired him. *Mein Kampf,* written in 1924, borrows its theories and sometimes its language from contemporary scientific and psychiatric books. Speaking of the future Nazi state like a psychiatric eugenicist, Hitler declared:

> It has to make the child the most precious possession of a people. It has to take care that only the healthy beget children. . . . Thereby the State has to appear as the guardian of a thousand years' future, in the face of which the wish and the egoism of the individual appears as nothing and has to submit. It has to put the most modern medical means at the service of this knowledge. It has to declare unfit for propagation everybody who is visibly ill and has inherited a disease and it has to carry this out in practice. . . .
>
> The prevention of the procreative faculty and possibility on the part of physically degenerated and mentally sick people, for only six hundred years, would not only free mankind of immeasurable misfortune, but would also contribute to a restoration that appears hardly believable today. [pp. 608–609]

American Psychiatry Encourages the Nazis

Rudin was not eager to gain the enmity of his English or American colleagues. He did not wish to alienate the American foundations, such as Carnegie and Rockefeller, that were so generous to him and German psychiatry during Europe's economic crunch. He sought precedents in America before laying his plans for Germany.

When Hitler's sterilization laws took effect in January 1934, the well-known California eugenicist Paul Popenoe quickly lavished praise on both the German dictator and his programs. While Popenoe was not a psychiatrist, he worked with and reported on the sterilization program carried out against mental hospital inmates in California. Writing in the *Journal of Heredity* in 1934, Popenoe quoted enthusiastically from *Mein Kampf,* stating "it is merely an accident that it happened to be the Hitler administration which was ready to put into effect the recommendations of the specialists." He opined that "the present German government has given the first example in modern times of an administration based frankly and determinedly on the principle of eugenics."

Popenoe viewed the Third Reich as an ideal—the world's first mental hygiene state. He had been to Germany to encourage them with their unfolding eugenic plans.

In 1936 Marie Kopp pointed proudly to the moral and scientific support the German authorities received from their American counterparts: "The leaders in the German sterilization movement state repeatedly that their legislation was formulated only after careful study of the California experiment. . . ." She correctly observed "the legal sterilization of mental incompetents originated in the United States."

Shortly after the promulgation of the Nazi sterilization laws, the *Journal of the American Medical Association* [30] published a lengthy report on the law and its many expected benefits. In a positive tone, it observed that 400,000 German sterilizations were soon expected.*

A year before war broke out between Germany and the United States, praise came in from American psychiatrist Aaron Rosanoff in his textbook *Manual of Psychiatry and Mental Hygiene,* in which he favorably compared the German and American sterilization programs. Rosanoff raises the question of whether eugenics smacks of "nazism and fascism" (p. 812), but concludes that eugenics is "scientific" rather than political in origin. Therein, to this very day, lies the great danger of eugenic theorizing.

In 1936, psychiatrist Leo Alexander—who, as mentioned earlier, would become the chief medical investigator at Nuremberg—was one of the authors of *Eugenical Sterilization,* an official report published by the American Neurological Association.[†] The senior author of the book was the famous American psychiatrist Abraham Myerson. Since Alexander was German-trained and German-speaking, he almost surely bore primary responsibility for the book's viewpoint on Hitler's program. The report is positive about the Third Reich's eugenical achievements, observing "the sterilization act is not a product of Hitler's regime, in that its main tenets were proposed and considered several years earlier, before the Nazi regime took possession of Germany." The authors praise Hitler's legislation, citing its legal "safeguards," "German thoroughness," and its close conformity with "knowledge of modern eugenics" (p. 22).

Alexander did not let his enthusiastic support for Hitler's eugenic programs disqualify him from becoming the official medical investigator at

---

*The final number fell a little short of that in part because euthanasia replaced eugenics.
†The report was supported by the Carnegie Foundation.

Nuremberg—the one man responsible for ferreting out psychiatric atrocities.[31] Few psychiatrists were brought to justice.

Robert Proctor pointed out in 1988 that involuntary sterilization was so common in America that it was impossible to consider it a war crime: "After the war, Allied authorities were unable to classify the sterilizations as war crimes, because similar laws had only recently been upheld in the United States."

America Leads the Way to Nazi Germany

Initially, America was ahead of Germany in its eugenical programs. According to Philip R. Reilly, "Between 1905 and 1922, thirty bills permitting the sterilization of institutionalized persons were passed in eighteen states."[32] By the end of World War II, the United States had perpetrated approximately sixty thousand sterilizations. While most were performed during the 1930s, some states continued widespread involuntary sterilization into the 1940s and 1950s. For many years, women constituted 60 percent or more of the victims. Often mildly retarded young women were admitted to institutions for the explicit purpose of sterilizing them.[33]

According to Reilly, "Revulsion over Germany's racist policies did little to curtail American programs before or after World War II. On the contrary, American advocates pointed to Germany to illustrate how an enlightened sterilization program might quickly reach its goals."[34]

Eugenical experts lobbied Congress to pass restrictive immigration laws and the banning of interracial marriages. By 1940, most states had laws barring marriage between blacks and whites, and the majority were not repealed until after the war. Robert Proctor (1988) points out that the Germans were in some ways "more lenient." In several U.S. states, people were labeled "colored" for possessing one part in thirty-two of African ancestry, while in Germany persons were considered German for most practical purposes even if they were as much as one-fourth Jewish.

Proposals Too Radical for the Nazis

In 1930 the California eugenicist Paul Popenoe called for more stringent measures than were subsequently taken in Nazi Germany—the involuntary sterilization not only of psychiatric inmates but of their families as well. America's most frequently cited genetic researcher, psychiatrist Franz Kallmann, also proposed programs for eugenical sterilization that were more radical than those legislated in Germany. Sterilizing every mental patient would not be enough to destroy the alleged recessive gene for schizophrenia,

Kallmann argued in 1938 in *Eugenical News.* He wanted both forced sterilization and the prevention of marriage between people considered "schizoid eccentrics and borderline cases."

As a psychiatrist in Nazi Germany a few years earlier, Kallmann had proposed similar sweeping sterilization measures that the Nazis considered too extreme.[35] Yet some modern biopsychiatrists continue to cite Kallmann's research as if it can be trusted.[36]

Throughout the 1930s, dozens of reports favoring eugenical sterilization appeared in American medical journals, often with favorable references to Nazi Germany. Steven Selden, a critic of eugenics, cites one American textbook of biology that continued to promote these concepts after World War II.

Eugenics in England

England rivaled America and Germany in its prewar enthusiasm for eugenics. As early as 1927, Charles Wicksteed Armstrong, in *The Survival of the Unfittest,* describes the eugenical debate as focusing on three potential practices: "the lethal chamber, segregation and sterilization."[37] He himself favored sterilization, and argued against segregation, while offering no discussion, pro or con, concerning the "lethal chamber."

As recently as 1974, John R. Baker wrote a detailed treatise entitled *Race* that resurrects the issue of racial superiority in a scientific guise. Baker summarizes Hitler's views in *Mein Kampf* in some detail, and finds that "The first part of the chapter dealing with the ethnic problem is quite well written and not uninteresting." But he goes on to criticize Hitler's discussion of the Jews as unscientific and abusive. He then laments that Hitler's excesses marked the end of the period in which "both sides in the ethnic controversy were free to put forward their views" and especially to "dare to suggest that any race might be in any respect or in any sense superior to another." Baker himself argues that blacks are intellectually inferior and suggests that some of their genetic subgroups are by nature predisposed toward being owned and enslaved.[38] Baker's book was published by the prestigious Oxford University Press.

The Eugenics Society in England, which flourished prior to World War II, still exists. At its 1962 annual meeting, Julian Huxley continued to argue that the problem of genetic differences among races was of "vital practical importance." Lamenting the Nazi extremes, which he calls "the *reduction ad horrendum* of racism," he yet promotes the fundamental principles of coercive eugenics, aimed not at Jews, but at England's inner-city poor. Huxley finds the inner-city poor to be "very low" in IQ, as well as "genetically subnormal in many other qualities. . . ." He calls for "public health measures" for sterilization, comparable to "compulsory or semi-compulsory vaccination, inoculation and isolation."

Medical Murder in America? A Close Call . . .

Not only eugenics, but medical murder of retarded children found support at the highest levels of American psychiatry. As in Germany, it began with those who initially supported eugenics. Foster Kennedy, an influential American psychiatrist and neurologist, advocated involuntary sterilization and castration in 1937. Then at the 1941 annual meeting of the American Psychiatric Association, Kennedy called for the extermination of incurable severely retarded children over the age of five. His goal was to relieve "the utterly unfit" of the "agony of living" and to save their parents and the state the cost of caring for them. He concluded, "So the place for euthanasia, I believe, is for the completely hopeless defective: nature's mistake; something we hustle out of sight, which should not have been seen at all."*

Another leading American psychiatrist, Leo Kanner, rebutted Kennedy, and the papers appear together in the 1942 *American Journal of Psychiatry.* Kanner warned against "haughty indifference toward the feebleminded." Citing William Shirer's 1941 report that an estimated 100,000 German mental patients had already been murdered, Kanner declared:

> Psychiatry is, and should forever be, a science dunked in the milk of human kindness. . . . Does anyone really think that the German nation is in any way improved, ennobled, made more civilized by inflicting what they cynically choose to call mercy deaths on the feebleminded?†

It's bad enough for individual doctors to debate mass murder. It's more menacing when the nation's leading psychiatric association supports it. An official, unsigned editorial in the same issue of the American Psychiatric Association's official journal supported Kennedy's position over Kanner's.[39] Using language indistinguishable from that of Hoche and the perpetrators of the German murder program, the editorial speaks of "disposal of

---

*Had Kennedy succeeded in promoting euthanasia in the United States, the German medical murder program would also have been exonerated, much in the same way as the German eugenical sterilization program.

†Kanner has the mistaken impression that the Germans were killing only the "feebleminded," but their program had a much broader sweep, including the mentally and physically ill, as well as criminals and other "unfit" people.

euthanasia," "merciful passage from life," "a method of disposal," and even facetiously "a lethal *finis* to the painful chapter."

To counteract mothers' feeling guilty over killing their children, the editorial suggests a public education campaign. The earliest Nazi exterminations had also begun with children, suggesting what may have lain in wait if this door had been opened.

Déjà Vu—It Began with Racism Against Africans

There's yet another parallel that connects the mere sixty years spanning 1934 and 1994. The German genetic researchers who supported Hitler and helped to bring about the Holocaust did not initially focus on the Jews. Their original interest—like some contemporary eugenicists—was to prove the inherent inferiority of Africans.* In *Toward the Final Solution: A History of European Racism,* George L. Mosse observed, "It was against the blacks, not Jews, that the ominous accusation of '*Kulturschande*' (rape of culture) was first raised after the war" (p. 176). According to Mosse, some Nazi racists originally warned about the "Negro-Jewish war" upon the Germans.

Two key German eugenicists, Theodor James Mollison and Eugen Fischer, were physicians and anthropologists.[†40] Both began their careers by proving that black people in the German colonies deserved their subordinate status. Mollison helped train Josef Mengele, who perpetrated the notorious Auschwitz twin experiments. Mengele's initial studies under Mollison also focused on supposed genetic inferiority of dark-skinned races.

While supporting Hitler's policies toward Jews, Fischer remained even more negative about blacks. Speaking of Africans as early as 1913, Fischer declared that European civilization "has suffered an intellectual and cultural decline as a result of the acceptance of inferior elements."[41] In 1939, Fischer declared in a speech, "I do not characterize every Jew as inferior, as Negroes are."[42]

The first illegal[‡] sterilizations in Nazi Germany were carried out against all of that country's black children—the offspring of French-African occupation troops, the so-called Rhineland half-castes.[43] With the participation of psychiatrist Ernst Rudin, formal planning for the program started in March

---

*The recurring connection between racism and anti-Semitism should not be forgotten. It recently resurfaced in Los Angeles with the arrest of a group of "white supremacists" who had targeted both African-American and Jewish leaders for assassination (Reinhold, 1993). Their main aim was to ignite a race war.
†Mollison and Fischer were trained in medicine and in anthropology, a professional combination that is uncommon in the United States. While they were not psychiatrists, their particular training and interests made them close allies of psychiatry.
‡The earlier mass sterilizations were legal. That is, they were authorized by legislation.

1935 and was first implemented in the spring of 1937. The ultimate fate of the approximately eight hundred children is unknown.

Racial policies against Gypsies also paved the way for the Holocaust. In November 1936 the psychiatrist Robert Ritter began working on the classification of Gypsies in the Section on Race Hygiene and Population Biology in the National Department of Health in Berlin. Eventually large numbers of them were sterilized and then murdered.

Frances Cress Welsing—an African-American psychiatrist and author in Washington, D.C.—emphasizes that the Nazi extermination policy was racial rather than religious in its aim, and was part of an international menace against all non-whites. Welsing believes that white racism is based on the fear that African genes are dominant and, with intermarriage, would overwhelm the white genetic pool.[44]

How and Why Psychiatry Would Become a Death Machine

Was psychiatry perverted and used by the Nazis? The data we have examined suggests instead that it spearheaded eugenics and mass murder and became the "entering wedge" into the Holocaust. But was German psychiatry essentially different from the remainder of Western psychiatry?

Britain and the United States during the 1930s benefitted from a longer tradition of political liberty than did Germany. These and other differences made the ascendancy of a totalitarian dictator much less likely than in Germany. By contrast, psychiatry differed little within the three nations. The only major difference—and a significant one—was the more open discussion of euthanasia in Germany. After the Jews were driven out of the psychiatric profession in Germany, there were greater numbers of psychoanalytically trained psychiatrists in Britain and America; but eugenical, biological psychiatry had always dominated the profession everywhere in the Western world. German psychiatrists like Rudin were considered world leaders.

Leading up to the German eugenics and euthanasia programs, Western psychiatry shared basic approaches that paved the way for the more radical German "solutions" and that continue to menace Western freedoms, most recently through NIMH's violence initiative. These principles are basic to institutional, biological psychiatry and include involuntary treatment, medical diagnosis, biochemical and genetic explanations, and eugenics. This is the array of principles that produces biomedical social control.

Selection in Psychiatry and the Holocaust

Selection was a major medical function in Nazi Germany and should be considered a general principle of psychiatry. At a 1988 conference in Cologne on medicine in Nazi Germany, firsthand accounts of Auschwitz by survivors Hermann Langbein and by Rudolf Vrba emphasized the role of medical doctors in "selecting" patients for death. Medical selection invested the Final Solution with scientific respectability.

When psychiatrist Alfred Hoche described the criteria for exterminating mental patients in his 1920 book coauthored with Binding, he extended the purpose of diagnostic selection to a new extreme. By the time Hitler wrote *Mein Kampf,* selection was deeply embedded in the future dictator's thinking. Ternon put it succinctly:

> All of racial hygiene, the whole platform of the Nazis could be summed up in two words: *Auslese* (selection) and *Ausmerze* (elimination). [p. 448]

Without being named as such, selection has always been intrinsic to psychiatry. In the 1930s selection within hospitals took on more dreadful meaning, as patients were chosen as targets for the various brain-damaging therapies. The victims were typically the less useful and more troublesome patients. Starting in the early part of the century, American psychiatry took the most active role in selecting patients for involuntary sterilization. The selection process had fewer legal protections than in Nazi Germany.

Today selection rears its head under another name, *triage,* in Frederick Goodwin's descriptions of screening children for the violence initiative. It is fundamental to all the ongoing research that aims at identifying genetic and biological markers for violence.

A Moral Flaw in Psychiatry

Psychiatry has not faced the role of the profession in Nazi Germany. In his 1986 book *Nazi Doctors,* psychiatrist Robert Lifton stresses the "Nazi" role, often to the exclusion of the psychiatric role. He gives the impression that psychiatrists were somehow twisted and turned to bad ends by the Nazis.

When it comes to research on electroshock treatment in the extermination camps, Lifton seems to waffle. In a section entitled "Genuine Research," he writes about Auschwitz: "Prisoner physicians could themselves sometimes initiate genuine research, like the program in electroshock therapy developed by a Polish neurologist." The shock program took "the unusual step of having female inmates brought there as well from Birkenau seven or eight kilometers away." Seemingly without skepticism or moral outrage, Lifton quotes his informant as saying the shock treatments were "genuinely therapeutic."

Lifton discusses whether or not the shock experiments were "tainted" by the Nazis and concludes that they were: "But overall the episode once more reveals the tendency for the Auschwitz environment to subsume virtually any medical effort to its relentless destructiveness." Thus, he seems to find nothing *inevitably* wrong in performing shock treatment within a totalitarian and even murderous institution. It is the potential misapplication of the treatment that seems to bother him—giving it to inmates who weren't mentally ill, or who were doomed for extermination anyway.

To forthrightly condemn the shock experiments, Lifton would have had to face the inherent abusiveness of the treatment, as well as its more obviously abusive applications in state mental hospitals throughout the Western world during the same era. In the 1940s in America in crowded state mental hospitals, whole wards of patients were shocked to keep them docile.[45]

Lifton is silent on the failure to bring many psychiatrists to justice at Nuremberg, an outcome due in part to Leo Alexander's exoneration of them. Alexander, before he died, was a primary source of information for Lifton's book.

We are not accusing Lifton or Alexander of any special moral deviation from psychiatric ethics or standards. Lifton, like Alexander in his day, is a respected, even a leading psychiatrist operating on a level consistent with ideals of the profession. That is the problem.

Human beings do not naturally view each other as objects, such as tables or chairs; the effort to do so results in their feeling disgust, revulsion, and hostility for the objects of their misbegotten attention. Thus psychiatrists treat human beings far worse than, say, mechanics treat cars or other machines. Psychiatrists inject toxic agents and inflict electric shocks on the brains of their patients. Sometimes they destroy parts of their patients' brains with psychosurgery. No sane mechanic or engineer would seek to disable further a malfunctioning machine in an honest attempt to fix it. The machine is treated with care, even though it cannot scream or otherwise protest.

The Biomedical Vision: Then and Now

The scale and the methodical ferocity of the Holocaust have tended to overshadow the murder of mental patients and others deemed by the Nazis unfit to live. Yet the Holocaust cannot be explained by anti-Semitism alone. As historian Henry Friedlander has shown, the Nazis were driven by a vision of biomedical social control toward the ideal society—a vision of "social planning" that drew heavily on medicine and especially on psychiatry:

Many groups and individuals shared their vision of a society racially homogeneous, physically hardy, and mentally healthy. Certain groups simply did not fit into this visionary society. They were the mentally disturbed and physically malformed, the criminal and asocial individual, and the racially alien peoples.

German psychiatry's key role in this master plan was determined by commonly accepted biopsychiatric basic principles and practices. When the Jews were exterminated or forced to flee from the Nazis, German psychiatry was stripped of its psychologically oriented leadership. We now have a similar situation in American psychiatry with the takeover of the profession by biologically and genetically oriented doctors. From the American Psychiatric Association to the National Institute of Mental Health, from Harvard to Johns Hopkins, biopsychiatry now dominates the profession.

America is not Nazi Germany. In this nation, individual rights receive greater protection, and the state is more gravely limited. Yet America is deeply enmeshed in racial conflict, and it has its own inherent tendencies toward oppressive biomedical solutions.

Genetically oriented psychiatry is enjoying a current propaganda resurgence, encouraging the psychiatric researchers and leaders to claim that crime and violence are genetic. There is a growing movement to ease the restrictions on involuntary treatment and to rejuvenate the state mental hospital system. Shock treatment—which was relied upon heavily in Nazi Germany—is in the midst of a resurgence in America.[46] The high cost of medical care and other economic and social factors have vastly increased current interest in euthanasia in America and elsewhere.[47] All these are ominous signs.

In America, psychiatry will not aim itself at Jews or Gypsies, but at this nation's most vulnerable and victimized minorities, especially young black men who live in poverty. It will not begin with a call for widespread involuntary sterilization or euthanasia, but with more subtle claims about the possible genetic and biochemical derangements in these youngsters.

As the violence initiative once again confirms, biopsychiatry is always ready to push the limits of biomedical social control. It is truly a case in which the price of liberty is eternal vigilance.

8

Racial Guinea Pigs?
Victims of Genocide?
Science and the African-American

A legitimate ethical foundation in medicine cannot be established until the profession has demonstrated the insight and capacity to acknowledge evil, to recognize its victims, and to commemorate their suffering.

—William E. Seidelman (1989)

[I]n a class conscious, sexist, and racist society, social scientists search for, identify and attribute pathology in the poor, women, and people of color.

—Ronald David (1992)

[M]any features of contemporary "civilized" society encourage the easy resort to genocidal holocaust.

—Leo Kuper, *Genocide* (1981)

WE WERE SITTING IN OUR PACKED HOTEL ROOM IN LOS ANGELES LISTENING to fears being expressed to us by residents and representatives from several "projects" in Watts—the subsidized low-cost housing units in South Central Los Angeles. We had come to L.A. to give a full-day seminar sponsored by the Watts College of Child Development, a community-based group that fosters the well-being and empowerment of black children and youth. The founder of the college, pediatric cardiologist Ernest H. Smith,* arranged for the more informal meeting with us to air concerns about research being conducted in the projects by the Centers for Disease Control and Prevention (CDC).

The CDC claimed to be studying hypertension in young African-American men, but its method of telephone canvassing seemed to suggest a

---

*Smith is a professor at Drew University's school of medicine, but the Watts College of Child Development is an independent organization.

hidden agenda. Anyone who answered the phone, including small children, was being asked about the whereabouts of young black men who might be candidates for the hypertension research.

The representatives from Watts saw sinister implications. At best, they believed, the hypertension study was a cover story for violence initiative research. At worst, the aim was to make a list of potential black resisters in preparation for a future police or army invasion of the projects, leading to their ultimate destruction. They feared that the iron fences erected around the project would ultimately be used to pen them in rather than to protect them.

Contrary to the public and media images, the project representatives felt grateful for where they are living. As fearful as they were about neighborhood violence, they were more afraid of the outside white community's intentions toward their homes and their children.* The bad publicity about the projects, describing them as nightmarish jungles, did not fit with their experience of community and their gratitude for an affordable place to live.

The uniformly negative public image of the projects among whites, they feared, is aimed at preparing the city to accept the demise of these communities. They felt sure that many white-owned businesses hunger to demolish the projects to make way for "progress" through economic encroachment. They also saw hints of genocide through the dismantling of yet another established black community and the possibility of the ultimate extermination of the project population. They uniformly believed that government policies are purposely fostering the lethal environment of drugs, guns, and gangs.

Innately Docile . . . or Innately Violent?

Do these African-Americans from Watts—many of them educated professionals—have reason to be so suspicious of medical research emanating from the federal government? Their concerns—and the reality of potential threats against their community—cannot be understood outside the context of medical racism. They are well aware that the last two decades in America have seen grand plans for programs of biomedical social control—the first and second violence initiatives. They know something about the role of biological psychiatry in the Holocaust. And they realize that the history of racist medicine and science has yet earlier and deeper roots.

For centuries, psychiatry and medicine have been used to rationalize

---

*Similarly, many black parents are more afraid of their children being hurt by the police than by neighborhood youth. Time and again, as I have traveled, mothers and fathers have told me stories about their teenage sons being arbitrarily arrested or brutalized by police officers.

slavery, colonialism, and racism. German scientists were preoccupied with justifying the colonial domination of blacks long before Hitler came to power (see Chapter 7). In America, scientists and intellectuals made the same rationalizations on behalf of slavery, and after the emancipation, on behalf of segregation and discrimination.

In America, Dr. Samuel A. Cartwright legitimized slavery through diagnoses like "Drapetomania," which "manifests itself by an irrestrainable propensity to run away," and "Dysoesthesia oethiopeca," which characterized the diseased person as "paying no attention to the rights of property," "breaking the tools he works with," and engaging in "idleness and sloth."[1] These slave-era diagnoses are similar to modern behavioral diagnoses, such as oppositional defiant disorder and conduct disorder in children and antisocial personality disorder in adults (see Chapter 4). The common purpose is the psychiatric labeling of resistive or rebellious activity in order to justify medical control.

Other physicians stated that the special care and supervision given to slaves benefited them. Statistics were compiled to show that slavery protected blacks from mental illness. Historian Melville J. Herskovits was among the first to debunk the myth of African docility. In *The Myth of the Negro Past,* published in 1941, he wrote that "It needs no great probing of the literature of slaving to become aware that, from the beginning, vast numbers of Negroes refused to accept slave status without a struggle." He added that revolts, uprisings, hunger strikes, and outright suicide were common.

If enslaved blacks were compliant, one wonders why there was such need for chains, whips, torture, and other brutal means of punishment. Black people clearly responded as any humans would. When possible, they rebelled and sometimes took over entire islands off the shores of the Americas. When they couldn't openly rebel, as Herskovits documents, they did as little as possible to cooperate with their enslavement. Slaves called lazy and stupid were often expressing passive resistance.

Slaves had much to resist—including their involuntary role as medical guinea pigs.

Jefferson's Slaves

Thomas Jefferson, U.S. president and founding father, was not a physician, but in an era when science was largely non-professional, he engaged in medical experimentation.[2] In the interest of public health, Jefferson tested a new smallpox vaccine on two hundred slaves, including eighty of his own.

No serious side effects became apparent, but many Virginians remained unconvinced about the vaccine's efficacy, so Jefferson exposed one of the vaccinated slaves to the live virus. When the man did not develop smallpox, white Virginians were vaccinated with matter drawn directly from the arms of the inoculated slaves.

The Dr. Mengele of Slavery

While Jefferson was no Josef Mengele, slavery did have its own versions of that infamous Auschwitz doctor. Only unlike Mengele, none of these practitioners were vilified. There was, for example, a little-known Dr. Thomas Hamilton who conducted tests "upon the slave John Brown in a makeshift open-pit oven in rural Georgia to discover the best remedies for sunstroke."[3]

Dr. J. Marion Sims was a nineteenth-century surgeon who is considered "the father of gynecology" for his invention of various surgical instruments, his belief in the importance of cleanliness, his founding of the New York Women's Hospital, and the discovery of a new vaginal surgical technique. In *Men Who Control Women's Health,* Diana Scully recounts Sims's various achievements as well as his violent experiments.

Dr. Sims began his southern medical practice in 1835. He became interested in a local slave, Anarcha, after he oversaw her difficult labor. Anarcha—whose last name remains unknown—suffered an injury called vesicovaginal fistula, after Sims damaged her during childbirth with his instruments.

Vesicovaginal fistula is the result of a puncture or tear between the vagina and the bladder, and leads to chronic bladder incontinence. Women with this condition became invalids and recluses. Enslaved black women were considered worthless since they could no longer "breed" or work.

Sims convinced plantation owners to give him, and in one case sell to him, seven young slave women who had the condition. He built a backwoods hospital where he experimented on the women from 1845 to 1849. Scully reports:

> [H]e performed repeated experiments on them in an attempt to find a way to close a fistula permanently. The operations were, in his own words, so painful that "none but a woman could have borne them." He operated on Anarcha thirty times without anesthesia and the others with "comparable frequency." As each experiment failed, the women's conditions worsened and became more painful. . . . [p. 42]

Sims was occasionally described as a "zealot" and his experimental zeal as "monomania," but colleagues also praised his courage and endurance. Sims's control over the enslaved women is discussed by Scully:

> [Sims] theorized that stoicism was part of the "negro racial endowment." [But] the explanation was simple. In addition to

the fact that it would have done a slave little good to resist a white man's orders, during the four years they were contained in his hospital Sims fed and sheltered the women and gave them "tremendous quantities of opium." Opium was used as a buffer against pain and "to prevent any activity of the bowels which might endanger the success of an operation." As a result of the administration of the opium, the women had "severe constipation," lasting up to five weeks; the tactic "nowadays . . . would be considered little short of murderous." Apparently the women became addicted to opium and were able to ensure themselves a supply of the drug only by submitting to Sims's continued experiments. [p. 43]

Sims succeeded in perfecting the operation in his thirtieth experimental surgery on Anarcha and made a name for himself in the history of gynecology. Scully comments that history tends to record "success," but not failure: "There is no record of the number of slaves like Anarcha who, because they were unprofitable for owners to keep, were used in medical and surgical experiments."

During the same period as Sims was active, the early 1840s, a physician in Prince George's County, Maryland, was subjecting enslaved women to the same type of experimental surgery. Dr. John Peter Mettauer operated numerous times on more than twenty-five women.[4] Although Mettauer reported his experiments in medical journals, he never achieved Sims's fame. Nor did he receive any censure.

The Myth of the Violent African

The myth of innate docility must have eased the consciences of experimenting doctors, slavers, and society in general. But once slavery was ended in America, the image of docility was completely transformed. The myth of the violent African now gained prominence to justify the continued oppression of black Americans.

In 1907 *The Negro: A Menace to American Civilization*, by R. W. Shufeldt, M.D., offered a quasi-scientific examination of biology and ethnology, claiming that the "negro" is closest to the apes. Indeed "he is untold ages nearer than is the typical representative of the best in the white race."*

---

*Another book from the same time period provides a stark contrast. *Is the Negro a Beast?*, an indictment of racism by William G. Schell (1901), describes the status achieved by blacks only thirty-four years after the end of slavery. Black America had already produced over 15,000 teachers, 17,000 college students, almost 1,000 doctors, and 1,400 books. At the time, $26,626,448 in church property and over 264,000 farms and homes were black-owned. Over the ensuing years, white racist policies would erode black ownership.

Shufeldt discusses African savagery as rooted in biology, quickly focusing on the central concern—the sexual craving of the "negro" for white women. He quotes another physician, Ellen Barret Ligon, who wrote a 1903 article titled "The White Woman and the Negro" for *Good Housekeeping*. Ligon warns, "The white woman is the coveted desire of the negro man. The despoiling of the white woman is his chosen vengeance." Shufeldt advocated complete segregation and the movement to re-colonize the black American race to Africa as the only permanent solution.

The view of Africans as dangerous beasts rationalized the extreme white violence leveled against them. Thousands of lynchings and untold numbers of other terrorist acts were committed against African-Americans, including beatings, cross burnings, and the rape of black women. Over many decades following the Civil War, blacks were driven from their land* and forced to migrate to major cities in search of industrial jobs and domestic work. They were segregated across the United States in ghettos—now called inner cities—and remain so to this day.

People as Objects

American anthropology contributed to the abuse and dehumanization of indigenous peoples by demeaning them as objects of study. Many indigenous people from around the world, as well as Native Americans, were brought captive to U.S. cities during the nineteenth and early twentieth centuries. Scientists of all sorts, including physicians, flocked to examine these people. The imported "live human specimens" were photographed naked, put on scientific and often public display, and housed under extraordinarily demeaning circumstances.

"Swallowing Other Beings Whole"

In 1903 a Congolese pygmy named Ota Benga was brought to the United States and placed on exhibit at the St. Louis World's Fair along with ten thousand indigenous people, including Japanese Ainu, Philippine Igorots, and Eskimos.[5] Prisoner of war Geronimo sold bows and arrows and was posed for photographs while on exhibit with Native Americans from more than fifty tribes.[6]

When the World's Fair was over, Ota Benga traveled with his white "sponsor," Samuel Phillips Verner, and the other pygmies, around the

---

*Black land loss exceeded six million acres by 1974. (Clift, 1974; Black Economic Resource Center, 1974).

United States and then returned to the Congo. But Ota Benga elected to return to America again.*

As Verner's finances disappeared, he sought shelter for Ota Benga by relocating him at the American Museum of Natural History in New York City, where Benga wandered at will among the tourists or through the silent nighttime corridors. P. V. Bradford and H. Blume's account of Benga's life describes him as being first fascinated but then disheartened:

> What Ota saw at the Museum of Natural History deepened an impression he had formed at the fair; the muzunga [white Americans] swallowed other beings whole. What they couldn't digest they deposited in fairs and museums. Totem poles, masks, pipes, hunting gear—the entire material world of the Kwakiutl Indians—were hanging from walls or the ceiling or displayed behind glass. It gave him a queasy feeling. . . . What had first held his attention now made him want to flee. It was maddening to be inside—to be swallowed whole—so long. He had an image of himself stuffed, behind glass, but somehow still alive, crouching over a fake campfire, feeding meat to a lifeless child. [pp. 165–166][†]

Ota Benga grew unhappy and became a potential embarrassment to the director, who was still coping with an earlier PR debacle surrounding captured Eskimos. Lacking funds to support Ota himself, Verner placed him at the Bronx Zoo.

Ota was initially allowed to roam throughout the zoo and its large woods. He adapted his native hunting style—to see but not be seen—but that created a problem, because zoo officials couldn't exploit him as a prize attraction. Zoo director William Hornaday arranged for Ota to live in the monkey house and posted a sign:[7]

The African Pygmy, "Ota Benga."
Age, 28 years. Height, 4 feet 11 inches.
Weight 103 pounds. Brought from the Kasai River,
Congo Free State, South Central Africa,
by Dr. Samuel P. Verner,
Exhibited each afternoon during September.

---

*Verner and Ota Benga developed a complex and lifelong friendship, although Verner eventually lost the financial means to be able to support and protect Benga.
[†]There is a brief mention in the Bradford and Blume book about a group of six Eskimos who were brought to the museum shortly before the time period that Ota Benga was living there. Their suffering (see ahead) may have affected Benga.

Thousands came daily to watch Ota through cage bars, and the New York media had a field day. Then members of the black clergy protested and eventually forced the liberation of Ota Benga from his display.*

Ultimately Benga sought refuge in Lynchburg, Virginia, among black friends. The newspapers continued to cover his life, indicating that although he was adapting, he wanted to return to Africa: "Speak of Africa, and there will come an indescribable longing in the jet-blacked eyes and a sort of droning like the sigh of an alien in a strange land."[8] Almost ten years later, still dreaming of Africa, desperate to return but lacking money, Ota Benga killed himself.

"Their Enlightened White Selves"

In 1897, renowned Arctic explorer Robert Peary brought six-year-old Minik and his father, Qisuk, along with four other Eskimos,† to New York City from Greenland. Peary was acting on the request of world-famous anthropologist Franz Boas to bring a live "specimen" for study.[9]

The six Eskimos were placed on exhibit and viewed by thousands before being turned over to the American Museum of Natural History. Housed in the museum's basement, they were frequently examined and observed by various scientists. The child Minik often slipped upstairs to play in the Arctic exhibit among the stuffed dogs and artifacts that reminded him of his homeland.

The basement grew overheated in the late summer and four Eskimos, including Minik's father and a young girl, died of tuberculosis.[10] Minik was adopted by the museum's building superintendent, William Wallace, and lived for a time on his farm. It was later discovered that Wallace had maintained a "bone-bleaching plant" on his farm, where numerous animals and the corpses of four Eskimos—including Minik's father—were "stripped of their flesh and forwarded to the [museum's] osteological department." Wallace confessed these activities haunted his dreams.[11]

Minik, while still a child, apparently learned that his father's skeleton was being kept at the museum. According to a recent recounting in the *Washington Post,* "Minik was stunned to come upon a display case housing the skeletal remains of his father—the father whose formal burial he thought he had witnessed years before."[12]

---

*The "Negro Clergy," members of the General Baptist Conference, were incensed at Benga's treatment. They gave daily interviews to the papers, attempted to get the mayor of New York to intervene, and eventually consulted a lawyer. An appendix in Bradford and Blume's book contains reproductions of a number of news accounts from that time period.
†Now known as Inuit.

The knowledge marked Minik forever, and he confronted the museum director who had arranged the sham burial of the boy's father in an attempt to placate him. One New York newspaper reported Minik saying, "I would shoot Mr. Peary and the museum director, only I want them to see how much more just a savage Eskimo is than their enlightened white selves."[13] At another point, according to Michael Kaufman, a despairing Minik stated:

> You're a race of scientific criminals. I know I'll never get my father's bones out of the American Museum of Natural History. I'm glad enough to get away before they grab my brains and stuff them into a jar.

After some years, Minik returned to Greenland, relearned the language and customs, and spent some years there before traveling again to New York State, where he became an itinerant sawmill worker until he died a year later in 1918 of the Spanish flu.

The museum, the anthropology profession, and Peary himself tried hard to expunge Minik's story from history, omitting it from descriptions and accounts of the time period. Minik was rediscovered and his story told by a businessman in the Northwest Territories, Kenn Harper, who spent eight years researching the Eskimo boy's experiences to report them in a book titled *Give Me My Father's Bones.*

Kenn Harper's efforts were eventually rewarded. After reporter W. Claiborne wrote a 1992 feature in the *Washington Post,* Wallace's great-great-granddaughter, Wendy J. Wallace, took up the cause. In a follow-up story, the *Washington Post* reported:[14]

> a precious cargo of century-old human bones will make its way in a few weeks from the bowels of the American Museum of Natural History in New York to a graveyard on the icy western edge of Greenland. A simple brass plaque will read: "They have come home."

The stories of Ota Benga and Minik have only recently been rediscovered. No one knows how many other human tragedies resulting from racist science are hidden away in the basement archives of our museums and universities.

The Infamous Tuskegee Study

Racism in America has continued to haunt science and medicine into the twentieth century. The Tuskegee Study that began in 1932 is among the most horrible examples of American medical racism.[15]

Tuskegee was a public health service project run by the Centers for Disease Control (CDC) that lasted forty years. Designed to examine the "natural" course of syphilis, the public health doctors advertised "special free treatment" and, after testing, selected 412 infected black men and a control group for study. Medical historian Bonnie Blustein notes that "the whole point of Tuskegee was racism pure and simple. There were already longitudinal studies of untreated syphilis in Scandinavia (from a time when there was no treatment of choice). The only point to Tuskegee was to look for racial differences: would it be the same in black people?"[16] In *Bad Blood: The Tuskegee Syphilis Experiment,* James H. Jones shows that the study was formulated within a general medical environment that encouraged racist speculation about supposed biological differences between white and black persons.

Over a period of forty years the infected men were not told they had syphilis, nor was the existing medical treatment for syphilis administered. Consequently, their entire families and any other contacts were placed at risk of acquiring the disease. Spinal taps were a part of the updated examinations given to the men, some of whom were left in pain for days afterward. Since examining the corpses of the men was important to the study, families were offered $100 in burial fees if they brought in the bodies.

When penicillin was discovered in the early 1940s, thousands of returning GIs were treated for syphilis, but the Tuskegee subjects were once again denied treatment. To prevent treatment, the public health service arranged for fifty of the infected men to be exempted from service during the war. It was, according to one CDC officer involved in the study, "almost like genocide."[17]

When Tuskegee doctors were interviewed in the 1970s, only one medical professional expressed qualms about the study's ethical implications—the black nurse who looked after the infected men for forty years.[18] More than thirteen articles about the Tuskegee study appeared in major medical journals, and dozens of young doctors participated for a time in the project while working for the public health service before going into private practice. No known protests were made within the profession. Despite an internal review in 1969, the CDC decided to continue the study.

The lid blew off Tuskegee in 1972 when a former public health service field-worker alerted the Associated Press. A lawsuit resulted in a government settlement of $10 million for Tuskegee survivors and their families. Nobody got rich: syphilis-infected persons received $37,500 each and non-infected individuals received $16,000. Only twenty-five men remained alive in 1992.

Tuskegee has been called "the most important event in the history of U.S. medical ethics," by Arthur Chaplan, director of the University of Minnesota's Center for Bio-Medical Ethics. Congressional regulations resulted, requiring new safeguards in cases of human experimentation. But as Blustein has pointed out, problems in medical ethics will remain as long as medicine is practiced within the context of a racist society.

Tuskegee still haunts African-Americans, hindering public health and CDC efforts to inform black communities on AIDS prevention. James H. Jones points out in *Bad Blood* that white America tends to ridicule black fears that AIDS is a conspiracy to wipe them out. Jones comments on the "singular lack of sensitivity" of those who use words like "bizarre," "astonishing," and "paranoia" to describe the African-American fear of an AIDS conspiracy.

"The Darkening Face of AIDS"

Recent developments are further inflaming fears of AIDS-related genocide in the black community. A *Washington Post* headline reads, "In Some Cities, AIDS Found Top Killer of Young Adults."[19] Among young black men, only deaths from homicide surpassed those from AIDS.[20]

A newspaper feature by Stephanie Mencimer, "D.C.'s New Death Row," discloses that AIDS is the leading cause of death among District of Columbia prisoners, nearly all of whom are black. In part because most are incarcerated for drug-related crimes, more than 20 percent of the inmates are infected with HIV. This compares with a rate of one-tenth of 1 percent for the public at large. Since many young men are raped in jail, exposing them to an extremely high risk of HIV infection, even a short prison term becomes a potential death sentence. Because America's justice system locks up black youths at a disproportionately high rate for drug-related crimes— while sending home white youths caught for the same crimes—the cry of genocide gains credibility.

First discovered as a disease among gay males, AIDS has made such massive inroads into black communities that African-Americans and Hispanics now account for 46 percent of AIDS cases although they make up only 21 percent of the population.[21] The National Commission on AIDS has declared that the disease must be viewed as a racial issue. One commission member who is black expressed fears about releasing the report. "I am terribly worried that, once it is learned that the face of AIDS is darkening, broad public support may fade."[22]

The commission also expressed fears that the disease could take hold quickly within the Asian and American Indian communities. Kevin Nephew of the National Native American AIDS Task Force pointed out that there are fewer than two million Native Americans and some tribes have memberships totaling only in the hundreds. He said, "If this disease infiltrates these communities, we are looking at the genocide of our people."[23]

The commission's concerns proved well-grounded when, in December 1992, the CDC cut funds for Washington, D.C. AIDS prevention, education, testing, and counseling services, including the only study in the country of HIV infection among adolescents.[24] The adolescent study was directed by Lawrence D'Angelo, chief of adolescent medicine at Children's Hospital. D'Angelo had found that only one in two hundred surveyed teens were infected with HIV in 1987, but that the figure had increased to one in sixty by early 1993.

When we spoke with D'Angelo, he confirmed that the early 1993 statistics on adolescent HIV infection rates are the last data that will be available. Due to the CDC cuts, he will have to abandon the study. Without any statistical barometer on increasing rates of infection among teenagers in the United States, how will Congress, federal agencies, and the American public be informed and galvanized into action? Should the CDC be funding controversial, questionable violence-initiative research while it cuts funding for AIDS projects that could directly save teenage lives?

Ethnic Weapons?

Is it possible that the U.S. military would try to develop a biological weapon that would target black people?[25] A fungus endemic to California's San Joaquin Valley produces coccidiomycosis, or "valley fever." It is disseminated by wind-blown spores, initially infects the lungs, and can be fatal when it spreads elsewhere in the body. The University of California's Naval Bio-Science Lab in Alameda discovered that the fungus interacts negatively with melanin.* Therefore African- and Asian-Americans are ten times more likely to die from the disease than are Euro-Americans.

As reviewed by Gerald Horne in *CovertAction,* Congressional hearings in 1977 disclosed that the Army had been experimenting with a supposedly harmless fungus that spreads in the same fashion as the lethal valley fever. Targeting African-American dock and warehouse workers at the Mechanicsburg, Pennsylvania, naval depot, the Army successfully contaminated shoes and naval stores with the benign fungus to study its spread. The real goal was to test the possibility of using the fatal fungus—with its special lethality for people of color—as a biological weapon. The article in *CovertAction* that tells this story was placed alongside an analysis of NIMH's proposed violence initiative.

---

*Melanin is the chemical substance responsible for skin pigmentation of human beings. It is also found in varying quantities in other parts of the body, including internal organs and the brain.

NIMH, Johns Hopkins, and the XYY Syndrome

A very small percentage of men have an extra Y chromosome, producing the XYY syndrome. On the basis of surveys of prison populations, it was erroneously concluded that these individuals are genetically predisposed to be impulsive, criminal, or violent.[26] By 1970, many geneticists already considered the XYY theory to be "scientific rubbish."[27]

A three-year NIMH-funded project aimed at locating XYY abnormalities in boys began in 1970. One part of the project targeted 7,500 East Baltimore children, "95 per cent from underprivileged Negro families enrolled in a free child care program at Johns Hopkins."[28] The blood was drawn as a routine check for anemia, and the samples were then sent, without parental permission, for examination by the staff of the Division of Medical Genetics at Johns Hopkins.

Another study group in the NIMH–Johns Hopkins project included 6,000 boys in Maryland centers for delinquent and neglected children, some younger than age fourteen. Maryland juvenile court probation officers were empowered to persuade reluctant parents to have the blood samples drawn from their children. The state director of juvenile services told investigative reporter Diane Bauer that the test results "will probably be passed on to the courts for whatever use they can make of it" and admitted it would expose the boys to the risk of being labeled biologically criminal for the remainder of their lives.[29] The population of these juvenile centers was 75 percent African-American.

As a result of adverse publicity, Johns Hopkins was forced to adopt a special consent form stating that the test results would be kept confidential, but otherwise the project was allowed to continue.[30] Johns Hopkins researchers described their project as a "free $100 medical bargain" to encourage impoverished families to submit their incarcerated children.[31] Meanwhile, the university refused to inform those previously tested that their rights had been violated and that a new consent form was in use.

Racism in Modern Psychiatry

The violence initiative itself provides confirmation of racism in contemporary psychiatry, but the problem reaches yet more deeply into the routine practice of institutional psychiatry. According to a recent survey reported in *Southern Exposure,*[32] "blacks are nearly three times more likely than whites to be locked up against their will in Southern mental hospitals." The hospitals are increasingly segregated, with blacks in public facilities and whites in private ones. The Mental Health Law Project of Washington, D.C. reported that "It is a fact of their everyday life that black and Hispanic consumers are underserved, misdiagnosed, segregated, and over-institutionalized."

Blacks are also more severely diagnosed and treated with heavier drug doses and lengthier hospital stays. *Southern Exposure* reports that African-American men in both public and private mental hospitals are diagnosed schizophrenic at almost twice the rate of whites. Black women fare even worse. Schizophrenia is the leading diagnosis for black women admitted to hospitals but the least frequent one for white women.

Southern Exposure reporter D. Ramm concludes that "states are using their authority to lock people up in mental hospitals as a powerful form of social control, creating a system of racial segregation."*

From the DBDs to Antisocial Personality Disorder

According to violence prevention researchers, psychiatric conduct disorders in children often turn into antisocial personality disorders in adults. This makes "early intervention" necessary to prevent adult violent crime. But this seemingly scientific observation has little basis. It also fits easily into racist programs.

Antisocial personal disorder is the extension of disruptive behavior disorders (DBDs—see Chapter 4) into adulthood. To be labeled antisocial personality disorder, the individual must first meet the childhood standard for conduct disorder, plus an additional four adult criteria. The criteria are selected from the following list: (1) "unable to sustain consistent work behavior," (2) "fails to conform to social norms with respect to lawful behavior," (3) "is irritable and aggressive, as indicated by repeated physical fights or assaults," (4) is financially irresponsible, (5) "fails to plan ahead," (6) lies and cons people, (7) reckless about safety of self and others, including drunk driving and "recurrent speeding," (8) if a parent, fails to function as a "responsible parent," (9) has never sustained a "totally monogamous relationship for more than one year," and (10) "lacks remorse (feels justified in having hurt, mistreated or stolen from another)."

Alan Stone, professor of law and psychiatry at Harvard, stated "there can be little question that the urban poor and racial minorities will be swept into this diagnostic category. *DSM-III* may well introduce . . . racism."[33] The profile for antisocial personality disorder fits many inner-city youths, as well as anyone living amid poverty, unemployment, violence, prejudice, and other demoralizing forces. And it is the impoverished and ethnic minorities who are most often caught up in the net of these psychiatric diagnoses.

---

*And despite mounting evidence of misuse of commitment laws, there is a "strong, national movement" to make involuntary commitment easier, according to Ramm (see also Breggin, 1991a).

However, as historian Bonnie Blustein points out, these same criteria, although not applied, would fit many more affluent members of society, such as financiers involved in the S and L crisis who are "financially irresponsible, fail to plan ahead, lie and con people, and lack remorse."[34]

Among the poor, some of these seemingly negative qualities are actually required for survival on the urban streets or in jail.[35] People often learn to lie and to con because it seems like the only way to survive. Similarly, people learn to focus on immediate satisfactions when the future seems to hold little hope. And we must also remember that social injustices can invite civil disobedience—admired in retrospect, but often considered lawbreaking when implemented.

How is it that mental health professionals so easily discount and ignore real-life stories in favor of abstract diagnoses? Why do we want to turn real people into stereotypes within categories? The Norwegian criminologist Nils Christie described how easy it was for World War II concentration camp guards in his own country to kill people whom they saw as a "grey mass" rather than as real people. In a concentration camp, according to Christie, "physical changes occur early and include malnutrition, edema, infection from the lowered immune systems, diarrhea" and various signs of apathy, listlessness, and numbness. People in charge, including commandants and guards, can interpret these signs of human degradation as barbarism rather than as a result of starvation, humiliation, and brutalization. The prisoners are ultimately viewed as being subhuman.

So it is in our inner cities, our barrios, our reservations, and in the Appalachian mountains—wherever ethnic enclaves struggle to scratch a living from their mean and meager surroundings. The cumulative physical results of malnutrition, exposure to toxic substances, poor health care, discrimination, unemployment, poverty, and segregation cause devastating psychological as well as physiological effects. A "scientist" or a psychiatrist examining these cumulative effects without taking the larger environmental context into account can erroneously conclude that this group of people is genetically or biologically deficient.

Racist Eugenics in America

The idea that blacks are biologically inferior has been promoted by Western eugenics from the very beginning. The widespread sterilization of inmates of mental institutions and facilities for the developmentally disabled undoubtedly affected blacks disproportionately, if only because of their higher representation among the poor who flood these institutions.

While Germany gave up eugenical sterilization after the war, America did not. In the early 1970s, it was disclosed that government-sponsored clinics sterilized more than eighty poor minors. During the same period, doctors in one North Carolina county had sterilized eighteen women—half the welfare mothers who had babies under Medicaid. Nearly all were black. Many major American teaching hospitals during the 1970s pushed poor and often black women into getting sterilized, sometimes encouraging hysterectomies over the safer and less traumatic tubal ligations.[36]

In 1974 Judge Gerhard A. Gesell concluded that between 100,000 and 150,000 low-income women had been sterilized annually over the last few years under federally funded programs. He wrote, "The dividing line between family planning and eugenics is murky."[37]

African-American women often bore the brunt of birth control research. When Upjohn's Depo-Provera—an injectable three-month contraceptive—was tested as an experimental drug, a disproportionate number of the subjects were "poor, black women."[38] This was done at a time when there was concern about potential dangers, including cancer. In another experiment, 55 percent of the women at a "ghetto clinic" in New York City were given an IUD when a clinic researcher was testing a new model. The IUD was eventually recalled.

Norplant, Teenage Motherhood, and Racism

It is no surprise that many African-Americans are suspicious of the introduction into their communities of Norplant, a surgically implanted contraceptive that prevents pregnancy for five years. First made available by the Baltimore public health service to urban black teens,[39] it is also being offered to teenage girls in the two poorest wards of the District of Columbia under a DHHS program, Healthy Start.[40]

The *Washington Post* reported that "the use of Norplant as a tool of social policy has drawn heated protests from critics who contend that encouraging long-term birth control—especially among low-income black women—is paternalistic and racist."[41] The controversy was sparked two years ago when an editorial writer in Philadelphia suggested giving "welfare mothers" incentives for using Norplant, an idea that continues to be floated in various states that are struggling with shrinking budgets. The American Medical Association has criticized judges who have ordered Norplant for women convicted of child abuse.[42]

While complaining about the high birth rates among inner-city teens, the Bush administration made abortion unavailable under health services offered to the poor. It is very likely that white teenager birth rates would more closely approximate the birth rates of minority youth if abortion were similarly unavailable to them.

The issue of abortion, Norplant, and overall birth control availability is controversial among African-Americans. Many black leaders, like Surgeon General Joycelyn Elders, are advocating the voluntary use of these measures by minority, and mainstream, youth. They emphasize *voluntary* use by teens to counteract the growing crisis of "children having children."

Genocide, eugenics, and population control of minorities are historical facts in the United States. Yet it is also true that the problems of black teenagers and their infants are immeasurably compounded by early parenthood. This is a controversy with convincing positions on both sides. White Americans can best assist the black community by frankly and directly addressing white racism and by leveling the playing field for all children and youths, while the black community develops its own positions on these issues.

Foster Care, Adoption, and the Fate of African-American Babies

There are thousands of black children in foster homes who need permanent families. But why have they landed in foster care? L. S. Richman points out in *Fortune:*

> [P]overty, along with the violence and hopelessness it breeds, has been the major factor in the staggering rise in the number of children removed from parental custody. In 1990 a record 407,000 minors were placed in foster homes—up 66% just since 1983. While some of the forced separations result from the physical or sexual abuse that grabs tabloid headlines, most stem from parental neglect—or inability—to provide basic food, clothing, or shelter.

These foster care children are not always better off away from their biological families. A New York study of children under the age of thirteen who ended up in mental hospitals showed that a whopping 70 percent of them had been in foster homes before being hospitalized.[43] Even children who have been physically or sexually abused can experience debilitating loss when separated from their families. A better solution often requires helping the whole family, and, through them, the child. The best family service approaches are exemplified by individualized, wraparound service programs that focus on the actual needs of the child and family (Chapter 9).

For some children in foster care, there is no going back to their biological parents, who may be dead or unable to care for them. The permanent adoption of black children by white families has been traditionally discouraged, but recently Senator Howard Metzenbaum introduced a bill to further accommodate transracial adoption. Supporters of the bill argue that there aren't enough black families to adopt all the available children.[44]

Many African-Americans have expressed deep concerns over transracial adoption, fearing that the removal of children from their cultural roots is genocidal. They cite racist barriers that prevent qualified and willing black families from adopting black children.[45] They believe the future existence of black America—its culture, its heart, its identity—lies within black families and their babies.

Taking Children Away

There are ominous calls for the wholesale removal of "at risk" children from their homes. Writing about the relationship between illegitimacy and violence in the "underclass," Charles Murray recently expressed fear over the growing numbers of "unsocialized male adolescents" whose "norms" are "physical violence, immediate gratification and predatory sex." Murray, a fellow of the American Enterprise Institute, wants to "end all economic support for single mothers" and thereby force many of them to give up their children for adoption or institutional placement in special government orphanages. He suggests calling the orphanages "24-hour-a-day preschools" and warns against "those who prattle about the importance of keeping children with their biological mothers." In his opinion, "The child deserves society's support. The parent does not." Murray's proposals are especially frightening in light of his own estimate that 68 percent of black children should be considered "illegitimate." That the *Wall Street Journal* would publish his op-ed piece is indicative of increasing hostility toward the black community among America's leaders, as well as a willingness to consider extremely repressive solutions.

In a *New York Times* column, John J. DiIulio, Jr., a Princeton University professor and senior fellow at the Brookings Institute, also focused on crime in the black community. He encouraged James Q. Wilson's concept of voluntary boarding schools for families in poor urban communities. These would promote "the good character traits of politeness, cooperation, kindness, hard work and self-control." Social consciousness and even leadership qualities are markedly absent from the description.

None of these authors mentions America's racist policies as a contributing factor to the plight of the inner city. Furthermore, they reject social transformation or safety-net programs. They promote their recommendations under the rubric of "save the children" and violence prevention. Like biomedical violence initiative advocates, they emphasize personality defects in vulnerable individuals whom they see as lacking impulse control. Their suggestions parallel Goodwin's interest in "highly structured environments with clear positive and negative reinforcers,"[46] as well as "day camps" for older children from "very disruptive environments."[47]

The War on Drugs and Operation Weed and Seed

We were on the air in Baltimore on a community talk show when the host asked us if we had heard about "Operation Weed and Seed"—a U.S. Department of Justice (DOJ) program that makes intensive interventions into designated areas of inner cities. We were sure our host had coined the phrase "weed and seed" to ridicule it. Then he pushed across the table an official DOJ document entitled "Operation Weed and Seed."[48] Only a profoundly racist federal bureaucracy could have allowed itself the luxury of comparing black youth to weeds.[49]

Operation Weed and Seed is a federal strong-arm program to "weed" criminals from targeted neighborhoods through coordinated police activity, afterward "seeding" the community with investment money, tax incentives, and federal funds. To date, there's been a lot of weeding, and precious little "seeding."*[50] Operation Weed and Seed parallels the psychiatric violence initiative, especially with its focus on identifying and targeting individuals, rather than ameliorating the overall situation of black youth.

The war on drugs also focuses upon individuals. As Elliott Currie noted in a 1993 critique of the war on drugs:

> most of our energy and resources have gone toward fighting the *symptoms* of the drug crisis, not its causes. Indeed the Bush administration explicitly rejected an attack on the causes of drug abuse—warning that we should not succumb to what it curiously called the "easy temptation" to focus our energies on the "chronic problems of social environment" that "help to breed and spread the contagion of drug use."

Operation Weed and Seed and the War on Drugs has contributed to the prison crisis which Congressman Don Edwards dates to 1981 with the Reagan-Bush "war on crime." Mandatory minimum sentences were established through legislatures, forcing judges to lock up convicted drug offenders for predetermined periods. Prisons have now become so overcrowded

---

*Copies of "A Call to Reject the Federal Weed and Seed Program in Los Angeles" can be obtained by writing the Labor/Community Strategy Center, 14540 Haynes Street, #200, Van Nuys, CA 91411.

that dangerous, hardened criminals are being released to make room for mandatory-minimum-sentence inmates, and the cost of new prisons is literally driving some states into bankruptcy. The prison population has tripled since 1980. Edwards says, "Three-quarters of new arrivals are drug offenders; by 1996, these offenders will comprise two-thirds of the prison population. Ninety-one percent of mandatory minimum sentences are imposed on non-violent first-time offenders."

And who is filling these prisons? In Baltimore, Maryland, 56 percent of black men, ages eighteen to thirty-five, "were under some form of criminal justice sanction on any given day in 1991." The study by Jerome Miller's National Center on Institutions and Alternatives found that most of Baltimore's black young men were "in jail or prison, on probation or parole, awaiting trial or sentencing, or being sought on warrants for their arrest."[51] By the age of thirty-five, 75 percent or more of all inner-city African-American men will be arrested and jailed. Most are convicted of non-violent drug-related crimes, usually involving the sale of drugs.

A black person is far more likely to be arrested on drug charges than a white person, and, once arrested, is far more likely to end up in jail than a white person engaged in precisely the same illegal activity. According to Miller, the African-American will most likely be charged with the sale of drugs, requiring a jail sentence, while the Euro-American, charged with the lesser crime of possession, goes home.

As a recent *Washington Post* editorial pointed out, possession of five grams of crack cocaine carries a federal mandatory minimum sentence of five years without parole for first offenders, while possession of powdered cocaine carries no mandatory sentence and offenders can get off with probation. The *Post* reported that a representative sample of federal drug cases for 1992 showed that "*all* defendants convicted of simple possession of crack during the time studied were black."[52]

The news of these injustices is at last getting around, and *USA Today*—"The Nation's Newspaper"—recently showcased a story by Sam Vincent Meddis entitled "Is the Drug War Racist?" The subhead concluded, "Disparities Suggest the Answer Is Yes." The feature reported that blacks and whites use illegal drugs in roughly the same proportions, while a *USA Today* computer analysis of 1991 drug arrests found that blacks are far more likely to be arrested and jailed. In at least thirty major cities, blacks were more likely to get arrested than whites by a factor of ten or greater.

The greater arrest rate of blacks is not due to stricter enforcement in the inner city. Blacks were even more disproportionately subjected to arrest in the suburbs, and increasingly Hispanics are being similarly targeted.

Nor is the great arrest rate of blacks for drug sales due to more drug traffickers among blacks. Drug Enforcement Administration (DEA) chief Robert Bonner told *USA Today* that white traffickers are in the majority.

What Works?

The punitive, law-and-order social policies toward street and especially drug crimes have been in place since the early seventies. They have done nothing but fill jails where the inmates become more hardened and crime-prone. Currie (1993) points out that the "correctional" approach—a law-and-order response to drug abuse—is at the least ineffective. At worst, it encourages drug abuse among disaffected youth by offering excitement and financial reward, an aura of illicit intrigue, and the "coolness" of being a gangster. The alternative traditional model—the "medical" model of addiction—also fails to address the underlying problem. Some individual addicts can be helped with treatment, but the social milieu from which the addiction grew continues to generate new addicts.

Currie's review of studies found that drug addiction is

> a particularly devastating syndrome that included relative poverty in a surrounding society and culture of affluence and mass consumption and a single-minded emphasis on material success; the bleakness of confinement in menial and futureless occupations; and the resulting absence of legitimate avenues for gaining either an adequate income (as the larger society defined it), or the less tangible but equally fundamental requirements of a sense of challenge, place, and purpose, a stable and respected identity.

Currie explains that national plans for community regeneration were derailed by the Nixon era and the redirection of federal funds into the Vietnam War. "As a result," Currie says, "by the seventies what we were doing in response to drug abuse in the cities increasingly diverged from what we knew about its causes, leading to the . . . divorce of analysis from strategy that has marked our urban drug policies ever since."

The result? Nowhere else in the world, including the old USSR and the old South Africa, is such a large percentage of the population subject to a criminal justice system. Far many more blacks go to jail than to college; in some communities, more go to jail than graduate high school. Prison has become the training ground for black youth in the inner cities.

American Apartheid

While this chapter focuses on racism in science and medicine, apartheid exists on every level in America, and multiple threats are aligned against the black community. A variety of books, including many recent ones, portray and analyze this tragic reality.*

Many of the African-Americans we have spoken with see America as fundamentally genocidal. They know that the country was built on the near extermination of the original inhabitants and the enslavement of captured Africans. They do not believe the European invasion was admirable, heroic, or edifying; and they doubt that white Americans have overcome the legacy. They think that the dominant society still lives by the principle "White Makes Right."

But genocide?

Many black community members we've spoken with feel there's no other possible explanation for the multiple escalating threats against the black community: the high rate of AIDS, the largely untreated epidemic of drug-resistant tuberculosis, the highest infant mortality rate among industralized nations, the lack of overall health care, the ongoing epidemic of lead poisoning,[53] poverty, unemployment, the deterioration and segregation of the schools,[54] collapsing inner-city infrastructure, disproportionately high environmental pollution,[55] police brutality, rampant violent crime, the avalanche of street drugs, the selective promotion of cigarettes and high-alcohol content drinks like malt liquor, government programs for long-term contraceptive medications for "welfare mothers" and teenage girls, utterly inadequate social welfare programs, corporate America's reluctance to make urban investments, deliberate and persistent financial and economic discrimination by banks and other institutions,[56] repeated failures to prevent or control riots before they spread, lack of rebuilding in the aftermath of riots, the criminalization of the great majority of black males, the murder and criminal conviction of black leaders, and finally, the refusal of mainstream white leadership to take a moral and political stand against racism.

African-Americans examine these realities and conclude, "This can't be all our fault; this can't be entirely accidental."

Everywhere we have gone, from Harlem to Watts and from Washington,

---

*Andrew Hacker, *Two Nations: Black and White, Separate, Hostile, and Unequal* (1991), and Douglas Massey and Nancy Denton, *American Apartheid: Segregation of the Underclass* (1991), explicitly describe apartheid. Elliot Liebow's *Tally's Corner* (1967), Jonathan Kozol's *Savage Inequalities* (1991), Alex Kotlowitz's *There Are No Children Here* (1991), and Derrick Bell's *Faces at the Bottom of the Well* (1992) portray the lives of black urban youths in human terms. Others, like Frances Cress Welsing's *The Isis Papers* (1991), Amos N. Wilson's *Black-on-Black Violence* (1990), and Cornell West's *Race Matters* (1993), analyze racism's painful social implications.

D.C. to Fort Lauderdale, from black universities to urban health clinics—African-Americans tell us that white America is increasingly genocidal toward them.

What Is Genocide?

Genocide is the ultimate expression of domination and exclusion. These two tendencies, to *dominate* and to *exclude,* are so closely related that they are nearly inseparable. To dominate others, we must first convince ourselves that they are sufficiently different and inferior from us to warrant "special treatment." We must be willing to exclude them from our personal version of the human race.

The term *genocide* was coined by jurist Raphael Lemkin before World War II to indicate the destruction of an ethnic or national group and was first officially used in the Nuremberg Nazi indictments.[57] On December 11, 1946, the U.N. General Assembly passed a resolution against genocide, and later a proposed international treaty, the Genocide Convention.

The final Convention on Genocide defines the crime of genocide as the intentional commission of "any of the following acts committed with intent to destroy, in whole or in part, a national, ethical, racial or religious group, such as":[58]

> (a) Killing members of the group.
> (b) Causing serious bodily or mental harm to members of the group.
> (c) Deliberately inflicting on the group conditions of life calculated to bring about its physical destruction in whole or in part.
> (d) Imposing measures intended to prevent births within the group.
> (e) Forcibly transferring children of the group to another group.

Genocide includes the intentional perpetration of *any* of these criminal acts whether or not a country is at war. Clearly all of them have been inflicted on the black community over the history of America. And a strong argument can be made that all or most of them continue to this day. Many African-Americans are especially certain about the first three in the list. They feel that the dreadful condition of black life in America is the direct result of racism as expressed through national policies and socially sanctioned racist attitudes.

The only defense America can hope to make is that it lacks genocidal *intent*—that its political and social policies are not intentionally aimed, for example, at creating the conditions of urban life that are destroying African-Americans and their communities. But can such a consistent and persistent policy have evolved by chance?

There seems little room for argument about whether American society is doing much to *prevent* the ongoing destruction of the lives and culture of the urban black community. The answer to that question must be a resounding "No!" We are doing very little to save the African-American community or, for that matter, to bring a halt to racism. These failures in themselves should be considered genocidal.

No More Mr. Nice Guy

While the African-American community says, "We're at the end of our rope; we can't stand any more," the white community responds, "No more Mr. Nice Guy." For fear of driving away the white electorate, even the "liberal" Clinton presidential campaign did not dare to make racism or the plight of inner-city children a campaign issue.

If white America cannot find the heart to empathize with the plight of its black children, and if the black community cannot find some hope for surviving and ultimately thriving in America, our society as we know it cannot be maintained. As journalist and author Sam Yette predicted two decades ago in *The Choice,* America will either fall apart or become a genocidal police state, or both, if it does not deal equitably with its black Americans.

The fate of the black child may turn out to be the single most important indicator of the future of America—a future that is inseparable from that of the black child.

How goes the black child? So goes America . . .

"I Never Did Anything to Black People. Neither Did My Parents."

Most white Americans seem to feel that they have no personal responsibility for the condition of black Americans. Given the chance, they express themselves with indignation about it: they don't owe anything to African-Americans, because they haven't personally done anything to them. In *Two Nations,* Andrew Hacker pointed out that "few white Americans feel obliged to ponder how membership in the major race gives them powers and privileges."

Nearly all white Americans benefit indirectly and often unwittingly from the violent legacy of slavery and ongoing racism. Because of the color of their skin, white people are born with an entitlement—to make the most of what the society had already developed over its several hundred years of history. They are born into or have arrived in this society as its chief benefactors. They enjoy the fruits of its historical crimes—Native American genocide, black enslavement, and continued racism—and continue to consume a disproportionate share of what the society has to offer. While it doesn't help to feel guilty, they should be aware of the injustice and unfairness, especially as these injustices continue to accrue to their benefit.

This nation cannot survive in relative freedom without the full inclusion of all races and social classes in whatever remains of the American dream. We cannot afford to discard any children.

In the words of Maya Angelou:[59]

> Sometimes I'm almost brought to tears when I wonder, what if all the vitality and insouciance and love of life of black America were openly included in the national psyche?

9

Ending Biomedical Child Abuse

In years to come, the United States will be less safe, less caring, less free, unless we act today. We catch glimpses of this future in the violence that stalks children in school-yards and neighborhoods, the homeless who crowd city streets, and prisons filled to capacity. We see it in the growing number of children without fathers, students without skills, teenagers without hope.

—Beyond Rhetoric, The Final Report of the National Commission on Children (1991)

I would not know how to be a human being at all, except I learned this from other human beings. We are made for a delicate network of relationships, of interdependence. We are meant to complement each other. All kinds of things go horribly wrong when we break that fundamental rule of our being.

—Bishop Desmond Tutu

A nation has a collective responsibility to provide hope and opportunity—or the promise of life and liberty is just a lie.

—Courtland Milloy (1993)

It takes a whole village to raise a child.

—African proverb

AMERICA IS A WONDERFUL PLACE TO LIVE.

America is a dreadful place to live.

It all depends.

What it depends upon is a matter of considerable controversy. Some be-lieve that it's a matter of circumstance, and that America is a wonderful place to live only if you have advantages, such as being white, educated, and male with a marketable skill. Others believe it's a question of personal responsibility, and that America is an ideal place to live if you are willing to take responsibility for yourself and your family.

Born in the USA

Both circumstance and personal responsibility are important in the lives of adult Americans, but a great deal happens along the way to becoming an adult. So let's rephrase the question.

Is America a wonderful place to be *born*?

If infants are innocent of personal responsibility, then being born is a matter of chance. You could have been born a rich Euro-American infant boy in the suburbs, a poor African-American girl in the inner city, or a stillborn fetus on a Native American reservation.

Few if any people would argue that America's children are born to a level playing field. The hope is that the tilt in the field is not unsurmountable, and that there's sufficient opportunity for almost any responsible adult to make a good, respectable life in America. But it has become increasingly difficult to believe that the ideal is being approximated. Especially if we consider children, the growing unfairness of life in America becomes all too apparent.

Personal Responsibility and Impersonal Handicaps

Successful living requires each person at all times to remain as responsible and self-determining as possible.[1] People should never allow themselves excuses for becoming helpless or for behaving unethically, and should always seek to triumph spiritually over temptation and adversity. Based on this philosophy, we do not hold that the environment alone determines the outcome of every adult individual's moral life. Why, then, place so much emphasis on the role of the environment in the lives of minorities, children, and other seemingly victimized groups?

While the environment probably cannot predetermine anyone's specific actions, it influences everyone's degree of suffering and distress, and can create overwhelming handicaps. Some people from very bad circumstances will turn out well, but they will not turn out unscarred. Poverty, racism, sexism, inadequate education, family violence, and other factors always make life difficult and produce misery. That some of the victims grow up to live honorable lives should not render us insensitive to their suffering, or to the suffering of others who fare less well.

In the instance of infants and small children, it becomes especially important to focus on their living conditions. From lead poisoning and physical abuse to chronic humiliation and rejection, there are negative influences that no small child can survive unscathed. Not only their minds, but their brains, can end up irrevocably impaired. (See Chapter 4 for the discussion of the effects of the environment on the developing brain.) These youngsters are not predestined to be violent, but they are compelled to struggle harder, longer, and more painfully in order to achieve the same results as others. Too many children are much too hindered in the process of growing up in America.

When women, children, racial minorities, or the poor are oppressed, their leadership must encourage a commitment to personal responsibility as well as social activism. But for those of us who are more advantaged, our responsibility lies in helping to lift the burden of prejudice and inequality off their backs. Justice requires, first and foremost, that we take responsibility for our contribution to the problem. If, instead, we focus our attention on the personal responsibility of the victims, we deny our own role in allowing the oppression to persist, and heap injustice upon injustice.

The Vulnerability of America's Children

Many Americans are vulnerable to biopsychiatry, including brain-disabling drugs and electroshock: women, minority groups, and the aged; the homeless; and people who lack education and technical skills, whose occupations are no longer needed, or who suffer from physical or mental challenges to their functioning in contemporary society. Typically, society invites psychiatry to step in, and to "treat" these people, instead of meeting their real-life needs.[2]

But no group is more vulnerable than America's children. The real problem in mental health care for children is not the one heralded by the profession. It's not the *lack* of traditional mental health services for our children. That's the last thing youngsters need. They deserve protection *from* much of what goes on in psychiatry, and they deserve empathic services that address their real needs.

Multiple indicators signal that America's children are suffering. Not unexpectedly, minority children are especially endangered, but so are all children. An advertisement by the Children's Defense Fund and the Robin Hood Foundation in the July 13, 1992, edition of *The New York Times* spells out their plight:*

---

*The ad does not exaggerate. See, for example, Carnegie Council on Adolescent Development, 1989; National Center for Children and Poverty, 1990; and National Commission on Children, 1991a, 1991b.

- More than one-fourth have no health insurance.
- One-fifth live below the official poverty line.
- A higher proportion of them die in infancy than in twenty-three other nations.
- One hundred thousand are homeless.
- Two and one-half million are *reported* abused or neglected yearly.

Some problems that we prefer to attribute to inner-city kids are actually worse in the suburbs, including alcoholism and drug abuse.[3] When high school students from Virginia talked to interviewers, they revealed:[4]

- More than one-fourth indulged in binge drinking.
- One-fourth carried a weapon to school in the prior several months, including guns, knives, and clubs.*
- Twelve percent used marijuana and 2 percent cocaine, during the prior month.
- One-quarter had seriously considered suicide in the prior year.
- More than one-half had engaged in sex.

Fear of disclosure probably led many students to underestimate or deny their participation in these activities.

Awareness Without Hope

I was conducting an all-day workshop for the Watts College of Child Development, an African-American group based in Los Angeles, when Virgil came up to me at break time. He was there with his grandmother and was understandably bored. I'd been talking about everything from the current violence initiative to the role of psychiatry in Nazi Germany. I asked him what he'd like to hear about. In a loud voice and without hesitation, he declared, "Trust and justice." He didn't mean trust and justice between the races, but between children and adults. He was only six years old.

Modern children seem to lack innocence. Their sophistication reaches beyond sex and drugs to concerns once reserved for older youths and adults. Often they are critically aware of racism, sexism, and economic injustice. Many realize there is a huge federal deficit hanging over their economic future and that the environmental fate of the planet is in doubt. They perceive that the world they are entering is threatening and filled with uncertainty.

---

*Starting in the fall 1993, our neighborhood junior high school is banning baggy clothing—to prevent youngsters from hiding weapons.

Although they are better informed and more aware than any previous generation, they are made more dependent than earlier generations by difficult economic times, declining stability and security in their families and schools, and the increasingly complex demands of growing up. Added to that, they cannot get us to respond to their plight.[5] As a result, many of America's children suffer from awareness without hope.

Given the situation of our children, it is no surprise that they have become psychiatry's growth industry.[6] But when anguish, despair, resentment, and rebelliousness are defined as psychiatric disorders, how can we expect children to develop courage and faith in themselves? When expressions of anger or emotional upset bring the threat of mind-dulling psychiatric drugs, like Ritalin and Prozac, how can they develop trust in their own intuitions and feelings?

Disaster Relief

During the Great Midwest Flood of 1993, *The New York Times*[7] carried a story about "black and Hispanic drug dealers from Chicago who tried to help 200 white farmers and factory workers save their town." The town was Niota, Iowa. The young men from the inner city were in a prison program. One young man said, "I felt like I was in a movie. In the city it's 'Look at John, he's trying to save his house.' But here everyone was helping each other." The men reported that not once did they run into racial slurs while they helped local residents in sandbagging Niota. And Niota? They sent a greeting card with a picture of roses that said "With warmest thanks to each of you, from your Niota family. You'll never be forgotten."

In Niota, Midwest farm and factory folk and young men from places like Chicago's Cabrini Green housing project found a caring relationship beneath all the apparent differences. It took a raging river to bring them together.

As we watched relief efforts mount for Hurricane Hugo and for the Great Flood of 1993, we were struck by an irony. Natural disasters that happen "overnight" get media coverage, national attention, and a quick infusion of billions in public funds. People may pour in from all over to lend a helping hand. But social disasters that grow slowly and inexorably don't receive the same support—even though the after-effects have become more physically and morally devastating and the death toll even higher.

The National Commission on Children compared the situation of America's children to a natural disaster. All our children are in crisis—and our minority and impoverished children are being destroyed.

Wrapping Around the Child

Disaster relief requires many forms of assistance. Housing has to be provided or repaired. Safe food and water must be made available. Clothing, household goods—the basics of living—must be provided. Employment, education, health care, and other more permanent features need to be established.

But something else goes on during disaster relief. It is the smile offered with a hot cup of coffee, a gentle word passed along with warm blankets and a cot, or the determination provided by a group of young men from Chicago as they sandbagged levees. That other people care—that "we are not alone"—makes a world of difference. And when the lives of children are at stake, comfort and empathy are as important as food and water.

Recently I was invited to Alaska by a state-funded patient-advocacy agency in Fairbanks led by Linda Linson. While in Alaska, I was also asked to provide consultation to a different kind of disaster relief program—this one aimed at reclaiming the lives of the most devastated children in the state. The program is called AYI—the Alaska Youth Initiative—and I worked with the groups in Fairbanks and Anchorage.

The AYI treats the most difficult and often violent youngsters in the state, many of them from the farflung Eskimo villages. For a child to qualify for the program, everything else must have failed, so that literally no other program feels able to handle the situation. In previous times, these children were shipped out of state for chronic institutionalization.

The AYI provides unconditional love and unconditional care. It never gives up. Determined to keep the child in the family if at all possible, and in the community for certain, the AYI is an example of a relatively new concept—individualized or wraparound services with flexible funding that can be adjusted to the child's needs.[8] It implements a philosophy long understood in social work and social services—the necessity of meeting the child's basic needs, including those of the supporting family and surrounding community.

A team of caring people is created around the child: parents, foster parents, teachers, neighbors, public agency representatives, and professionals when necessary—anyone and everyone who matters in the child's life. The team has a fixed amount of money to spend in any way that it deems useful for the child: money for rent, for a therapist for the parents or the child, for a mentor or big brother, for a parenting course, for tutors for the child, for round-the-clock supervision in crises to prevent psychiatric hospitalization, for a baby-sitter to give the parents some relief, for job training for a parent . . .

Instead of paying for fixed bureaucratic services—welfare or child services, mental hospitalization or special education—flexible funding can be directed toward satisfying the particular necessities of the child and family.

The goal is to identify and to meet the particular child's needs, rather than to fit the child into the existing framework of an agency or service provider.

The results of the program are astonishing. Most of the children no longer require any institutionalized care, most stop being so difficult and violent, and many begin to meet the goal of "normalization"—entering society like anyone else.

There are dozens of wraparound programs in the United States, and they work. While they seem to cost a lot of money, they are in reality much cheaper than the alternatives, such as jail and psychiatric hospitalization. A month in a private psychiatric hospital, for example, can cost $30,000 to $50,000. With flexible funding, that amount could provide the child's family two or three full-time support persons for an entire year. If the support persons are selected for their personal qualities, such as empathy, and trained in the program itself, they are likely to be less costly and much more effective than typical mental health professionals.

Just Say No to Drugs

The AYI program, and wraparound programs in general, do not in principle reject psychiatric diagnosis and medication, and psychiatrists often participate on the teams. But wraparound principles are, in reality, incompatible with biopsychiatry. Diagnoses and medications cannot meet the basic needs of children or replace components missing their lives. Almost invariably psychiatric interventions suppress the child and substitute for resolving conflicts in mutually satisfactory ways. And they are not good for the brain.

Too often the children arrive in the AYI on multiple medications, any one of which could stupefy the average adult. Even if the child's psychiatrist wants to help taper off the drugs, he or she may not have much experience or know-how in doing so. I am not aware of any professional seminars—except my own—on the subject of withdrawing children from psychiatric drugs. The drug companies, who sponsor everything else, won't sponsor anything like that; and the psychiatric establishment is pushing for more long-term drugging, not for drug withdrawal.

I evaluated an eight-year-old AYI boy who was already developing a permanent drug-induced neurological disorder that his psychiatrist hadn't noticed. To take the child off drugs, the team worked with me to develop a home-based program with full-time round-the-clock practical nurses and a pediatrician on call. It was a lot cheaper than sending him to the mental hospital for drug withdrawal, and it was successful. The team had already tried hospitalization, but it had led to an increase in the doses.

Behavioral Control

Without relying on drugs for behavior control, what can be done when confronting an angry and potentially violent youngster? In addition to drugs, the mental health system advocates behaviorist methods of control—the use of rewards and punishments, and especially the imposition of "consequences" for "negative behavior." But every child's hostile act *is* a negative consequence—usually a consequence of feeling worthless. Every child's hostile act automatically generates new negative consequences, making the child feel yet more worthless.

In behavior modification, the consequences do not flow naturally as the inevitable result of conduct, such as failing grades from shirking homework or a headache from binge drinking. The so-called consequences are contrived punishments, such as withholding privileges or sending the child into seclusion.[9] It is systematic manipulation based on threat and coercion.

In such a tightly managed system, the withholding of rewards becomes a punishment. These methods enforce humiliation, teach a child to resent authority, and encourage deception. People differ in their philosophy of punishment, and while a humane and limited punishment may occasionally be useful, reliance on it breeds rebellion, submissiveness, or both.

Systematic punishment and/or behavioral management cannot be the basis of a truly therapeutic program—one that builds self-esteem and personal responsibility. Every act of violence by a child is motivated by futility and self-hatred—inspired ultimately by feelings of worthlessness and humiliation. Punishing the act often increases the child's feelings of helplessness and self-hatred or shifts the child's focus to blaming the source of punishment. Helping the child learn to resolve conflicts before they escalate into violence is a much more positive approach, leading to a sense of efficacy and worth.

Accordingly, the second purpose of my Alaska consultations became teaching and applying non-violent, non-coercive methods for dealing with severe conflict, including those children who perpetrate violent acts against their families, foster parents, caregivers, or peers. It was a straightforward extension of the basic principles already inherent in the AYI program: unconditional caring and unconditional love. Most mental health professionals teach and use approaches that don't mention the word *love*.

A Loving Response to Violence

What do we mean by love? Love is "joyful awareness"—delight in the child's existence.[10] When we love, we reach happily toward an understanding of the other's essential beauty—his or her enduring value. We feel inspired with what Albert Schweitzer called "reverence for life" and we treasure the person.

A loving attitude helps us overcome our tendencies to react with hostility when we feel rejected or threatened. It encourages us to abhor the use of force in favor of unconditional love and mutuality. It leads us to reason and to act from humane and caring values when we are tempted to do otherwise.

The AYI teams intuitively knew it was ideal to rely on relationships—on love and caring—as the ultimate solution to violence; but they needed a professional to confirm it. The approach requires personal self-restraint on the part of the adult, rather than restraint of the child. The aim is to break the cycle of unfulfilled needs and mutual coercion, by reaching out with love against the onrush of anger and violence.*

Under the stress of conflict, the goal is to work yet harder to create relationships and love—to show that a child's violence does not beget adult violence, but that it brings forth understanding and renewed devotion to fulfilling the child's needs. This doesn't "spoil" the child—it liberates the child from the need to express himself or herself through helpless violence. A punishing milieu encourages a child to continue blaming and hating; a loving one promotes personal responsibility for acting in a more ethical and productive manner.

If a child cannot get attention without becoming disruptive or violent, then something is probably the matter in the adult world that surrounds the child. Certainly, something has been the matter in the child's earlier experiences with adults. The child does not need to be "taught a lesson." Almost all deeply distressed children have already been taught too many horrible lessons—including the capacity of adults to react to their outbursts with even greater violence. These children need a loving outreach that addresses their basic needs for attention, security, esteem, and love.

If a child has intentionally threatened or injured someone, it remains crucial to help the child stop withdrawing in fear and humiliation. The goal is to maintain a loving attitude, to treasure the child, even as measures are taken to prevent further bloodshed.

Setting Limits in a Loving Context

All professionals who work with children acknowledge that the youngsters need help in setting limits. With wide variation among children, they need help in regulating their dietary habits, sleep schedule, and school attendance, as well as learning to do chores. They usually require guidance in maintaining respectful relationships with their peers and adults. Good parents or mentors frequently offer help in working out conflicts about rules and regu-

---

*As described in *Beyond Conflict,* this is the application of Gandhi's philosophy to interpersonal conflict. Also see Bondurant, 1988, and Gandhi, 1957.

lations. But children's needs for limits should not become an excuse for arbitrary or escalating punishments. As much as possible, parents and children should cooperate to arrive at mutually satisfactory rules and regulations. The more a child understands and participates in formulating these necessary limits on freedom, the more likely he or she will develop rational autonomy rather than reflexive rebelliousness or submissiveness.

The more the child senses that the parent is genuinely concerned about her or his well-being, the more probable it is that conflicts will be resolved. It won't help for parents to repeat slogans, such as "This hurts me more than you" or "I'm doing this for your own good." A child is much more able to trust a parent's good will when the parent communicates happiness over the child's existence. Although it is a difficult ideal to live by, the key is maintaining unconditional love through the thick of conflict.

By the time parents come to me for help, or seek out other mental health or rehabilitation approaches, they have often become so frustrated that they would do almost anything for a few moments peace in the home. Sometimes they have already tried drugging and hospitalizing their child. Now the youngster is threatening to fight back physically or to run away. The parent's feel they have "tried everything." My task is to get them back in touch with the one thing that matters the most—loving their child.

Usually these parents want to discuss strategies. "What do I do if she runs away again or threatens us?" Consistent strategies can be useful, but only if the child comes to feel that they are born from love. Tough love? Permissiveness? There's a wide range of acceptable parental authority. There's little or no range in regard to love. When a child doesn't feel loved, all other interventions lose their usefulness. When a child feels treasured, he or she will learn to accept a wide range of parental authority, while learning more about personal responsibility. This is equally true in foster homes or other alternative placements for children. Nothing matters as much as the loving attitude of the caregivers, and nothing can compensate for the lack of it.

Facing Extreme Situations

Children rarely lash out at themselves or others when they feel themselves in a secure, trustworthy relationship. When they do act in such a self-defeating matter, they are responding to past experiences of abuse. They have not yet learned to trust. I've never seen a child say to himself or herself, "I really love and trust this adult, I think I'll have a temper tantrum, start a fight, or kill myself."

If children do become destructive under loving conditions, they usually feel so remorseful afterward that it would be distracting to impose a punishment on them. It's better for everyone involved, including children and adults, to recognize the hurt that's been engendered and to work toward the repair of the relationship.

The principles of loving conflict resolution begin with restraint: first and foremost, do nothing to the child except in self-defense and then limit self-defense to the very minimum. It's one thing to raise one hands in self-defense, and another to overwhelm the child with a takedown to the floor. It's one thing to back away from an enraged child until he calms down, and another to send him off to an isolation room.

Caregivers should not persist in negative activities or attitudes toward the child once the immediate threat has passed. The moment that self-defense is no longer required, all punitive measures should usually stop. This effectively rules out typical mental health responses, such as increasing drug dosages, putting the child in confinement, taking away privileges, and so forth.

The second basic principle is to remain empathic toward the child and to find ways to resolve the conflicts and frustrations that are driving the underlying rage. An "out-of-control child" needs more security, more trust, more love—not medication or isolation. Caregivers should begin rebuilding the caring relationship the instant it is possible, typically in the midst of the conflict.

Keep in mind that you are offering more than a loving relationship— you are paying attention to every hint about what the child needs. Most importantly, every child needs a loving, secure, and trustworthy connection with at least one adult. Compared to that need, all others pale. When a positive relationship is made with a mature adult, most other things begin to fall into place.

The same principles apply to the treatment of angry, upset adult patients. When speaking and consulting recently at a medical center in Canada, I reviewed the use of restraint and seclusion with psychiatrists from two different mental hospitals. Although the two facilities served the same kind of adult patients, including very disturbed "schizophrenics," one hospital never used physical restraints or an isolation room, while the other relied heavily on both. The dramatic difference was the product of differing staff attitudes. The less coercive facility emphasized closer, more caring, and more frequent contacts between the staff and patients. It also tended to use somewhat lower doses of drugs.

The Effect of Biopsychiatry on Otherwise Ideal Programs

For the most disturbed children and adults, including those who get labeled schizophrenic, there are alternatives to diagnosis and mental hospitals. These caring solutions, often involving safe havens, have proven themselves superior, even without the use of psychiatric drugs.[11] These options are rejected by a biopsychiatric establishment that will not tolerate non-medical competition. Yet it's impossible to provide optimum services to a child who is being diagnosed and drugged. The label sets the child outside the human circle and makes it difficult for the caregivers to remain fully empathic. It stands in the way of "normalizing" the child—treating him or her as any other child. The prescription of the drug distracts adults from ascertaining the child's real needs, and the toxic effects render the child less able to feel or to express those needs. To make matters worse, the drugged child is in effect told that personal feelings or responses are dangerous and that conformity is the rule of life. At the same time, the adult suppresses his or her own human tendency to remain open and caring toward the "patient."

At those critical moments, when painful emotions have reached a peak, breakthroughs of understanding and relationship can result; but not if the child's responses are flattened. If the drug itself doesn't prevent meaningful communication and human connection, the decision to use it surely will. Ironically, then, drugs are given at exactly the wrong moment—when the most painful internal issues and interpersonal conflicts are surfacing. At the very time that the caregiver needs to dig deeper into his or her own personal resources, he or she instead reaches into the medicine cabinet. It's a prescription that's guaranteed to fail.

Individual Programs Are Not Enough

Wraparound programs—family- and community-oriented—are among the most desirable approaches for helping children and their families. But they cannot solve the systematic kinds of abuse that abound in our society based on sexism, racism, pedism, and economic injustice.

So many good reports have now been produced on child-oriented reform that books could be written about them. One such report stands out and is readily available. In 1991, the bipartisan National Commission on Children, although loaded by the conservative Bush administration, came up with sweeping reforms for improving the lives of America's children.[12]

The commission came to a striking consensus that no matter how hard families try, many can no longer take care of their own children; that society needs to help these families provide for the basic needs of their offspring; and that specific and yet general policies can be agreed upon for immediate implementation.

The consensus reached by the commission suggests that the failure to act on behalf of children is not caused by insurmountable differences of opinion in regard to potential solutions. While controversies over policy are inevitable, there is sufficient agreement on the plight of children and on basic approaches to helping them. Many of these approaches have already proven successful in other Western nations that provide a more level playing field and a better safety net for children and youth. They include an income floor and other supports for poverty-level families with children, improved educational opportunities for small children, greater protection from child abuse, and universal prenatal and child health care.*

Americans will be able to reach a working consensus on many of the required policies, if and when they can overcome the barriers within their hearts. The nation needs to shed the old values that impede progress, and to develop a new set of more positive ideals based on empathy for all citizens and especially for children of all races and economic status.

How Goes the Black Child?

Not enough can be said about racism as an impediment to improving the condition of all of America's children. From the Native American reservations to the mountains of West Virginia and the suburbs of New York and Chicago, our children are suffering. But if we cannot face the plight of the urban black child, we will remain stymied in our efforts to help any of our children, because we will go on imagining that the more serious problems belong exclusively to "their" community and not to "ours."

America's white majority so fears and rejects the black community that it will withhold help from all children for fear of handing an undeserved or unwarranted benefit to the black child. When white Americans think about the cost of programs to help children, we often forget that vast numbers of children of all races are suffering from poverty, hunger, ill health, poor housing, inadequate education, parental neglect, and fear of the future. Instead we focus on black or Hispanic children and their parents, invoking images of "welfare mothers who are too lazy to work." Or, like Frederick Goodwin, we picture young black men obsessed with sex and violence.

Too many of us hold these stereotypes to our hearts. We like to imagine that problems in the inner city stem more from "bleeding-heart liberalism" than racism and neglect. We want to cut back on what we are giving, instead of finding more effective ways of caring and sharing. We think that the deterioration of life in the inner city is due more to the "lack of moral fiber" and "easy living" of the adults on welfare programs than to the dreadful deprivations imposed upon them and their families. We do not realize that our eco-

---

*The modest health care proposal has, of course, been supplanted by current federal plans for universal health care for all ages.

nomic safety net is one of the least adequate in the Western world and that the poor escape from welfare much more frequently in countries that treat them with greater compassion.[13]

The White Community's Responsibility

From Harriet Tubman, Frederick Douglass, and Marcus Garvey to Malcolm X and Martin Luther King, Jr., African-American leaders have historically emphasized the importance of self-help and personal responsibility.* Today, many groups are attempting to encourage the self-empowerment and self-determination of black youth.

In Los Angeles, for example, The Watts College of Child Development for many years has conducted seminars and week-long workshops to encourage the positive growth and development of black children.[14] More in the mainstream, the Reverend Jesse Jackson is encouraging a program to divert non-violent first offenders away from the criminal justice system and into the churches. According to William Raspberry, "The immediate target is to get 1,000 churches to rescue 10 children each." These, and innumerable other programs, inspired by African-Americans, offer hope to inner-city youth. A list of these efforts within the black community would be endless, because more of them are appearing all the time.

But self-help programs among the poor in inner cities are stymied by broader social policies and prejudices beyond their control. Without a transformation in white attitudes toward minority citizens and all children, the situation can only grow worse. But if we act with greater empathy and justice, then those on the margins of our society will surely find it easier to take responsibility for themselves.

A True Public Health Approach

We have seen how the government misdefined public health as a method of singling out individuals for treatment. Imagine what it would be like if, instead, federal agencies took a genuine public health approach to violence. The nation could be taught to focus on those environmental influences—especially widespread public attitudes—that suppress our children and minorities. Our society must realize that it is morally contaminated by prejudice and indifference, and that this contamination causes the humiliation and oppression of most black children in America—and most other children as well.

---

*The white community, in fact, has often seemed most threatened by black leaders who espouse self-determination and responsibility.

As the ultimate source of the problem, white leadership is essential to ending racism and discrimination in America, and to bringing about a more empathic society. This leadership will not come forth until a sufficient number of Americans are ready to welcome it, and that will never happen as long as we harbor beliefs about the genetic or biological inferiority of rebellious, upset children of any race.

High-Tech Child Abuse

Children who are in conflict with their families, schools, and society rarely have anything wrong with their brains, and when they do suffer from brain dysfunction, it does not by itself make them unruly or dangerous. Children in trouble are typically the victims of emotional, physical, and sexual abuse. If we include neglect, abandonment, poor parenting, inadequate schooling, and the effects of poverty, sexism, and racism, then almost all children seen by mental health professionals are victims of child abuse.

We have seen how these children are subjected to intrusive physical interventions—including spinal taps and brain scans—as a routine part of biopsychiatric research at major universities and in federal agencies, such as the National Institute of Mental Health (NIMH). Such research on children should be labeled child abuse and stopped.

We have seen how millions of other children in conflict with authorities, such as parents and teachers, are psychiatrically diagnosed to justify drugging and hospitalization. There is no excuse for subduing children with brain- and mind-disabling medications or psychiatric incarceration. The biopsychiatric treatment of children constitutes high-tech child abuse and it too should be stopped.

Even the most seemingly benign mental health approaches to children are likely to be abusive. When a ten-year-old boy is brought to "therapy" because he is considered too difficult or disruptive in the home or school, most mental health professionals proceed on the principle that there is something "wrong" with him. He is diagnosed and the treatment is directed at his presumed problems. In reality, the major source of difficulty and most of the potential for ameliorating it lies outside the child's control. Labeling the child as the core of the problem is unjust and does more harm than good.

Practical Approaches When Children Are
Endangered by Psychiatry

When a child is in danger of being labeled or drugged, there are a variety of actions that a parent or child advocate can take, including negotiating with the schools and mental health professionals, getting family therapy, obtaining a lawyer, and organizing the community.

If the school threatens parents by linking the educational program to unwanted treatment, then the parents need to make a carefully planned response. As one approach, the parent can seek a second opinion from psychologically oriented and family-oriented therapists. They can be found through the yellow pages, sometimes under family therapists, or under other non-medical headings, such as "psychologists," "social workers," or "counselors." Sometimes names can be obtained from the American Academy of Psychotherapists.[15] If parents can find a mental health professional to work with them without drugs, the school will usually back down. The therapist should also be able to help the parents improve their methods of relating to their children.

Rarely should a consultation be sought from an ordinary psychiatrist or pediatrician, or from any mental health professional considered an expert in ADHD or other childhood "disorders," since people who specialize in them are usually biased toward diagnosis and medication. Before making an appointment, the parent or caregiver should query professionals about their views on topics like ADHD and Ritalin.

In evaluating professionals, effective test questions include "How many children do you treat with Ritalin?" or "How often do you refer children for possible treatment with Ritalin?" or "Is ADHD really a disease?" or "Is Ritalin or ADHD controversial?"

The parent or caregiver should try to locate a non-pedist therapist—one who cares about children and doesn't blame them for problems in the adult world. The therapist should feel competent in working with families and with schools, if necessary acting as a consultant to the teacher or school counselor.

In general, it is not a good idea to remove the child from the regular classroom. There are exceptions to this, however, when the alternative classroom or school provides improved services and opportunities for children. The teachers may be more caring or more able. The class sizes may be smaller, allowing for greater attention and more individualized instruction.

Before assignment to a special program, classroom, or school, regulations often require the rubber-stamp testing and labeling of the pupil. Whenever possible, parents and caregivers should politely refuse to have their children subjected to psychiatrically oriented tests; they should try to keep any and all diagnoses out of the official school record.

While advocating for a child, it is helpful to maintain a cooperative, mutually respectful relationship with the teacher and the school. When rejecting diagnosis and drugging, it can be useful to provide supporting professional opinions and publications.[16] Many people of good will are misled by biopsychiatric propaganda, and may be grateful to be educated.

If a child is "difficult" to relate to, then the parent should admit it, and work with the school and perhaps with other professionals to help the youngster learn to be more cooperative. Invariably, however, the problem originated outside the child, and requires a non-punitive approach on the part of supportive adults. Most of the "child's problem" can usually be cleared up by improving his or her surroundings, especially the attitudes and practices of the adults.

If financing is available through the family or the school system, child-oriented private schools can sometimes change a child's life for the better. When the school system fails to offer what the child needs, it can be legally required to provide the funds for alternative schooling.

In selecting an alternative school, the parent or caregiver should find one in which biopsychiatry is not favored as an option. Schools with several children on medication should probably be avoided. If *any* of the school's children are on Ritalin or other psychiatric drugs, the parent should find out if the school recommended or approved the treatment.

Under no circumstances should a child be told that he or she is suffering from "cross-wires in the brain," a "biochemical imbalance," "hyperactivity," "ADHD," a "learning disability," or other concocted diagnoses. Children should be forthrightly told that they are having conflicts with their teachers, school, or family, and that the adults will work to resolve these conflicts in a mutually beneficial manner. It should be made clear that the adults have the largest burden of responsibility for helping make the environment safe, interesting, and educational. In that context—and only in that context—is it rational and fair to ask the child to work on improving his or her conduct as well.

If children have already been labeled, they should be told that it was a mistake and that there is nothing wrong with their brains—that they have a wonderful brain and mind, and that the problems in their lives did not originate within them.

Parents frequently obtain lawyers in order to force school districts to provide their children with specialized mental health services. It is less common to use the legal system to protect children from biomedical social control. Legally, school districts cannot force a child to take medication as a condition of the educational program, but they often act as if they can. When the parent or child obtains the assistance of legal counsel, the school will often back down. State Protection and Advocacy Offices and Legal Aid

Agencies will sometimes represent children on this issue.[17] We are hopeful that class action suits may develop in the future aimed at protecting children and their parents from the threat of forced diagnosis and medication.

Children First!

Despite their best personal efforts, professionals, concerned parents, and other advocates for children are often stymied by the biopsychiatric monopoly and its parent-support groups, such as NAMI and CH.A.D.D. (see Chapter 5). While many grassroots committees have been developed to fight the violence initiative, they lack organizational structure and a national leadership or forum.

In response to these needs, the Center for the Study of Psychiatry has recently created a new program, *Children First!* with a membership that is open to the public. *Children First!* of the Center for the Study of Psychiatry is critical of biomedical control and promotes more caring approaches. In addition to *Children First!,* several other psychiatric reform groups focus in part on children and publish newsletters or newspapers (see Appendix for how to join or subscribe).*

A Different NRC Report

The National Research Council (NRC) report *Understanding and Preventing Violence* supported the biomedical approach to crime control.[18] But in the summer of 1993 a different NRC panel released another report, *Losing Generations,* which took an opposite viewpoint.[19] The slim volume gave a deceptively simple message: the environments of our children have continuously deteriorated to the point where they no longer support them, and consequently whole generations of American children are being lost.

Losing Generations diverges dramatically from the earlier NRC report with its biomedical, individual-vulnerability approach. It states that "the highest priority for future research should shift to studies of the contexts and settings of daily life, especially for adolescents from low-income and disadvantaged backgrounds."

The panel explained that their work "began as an attempt to better understand why some adolescents are drawn to risky life-styles while others, similarly situated, engage in only normal adolescent experimentation." This

---

*These reform groups are not set up to offer therapeutic alternatives for children, such as a psychosocial haven or clinic free of biopsychiatric domination. Alternative service institutions are not likely to prosper until the psycho-pharmaceutical monopoly is made to loosen its grip on America (Breggin, 1991a, Breggin and Breggin, 1994).

initial focus corresponds with the NIMH focus on individual vulnerability. But this panel ended up rejecting victim-blaming under any guise, biological or psychological: "We concluded that it was important to right the balance by focusing on the profound influence that settings have on the behavior and development of adolescents." The report called for addressing the effects of "class, race, gender, and ethnicity on adolescent development."

Losing Generations swam against the tide of biopsychiatry and the psycho-pharmaceutical complex. It also swam against the media tide and got almost no publicity. In America today, unfounded biological claims make headlines while sound psychosocial analyses go unnoticed.

Rejecting the Psychiatric Approach to Children

Biopsychiatry appeals to people who feel so helpless that they want to give up responsibility for themselves, and to parents or teachers who feel so frustrated or baffled that they uncritically turn to the experts. It appeals to people who want to take control of others, sometimes for racist or pedist motives, and to psychiatrists who are trained and empowered to be agents of control.

But biopsychiatry has no place in a world in which children need attention, love, improved parenting, better schooling, and more equal opportunity. It has no place in a society in which adults take responsibility as parents, teachers, or child advocates.

As long as biobehavioral control remains an option, we will end up repeating the same old mistakes. Renouncing racist, pedist medical control comes first; creative solutions follow. Stopping coercion is the starting point. Once biopsychiatry is rejected as an alternative, people will be freed to think creatively on behalf of children.

The controversy surrounding the federal violence initiative drew attention to the threat to minority children, but all of our children are increasingly subjected to the danger of biomedical abuse. We have handed over responsibility for too many of our children to psychiatry; now we must begin to take it back.

No child deserves to be psychiatrically diagnosed and drugged, or locked in a mental hospital. No child should be subjected to intrusive research techniques aimed at proving a biological origin for psychological and social conflict. We must stop acting as if we cannot help our children without coercive biological psychiatry. Until we give up relying on the easy way out, we will have no motivation to come up with better, more humane, and caring approaches.

Whatever we do must be characterized by *unconditional love* and *unconditional caring*. Biological psychiatry sidesteps or ignores these two principles, and frequently undermines them. We must start by saying no: no to racism, no to pedism, no to abusive biopsychiatry. Then we can say yes to our children's needs.

A p p e n d i x

To Learn About or to Join the Psychiatric Reform Movement

(1) *Children First!*, Center for the Study of Psychiatry, 4628 Chestnut Street, Bethesda, MD 20814

Children First! is the only national program that focuses on the dangers of biopsychiatric interventions into the lives of children while supporting more caring alternatives. It needs your support to enlarge its national educational campaign against the wholesale diagnosing and drugging of America's children.

Children First! is a newly developed activity of the Center for the Study of Psychiatry. The center itself was founded in 1971 and is a non-profit, tax-exempt research and educational institute devoted to reform in mental health. The Center's Board of Directors and Advisory Council include more than one hundred leading psychiatrists and other mental health professionals, attorneys, patient advocates, psychiatric surivors, and members of Congress.

Peter R. Breggin, M.D., is the Center director and Ginger Ross Breggin is the director of research and education. John George, Ed.D., and Michael Valentine, Ph.D., are co-directors of *Children First!* and can be reached through the Center.

Members receive a newsletter and the satisfaction of supporting these reform efforts on behalf of America's children. The annual membership fee for *Children First!* is $25.

(2) *National Association for Rights Protection and Advocacy (NARPA)*, 587 Marshall Avenue, St. Paul, MN 55102. Phone (612) 224 -7761.

NARPA is open to all people interested in supporting advocacy of patient and inmate rights, including both adults and children. You do not have to be a mental health professional or an activist in order to join. NARPA publishes a newsletter, *The Rights Tenet*, and holds an annual convention on patient rights and psychiatric reform, with workshops by lawyers, advocates, survivors, and reform-minded mental health professionals. It's worth joining to get the newsletter and to be reminded of the yearly conference, which is the best in the field. The Center for the Study of Psychiatry publishes a report in each NARPA newsletter, and many Board and Advisory Council members usually give presentations at each annual conference. The annual NARPA membership fee is $20.

(3) *National Empowerment Center (NEC)*, 20 Ballard Road, Lawrence, MA 01843-1018. Phone 800-POWER-2-U. Fax (508) 681-6426.

NEC is a new resource and information center for individuals and organizations concerned with empowering psychiatric survivors. It believes that all persons can take over and improve their lives. You can contact NEC to learn about the survivor movement and to locate resources in your community.

(4) *The Prozac Survivors Support Group, Inc.*, Guy McConnell, National Director, 3080 Peach Avenue, No. 104, Clovis, CA 93612. Phone (209) 291-8661.

This organization brings together hundreds of victims of negative effects from Prozac and related drugs, like Zoloft and Paxil. Concerned families and friends also become members. It provides information, self-help, a support network, and conferences.

Ann Tracy, the Utah director, has written and published *The Prozac Pandora: The Rest of the Story* (1994). It can be obtained from her at 3851 Saddler Drive, West Jordan, UT 84088 for the cost of $22.95.

(5) *Dendron*, P.O. Box 11284, Eugene, OR 97440. Phone (503) 341-0100.

Founded, edited, and published by David Oaks, this psychiatric-survivor newsletter offers articles on psychiatric oppression, human rights, and self-help alternatives. It is highly recommended for staying in touch with what's happening in psychiatric reform and the survivor movement. The subscription rate is $12 for four issues.

(6) *The National Association of Psychiatric Survivors (NAPS)*, P.O. Box 618, Sioux Falls, SD 57101.

If you have been damaged by psychiatry and want to join other survivors for moral support, political action, and the development of client-run alternatives, this is your organization. Even if you are not a former patient, both your membership and support are welcome. NAPS publishes a newsletter and can provide the addresses of local survivor groups around the United States and in many other countries. The NAPS annual membership fee is $25.

Joining *Children First!*, NARPA, and NAPS, and subscribing to *Dendron*, will keep you up on the latest activities in the psychiatric survivor and psychiatric reform movement.

To Obtain Legal Aid Against Psychiatric Abuse

The National Association of Protection and Advocacy Systems (NAPAS), 220 Eye Street, NE, Suite 150, Washington, DC 20001. Phone (202) 546-8202.

If you are or have recently been an inmate subjected to abusive psychiatric treatment in any institution, public or private, and need help in protecting your rights, you can contact NAPAS. It can provide you with the address and phone number of federally funded Protection and Advocacy agencies in your state. Many of these state agencies are doing good work supporting patient rights and investigating violations. The services are free. They may be able to provide referrals to sympathetic private attorneys as well.

To Find a Psychotherapist

The American Academy of Psychotherapists (AAP), P.O. Box 607, Decatur, GA 30031. Phone (404) 299-6336.

The AAP central office can provide names from among its several hundred members, some of whom may live in your area, including psychologists, psychiatrists, social workers, counselors, and other professionals. AAP members are trained and experienced in psychotherapy and have themselves undergone psychotherapy. Get several names and shop carefully for a person with whom you feel comfortable and confident. Membership in any organization does not guarantee that an individual is ethical or competent. The AAP is not affiliated with the Center for the Study of Psychiatry, NAPS, NARPA, or any other psychiatric reform organization, and membership in the AAP indicates nothing about a psychotherapist's views on psychiatry. It is up to the individual seeking help to question any potential therapist about his or her orientation and values (for further suggestions, see Chapter 9 as well as Breggin, 1991a).

Notes

Chapter 1

1. Ronald David helped us to appreciate this. In a personal communication in September 1993, he wrote: "It is easier for us to imagine that certain problems are confined to black and/or poor communities—we can then deny or ignore their occurrence in more privileged communities. We are blind to the realization that we have even failed to meet the basic material, psychoemotional and spiritual needs of white children."

2. *U.S. News & World Report,* November 8, 1993.

3. This conclusion is based on the total consumption of Ritalin in these communities, as well as on our personal experience. See Chapter 4.

4. Franklin, 1984, p. 4.

5. In a letter to Secretary Sullivan (Adler, 1992).

6. American Psychological Association, May/June 1992.

7. Breggin, 1992b; Isikoff, 1992; Leary, 1992; Rensberger, 1992; Rich, 1992.

8. Herman and Newberger, 1992.

9. Also see Miller, J. J., 1992, for a discussion of Goodwin's letter to Bush.

10. In parentheses, the letter summarized the earlier incarnations:

    (Notable among these have been the proposal by President Nixon's personal physician that all five year olds be tested to identify potential presidential assassins; the highly publicized and ultimately futile efforts to link XYY chromosomes to hypermasculinity and violence; and the hypothesis preferred by several psychiatrists during the civil disorders of the '60s that participants in the inner-city uprisings were suffering from "temporal lobe epilepsy." It is more than just ironic that the definitive refutation of these endeavors came from careful studies conducted at NIMH in conjunction with the Kerner Commission, which concluded that the disorders were deeply rooted in social and economic conditions and which found no evidence that riot participants were more "pathological" than nonparticipants.)

11. Leary, 1992.

12. Phillips, 1992. In an April 1992 commentary in *Psychiatric News,* Robert Phillips, chair of the APA's Committee of Black Psychiatrists, said he was "appalled" by his association's decision to support Goodwin's appointment.

13. The Center for the Study of Psychiatry is a nonprofit research and educational network founded in the early 1970s by Peter Breggin with the support of twenty other individuals, including reform-minded mental health professionals and members of the U.S. Congress and Senate. It now has more than a hundred members on its board of directors and advisory council. Some of the earliest re-

form activities were aimed at stopping racist psychiatric theories and practices (Chapter 5), and African-American congressmen Louis Stokes and Ronald Dellums, founding members of the Board of Directors, remain on the board to this day.

We began the campaign against the violence initiative by sending out hundreds and then thousands of critiques of the planned government program and biomedical social control in general. (See Breggin, 1992b–g, and Breggin and Breggin, 1993a&b.) Most of these packets included the transcripts of Goodwin's remarks to the National Advisory Mental Health Council and the American Psychiatric Association, as well as other background materials. The campaign was paid for from our personal finances with a little help from small donations by individuals around the country. It is now possible to join and to support the center through its division, *Children First!* (see Appendix to this book).

14. In the audio version, Goodwin seemed to us to say "any social personality disorder" (Goodwin, 1992b, p. 9) rather than "antisocial personality disorder" as indicated in the official transcript (Goodwin, 1992c, p. 8). He probably meant "antisocial personality disorder." For the purposes of this discussion, there is little or no difference.

15. See *Jensvold* v. *Sullivan*. Also based on interviews of Jensvold by Ginger Ross Breggin, including August 28, 1993. Jensvold recently won her case in court before a jury.

16. Loren Mosher, interview with Peter Breggin on August 27, 1993.

17. See Alcohol, Drug Abuse, and Mental Health Administration, 1992. We were refused access to materials such as this under the Freedom of Information Act on the grounds that planning documents are exempted from the act, and did not obtain this one through other sources until late in 1993. Elliot Currie (January 1993a) bases his criticism of the violence initiative on this document. In rebutting Currie, Louis Sullivan (March 1993) confirmed that the document represented ADAMHA's proposed "*new* initiative" and "plan" for violence prevention incorporation into the 1994 budget.

18. Our copy had facsimile transmission markings showing that it existed in October 1992, but it was probably written much earlier. Its somewhat rough form indicates that it might be an early draft. We received it in the fall of 1993.

19. A project was submitted in 1983 to the DOJ's Law Enforcement Assistance Administration (LEAA) by genetic researcher Sarnoff Mednick, along with Katherine Van Dusen. It proposed the biomedical screening of two thousand 9- to 12-year-olds to identify potential offenders. Entitled "Early Identification of the Chronic Offender," it included physical exams, brain-wave studies, skin electrical conductance tests, IQ tests, neuropsychological tests for brain dysfunction, psychological tests of impulse control, and testosterone blood levels. One of the suggested test stimuli was the unexpected firing off of a gun behind the child's back. The grant was turned down because, following criticism of earlier,

similar proposals in the 1970s, LEAA no longer funded medical experimentation (see Chapter 6).

20. The ongoing DOJ project is led by Felton Earls at Harvard (see Chapter 2).

21. Office of Minority Health, 1989.

22. The mammoth seven-hundred-page federal report laid the early groundwork for NIMH's later proposals. Published in 1991 by the Department of Health and Human Services and the U.S. Public Health Service, it is the product of twenty-two "expert working groups," a consortium of three hundred national organizations, and extensive review and commentary from "more than 10,000 people."

Despite the participation of innumerable citizens, with their more social orientation, the task force reports are written to meet the needs of its federal sponsors. The report was submitted to DHHS secretary Louis Sullivan by Assistant Secretary for Health James O. Mason, who would become a vocal supporter of the violence initiative.

23. Department of Health and Human Services, 1991, p. 244.

24. The government seemed most affected by the response to two talk shows, *Lead Story* and *Our Voices,* on BET.

25. The twenty-six members of the Congressional Black Caucus sought Goodwin's ouster from ADAMHA, and they also protested his appointment as NIMH director (Wagner, 1992). The Association of Black Psychologists (ABPsi), Blacks in Government (BIG), the Black Business Alliance, the American Counseling Association (the largest in the world), and the National Association for Rights Protection and Advocacy (NARPA) also took strong stands against Goodwin and the proposals for biopsychiatric interventions into the inner city.

26. Documents obtained under the Freedom of Information Act.

27. Butterfield, 1992a. Sullivan repeated similar remarks to other members of the press who interviewed him and who then called me for rebuttal.

28. It was hard to get answers to two basic questions: "How much money has already been spent on violence prevention?" and "How much of that money was devoted to biomedical research?" The biomedical research would largely be conducted through the medically oriented institutes ADAMHA and NIH, rather than the CDC, which was also involved. Finally, the government released data stating that expenditures on youth violence prevention in 1992 totaled more than $53 million, mostly from the CDC, with very little from the biomedical agencies. The figures were used to disprove the suspicion that the government was already spending heavily on biomedical research for the control of violence.

Through Freedom of Information Act requests, we obtained an earlier version of the same financial tally in a document entitled "Ongoing PHS [Public Health Service] Activities Directly Related to Youth Violence

Prevention." This document indicated that an additional $45 million had been spent on violence prevention by the biomedical agencies. But the $45 million was deleted from this document by handwritten editing. In each case the original amount was crossed out and a new figure inserted, representing reductions of 37 to 50 percent. All the reductions were in biomedical agencies and none in the CDC. The edited version became the official statement on government expenditures for violence prevention.

29. Stone, October 9, 1992a.

Chapter 2

1. Reiss and Roth (eds.), 1993. It was released in October 1992 with a 1993 publication date.

2. Butterfield, 1992b.

3. Miller, J. J., 1992.

4. Touchette, January 1993.

5. The National Academy of Sciences, the parent group of the National Research Council, was chartered by Congress in 1863 as "a private, nonprofit, self-perpetuating society of distinguished scholars engaged in scientific and engineering research, dedicated to the furtherance of science and technology and to their use for the general welfare." The final report exemplifies the dangers of applying a "scientific" and "engineering" mandate to social problems and political policy.

6. For its study of violence, the NRC created a "Panel on the Understanding and Control of Violent Behavior," consisting of twenty members from a variety of disciplines, including public policy and law; sociology and social psychology; developmental psychology; criminology; medicine, psychobiology, and psychopharmacology; and behavioral genetics.

7. Reiss and Roth (eds.), 1993, pp. 160–161.

8. P. 24.

9. Pp. 341–342.

10. P. 159.

11. P. 158.

12. P. 382.

13. References can be found in Reiss and Roth's index under "pharmacological interventions."

14. P. 12; also see p. 300.

15. P. 24.

16. P. 25.

17. P. 380.

18. Pp. 70–71.

19. Touchette, November 1993 describes the history of how our campaign against the violence initiative caused Bernadine Healy, then NIH director, to convene the panel. We were sent invitations to present at the public testimony phase of both sets of hearings (Breggin and Breggin, 1993c&d).

20. Touchette, November 1993; the bracket is in the original.

21. Gubin, 1993.

22. The *Wall Street Journal* has tried to dismiss attacks on Prozac. It has also tried to bring good news to industry, for example, that Lilly's Prozac and Pfizer's Zoloft might eventually be seen as drugs that people safely take for an entire lifetime (Tanouye 1993).

23. It is unsigned. See "Critics See . . ." in the Bibliography.

24. "National Effort . . . ," 1993.

25. The FAES provides a variety of services to NIH—courses, special awards, music and lecture series, artwork displays, and salary supplements (drug company funded) to postdoctoral level scientists "whose stipends are otherwise inadequate." The four courses the FAES sponsored confirm its biomedical orientation: endocrinology, pathology, medical genetics, and psychopharmacology. The relative absence of psychosocial approaches is noteworthy. The FAES also provides a "social and academic center" on 1.5 acres of prime land adjacent to NIH.

26. Carrie Lee Rothgeb, Freedom of Information Coordination, DHHS, letter to Ginger Ross Breggin, Center for the Study of Psychiatry, September 28, 1993. By charging us this astronomical sum, NIH displays its need to cover up the facts. Previously NIH had determined that the Center for the Study of Psychiatry was exempt from such charges for its FOIA requests in these and related matters of public interest.

27. This is a recent discovery. We are looking into the total amounts awarded by drug companies to Rapoport and others.

28. See Breggin, 1991a, for documentation.

29. Karel, 1993. William Styron (1993) describes how "a gentleman who identified himself as the acting director of the National Institute of Mental Health" edged him away from the microphone at a press conference following his presentation during "A Conference with William Styron." Styron had begun to criticize Prozac, and Eli Lilly was sponsoring the conference.

30. "Paradigms of Power," 1993.

31. Schwartz, 1993.

32. See, for example, Graedon and Graedon, 1985, who strongly recommended it for sleep before the ban.

33. We have reviewed the subject in *Talking Back to Prozac.*

34. Marcus, 1991.

35. Marcus, 1991.

36. In *Toxic Psychiatry,* for example, I focus on Upjohn rather than Eli Lilly.

37. Baughman, 1992; Jonas, 1992.

38. Kolata, 1992.

39. The nurse, with her back to the camera, is on her knees with her hands and face in the fly of the man, who is standing erect holding the symbolically huge syringe as if it were a rifle. A bandolier of ammunition is strung over his shoulder. Beneath the picture, it says "Season's Greetings." The card is exhibit "Rubinow 33, 3.26.92" in *Margaret Jensvold, M.D., Plaintiff,* v. *Louis W. Sullivan, M.D., Defendant,* in the U.S. District Court for the District of Maryland, Civil No. L-90-3123.

40. The information and quotes are taken from a two-page flyer put out by the DOJ's National Institute of Justice (DeWitt, circa 1991).

41. Earls as a panel member and Reiss as the panel chair and senior editor of the report. In addition, Earls chaired the Violence Prevention Panel of the Centers for Disease Control and Prevention (CDC).

42. The phrase is from Earls, 1991. The other material is from DeWitt, 1991.

43. Mednick, Brennan, and Kandel, 1988. Earls's complete misrepresentation of the article is reminiscent of a similar misrepresentation of another Mednick article by Frederick Goodwin in his speech to the American Psychiatric Association (Chapter 3).

44. We are attempting to confirm the NIH source.

45. See Bush, October 12, 1993. Entitled "Conference on Psychopathology, Psychopharmacology, Substance Abuse, and Ethnicity," it took place October 14–16, 1993, and was sponsored by NIH, the National Institute of Drug Abuse, the American Psychological Association, Drew University School of Medicine and Science, and the Upjohn Company. Goodwin was scheduled as the lead-off speaker on the subject of "Overview of the Role of the National Institute of Mental Health's Commitment to Clinical and Biobehavioral Research and Treatment." The conference was opposed by a coalition that included three related grassroots organizations—the Compton Pediatric School of Health Association, Inc., the Ann Frank Memorial Committee, and the Watts College of Child Development, Inc.—led by Drew University professor Ernest Smith, M.D.

46. Bass, 1993.

47. "Clinton proposes . . . ," 1993.

48. Rhein, November 1993.

49. National Advisory Mental Health Council, October 1993.

50. For example, by giving unqualified support for antidepressants and electroshock in the elderly, with no mention of the ageist implications or extreme hazards involved in giving these treatments to older people (Breggin, 1991a).

51. Agnew, November 1993.

Chapter 3

1. Anderson, 1992.

2. Institute for Philosophy and Public Policy, 1992.

3. Annas and Elias are referring to two astonishing editorials by Daniel E. Koshland, Jr., in *Science*. Koshland began a 1989 editorial, "Last week a crazed gunman terrorized hostages in a bar in Berkeley, killing one and wounding many others," and then went on to suggest that such brutal crimes might be caused by "hereditary defects utterly unrelated to environmental influences." In a 1990 *Science* editorial, Koshland cited a spectrum of psychiatric disorders, stating "these diseases are at the root of many current societal problems," including homelessness. For more on the controversy, see Annas and Elias, 1992, as well as Kevles and Hook, 1992. Müller-Hill, April 8, 1993, a genetic researcher, supports the project but warns of potential political and social abuse based on the information it generates.

4. A sample of publications includes Anderson, 1992; Babington, 1992; Bielski, 1992; Breggin, 1992c–f; Gilliam, 1992; Hilts, 1992; Palca, 1992; Stone, 1992a&b; Talan, 1992, 1993; and Wheeler, 1992a–e. A key television event involved my appearance on the cable Black Entertainment Television (BET) program *Lead Story*, a news interview show, on July 4, 1992 (Palca, 1992).

5. The blocking of the conference was fully documented with copies of Torrey's letter, and a variety of other confirmatory materials (e.g., Gil, 1989), including a letter—written by NIMH director Lewis Judd—justifying the funding cutoff. But outside of Kentucky itself, there was no media interest in the canceling of this conference, perhaps because the ultimate victims were indigent "mental patients." While the cancellation of the conference had relatively little personal impact on us, it was extremely demoralizing to the Kentucky psychiatric patients. Consumers and survivors of psychiatry throughout the country expressed their hurt, grief, and outrage at being stymied once again by NIMH.

6. Prior to this, the National Advisory Mental Health Council itself published a *National Plan for Research on Child and Adolescent Mental Disorders,* calling for research to discover "genetic markers" for mental illnesses. It did *not* discuss crime or violence.

7. In testimony at the Congressional Black Caucus Legislative Weekend, I wrote, "Goodwin stated that no one becomes violent without being genetically predisposed to do so." The Department of Health and Human Services, 1992 (p. 6), responded to my criticism by claiming that "Dr. Goodwin did not say this"; but my observation seems to me like little more than a paraphrase of his remarks.

8. Alcohol, Drug Abuse, and Mental Health Administration, 1992. Also see Chapter 1 and Currie, January 1993, for further discussion of genetics in the ADAMHA plan.

9. Reiss and Roth, 1993, pp. 116–117.

10. See Fausto-Sterling, 1985; Tardiff, 1988.

11. Tardiff, 1988, p. 1038.

12. Marshall, 1993. The letter was written by John Diggs, then deputy director of NIH for extramural research.

13. Goleman, 1992b.

14. See Goodall, 1986; de Waal, 1989. I use films and studies of primates in teaching courses on conflict resolution at George Mason University, as well as in my books, *Toxic Psychiatry* (1991) and *Beyond Conflict* (1992); but the lessons I find are very different from those drawn by biopsychiatrists from rhesus monkeys.

15. de Waal, 1989, p. 49.

16. Early in the century, Petr Kropotkin wrote *Mutual Aid* to dispel the myth that animals or indigenous peoples live in fierce competition within their own groups.

17. Mydans, 1993.

18. In addition to the many citations in *Toxic Psychiatry*, Pam's (1990) lengthy analysis is worth studying.

19. The public has especially been led to believe that a biological basis for schizophrenia has been found, but as Seeman et al., September 1993, recently declared, "The biological basis of schizophrenia is not known." Like most biomedical researchers, these authors assume, without basis, that there is a biological origin.

20. Breggin, 1979, 1983c, 1990a, and 1991a.

21. Quoted in Maugh, 1989.

22. "Confidence Wanes . . . ," 1989.

23. "Twin Studies . . . ," 1992.

24. Bower, 1988.

25. Newman, 1993.

26. Eichelman and Hartwig, 1990.

27. Athens, 1989, does not set the stage in the larger world of racism, poverty, and hyper-masculine values; but one can infer these factors from the biographies.

28. If psychiatrists cannot predict violent behavior, then how can they justify committing people to mental hospitals on the grounds that they are "a danger to others"? A politically pragmatic organization, the APA argues that it cannot predict violence in order to protect its members from lawsuits, but forgets the argument entirely when it supports the right of psychiatrists to lock up people against their will.

29. Quoted in Coleman, 1984.

30. The books include a socially and environmentally oriented program (Currie, 1985); Wilson and Herrnstein's 1985 biologically oriented *Crime and Human Nature;* and several comprehensive critiques of the genetic-biological

viewpoint, including Gould's 1981 *The Mismeasure of Man,* Lewontin et al.'s 1984 *Not In Our Genes,* and Kevles's 1985 *In the Name of Eugenics.*

31. Toufexis, 1993.

32. See Duster, 1990, for citation and discussion.

33. Brimelow, 1993.

34. Rich, 1993. The unpublished studies by Greg J. Duncan and others at the University of Michigan were reported at the national meetings of the Society for Research in Child Development. Not unexpectedly, poor children also showed more signs of both emotional suffering and negative behavior.

35. Gelles and Cornell, 1990; Yllo and Bograd, 1988.

36. Burton, 1990a&b; Breggin, 1992a; Coate and Rosati, 1988.

37. For discussions of the relationship between humiliation and violence, also see Breggin, 1991a, 1992a.

38. See Breggin, 1992a, for an analysis of shame and violence.

39. Escobar and Greenberger, 1993.

40. Angier, 1993; Stolberg, 1993.

41. Tardiff, 1988, p. 1038.

42. The underlying biochemical defect is described as a deficiency in monoamine oxidase, an enzyme that facilitates the breakdown of three of the most widely distributed neurotransmitters in the brain—dopamine, norepinephrine, and serotonin. While such a widespread and potentially devastating impairment could reduce overall brain function, producing mental retardation, it seems unlikely that it could selectively cause antisocial or violent behavior.

43. Marshall, October 1, 1993. The appeals board found that NIH erred in claiming that the university had "significantly misrepresented the objectives of the conference" in its brochure. In fact, the genetic and biopsychiatric themes were expressed in even more detail in the application than in the brochure.

Chapter 4

1. Begley, 1993.

2. The *DSM-III-R* (American Psychiatric Association, 1987) observes, "Studies have indicated that in both clinic and community samples, the symptoms of these disorders covary to a high degree." A recent NIMH study of DBDs (Kruesi et al., 1992) similarly observes, " 'Pure' conduct disorder or 'pure' opposition disorder are relatively rare in clinical samples, with most cases also qualifying for an attention-deficit disorder diagnosis."

3. Barkley, 1981, p. 13.

4. Fasnacht, 1993.

5. See Gaines, 1991, concerning special education.

6. Smith, B. D., 1993.

7. According to Richard E. Vatz of Towson State University, "Attention-deficit disorder (ADD) is no more a disease than is 'excitability.' It is a psychiatric, pseudomedical term." Frank Putnam, a director of one of NIMH's research units, recently applauded "the growing number of clinicians and researchers condemning the tyranny of our psychiatric and educational classification systems." Putnam finds that it is "exceedingly difficult to assign valid classifications" to children, and yet "children are by far the most classified and labeled group in our society." He warns against "the institutional prescriptions of a system that seeks to pigeonhole them."

8. For example, Golden, 1991, says "the response to the drug cannot be used to validate the diagnosis. Normal boys as well as those with ADHD show similar changes when given a single dose of a psychostimulant."

9. Grahame-Smith and Aronson, 1992.

10. Compare this to the more familiar range of variability in response to coffee. Some people seem more relaxed after a cup or two; others quickly get too "hyper."

11. Citation numbers removed from the quote.

12. Reviewed in Breggin, 1991a; Coles, 1987; McGuinness, 1989; and Swanson et al., 1992.

13. Regier and Leshner, 1992. Discussed later in chapter.

14. *Physicians' Desk Reference,* 1993.

15. American Psychiatric Association, 1989, p. 1221. Also see Breggin, 1991a. Advocates of Ritalin point out that addiction is rarely if ever reported in the literature, but the same literature also fails to emphasize *any* Ritalin side effects, including withdrawal symptoms, which are relatively common in clinical practice.

16. Spotts and Spotts, 1980. Some of the medical reports in the compendium point out that taking Ritalin once a day to deal with personal problems or conflicts constitutes an abuse.

17. Goodman et al. (1991, p. 78) observe, "Over 40% of physicians are not aware that the FDA has a reporting system for adverse drug reactions. . . ." Also see Breggin, 1993a, and Breggin and Breggin, 1994.

18. Nashrallah et al., 1986.

19. John George provided us with these figures. Within the United States in 1991, the dozen states and territories with the highest per capita use of Ritalin, in descending order, were Idaho, Michigan, Utah, Ohio, Iowa, Alaska, Montana, Georgia, Indiana, Wisconsin, Maryland, and Virginia. The lowest in descending order were New York, South Dakota, California, Hawaii, Maine, Puerto Rico, Guam, and the Virgin Islands.

20. According to the *DSM-III-R,* ADHD occurs in boys up to six to nine times more frequently than in girls and conduct disorder occurs in 9 percent of boys and 2 percent of girls.

21. About schools, see Kozol, 1991, and Armstrong, 1993.

22. For girls who grow up to become caricatures or exaggerations of the expected female role, psychiatry has proposed a controversial adult diagnosis: self-defeating personality disorder. This is an extension of Freudian ideas of "women's masochism" into modern psychology. It blames the tendency to fail on the women themselves when failure is in reality desired and even demanded of them by the male-dominated society. We shall never have a *DSM-III-R* diagnosis of "male dominator syndrome."

23. Breggin, 1991a.

24. Documented in Breggin, 1991a.

25. Armstrong, 1993.

26. See Breggin, 1991a. For example, NAMI's national director is officially invited to attend the closed board meetings of the American Psychiatric Association, and NAMI lobbies and promotes "mental health" in partnership with the association.

27. Fowler, 1992.

28. Material for this section was taken from Kotulak, 1993. I have attended scientific conferences in which unpublished research presentations have confirmed these findings.

29. The brain scan findings require confirmatory research.

Chapter 5

1. Wender, 1973, pp. 8–9.

2. Rapoport, 1989, p. 39.

3. The journal volume on violence resulted from "the challenge by George Lundberg and C. Everett Koop to the American Medical Association family of journals to address their June issues to aspects of violence that are medically relevant . . ." (Freedman, 1992, p. 485). The violence initiative was an interagency plan. The AMA's choice of articles reflects Goodwin's violence initiative.

4. To their credit, the authors acknowledge that their findings, even if confirmed, do not prove a causal relationship between serotonin levels and aggression, and may reflect correlations with stress. Consistent with this, steroid levels, which are known to increase during stress, were elevated in the multiply-wounded monkeys.

5. *All Things Considered,* 1992, p. 10. In the transcript, Markus Kruesi's name is misspelled "Marcus Cruzy."

6. Information from the study abstract only.

7. Judith L. Rapoport, Markus J. P. Kruesi, William Z. Potter, Josephine Elia, B. J. Casey, Theodore Zahn, and Thomas Cooper: "Notice of Intramural Research—Neurobiology of Disruptive Behavior Disorders" (October 1, 1990–September 30, 1991) (Z01-MH-02240-03 CHP) (Child Psychiatry Branch).

8. Leonard et al., 1991.

9. Reiss and Roth, 1993, p. 127.

10. Adams and Victor, 1993.

11. Lately it has been found that nitric oxide and carbon monoxide play major roles throughout the brain, but their action differs greatly from typical neurotransmitters (Kolata, 1993).

12. There are many reasons to suspect that the serotonin theory of impulsivity is a gross oversimplification and that it will eventually fall into the same obscurity that has afflicted every other biological theory of "mental disorder" and criminality. The nerve cell bodies that produce serotonin originate deep in the brain within the raphe nuclei and then radiate upward to almost every other part of the higher brain. A schematic of the serotonin nerves (see Breggin and Breggin, 1994) shows a trunk that branches upward into every lobe and then into nearly every nook and cranny of the great organ in the skull. These nerves then interact with innumerable other systems in the brain, producing still more complex relationships and effects.

Serotonin is thus involved in the overall function of the brain and the person. It is a very long reach to imagine that gross variations in the activity of such a vast system would be causative of an isolated behavioral effect, such as "impulsivity," or, more specifically, violence in inner-city children.

As an example of a similar futile effort, hundreds of papers once aimed to prove that an abnormality in the brain's steroid (cortisol) regulation causes depression. In simplified terms, in chronically depressed patients cortisol would be put out despite contrary signals from the feedback mechanism. Yet this is a natural reaction to almost any kind of stress, from emotional trauma to a blow on the head (Breggin, 1991a).

13. The spelled-out name of the drug is m-chlorophenylpiperazine; it is a serotonin agonist. For its marked tendency to cause anxiety and panic, see studies cited in Brown and van Praag, 1991 (see "MCPP" in their index).

14. See Talan, October 11, 1993. For the research she cites, see Higley et al., 1993. She quotes Higley as claiming that his research "provides insights we've never had about how chemistry can govern behavior."

15. In reality, NIMH's overall research is unbalanced. During a reorganization that was made into law in 1992, the service components of NIMH were split off, leaving it a pure research institute under NIH. Congress was sufficiently concerned about NIMH's low level of psychosocial research funding that it required the institute to spend a minimum of 15 percent of its budget in this area, a standard that NIMH has had difficulty meeting.

16. For example, in 1992 the National Institute of Drug Abuse (NIDA) awarded $1,266,157 as part of a five-year grant to Thomas J. Crowley. Among other things, he will test the efficacy of lithium and carbamazapine (an anticonvulsant, brand names Tegretol, Epitol, Atretol) on aggressive adolescents.

17. The following is a partial list of grants that we located that (unless otherwise indicated) involve giving stimulant drugs to children. Each is being funded

as of 1992 and the dollar amounts are for that year only, although most of the grants extend for several years or more. The information is more complete in some of the citations than others:

Rapoport, J., "Neurobiology of Disruptive Behavior Disorders," intramural (at NIMH), $424,700, children and adolescents; Deborah Ann Pearson, "Attention Deficits in Mentally Retarded Children," ages 9–14; Jan Loney, State University of New York at Stony Brook, "Child Disruptive and/or Mood Disorders," ages 7–11, $281,484; Kevin MacDonald, "Effects of Ritalin on Play in ADHD," ages 5–9; Marcel Kinsbourne, untitled (R01 MH37578-09), ages 6–12; Jeffrey Halperin, "Validation of Inattention and Aggressive ADHD Subtypes" (no stimulant drug treatment but uses medication in the form of a fenfluramine challenge test); Stephen Pliszka, University of Texas, Health Sciences Center, Medical Center, Texas, "Clinical and Neurochemical Subtypes of ADD," ages 6–12; Rachel G. Klein, Long Island Jewish Medical Center, "Prospective Longitudinal Study of Hyperactive Children," $205,850; Rachel G. Klein (second grant), "Methylphenidate in Childhood Behavior Disorders," ages 13–16, New York State Psychiatric Institute ("a substantial portion of subjects will be from the minority community"), $181,363; Magda Campbell, "Research Training in Child Psychopharmacology" (unlike others, training only without drug administration), New York University, $190,757; Rafael Klorman, "Stimulants and Adolescent Attention Disorder," 25 percent African-American, ages 12.5–16, $190,850; Paul Wender, University of Utah, "Further Studies of Attention Deficit Disorders" (unlike other studies this is confined to adults), $182,361; Michael G. Aman, Ohio State University, "Fenfluramine and Methylphenidate in Mental Retardation," ages 5–13, $132,837; Kenneth D. Gadow, State University of New York, Stony Brook, "Methylphenidate Treatment of ADHD in Children with Tourette's Syndrome," ages 6–12, $161,477; William E. Pelham, University of Pittsburgh at Pittsburgh, "Methylphenidate Effects in ADHD Adolescents," ages 12–15, $211,382; William E. Pelham, University of Pittsburgh at Pittsburgh, "Pharmacological and Psychosocial Treatment for ADHD," $186,098; William E. Pelham, University of Pittsburgh at Pittsburgh, "Pharmacology and Cognitive Motivation in ADHD," ages 8–13, $303,784; Russell A. Barkley, University of Massachusetts Medical School, "Multi-Method Intervention with Aggressive ADHD Children," 5-year-olds, $662,718; Robert K. McBurnett, University of California, Irvine, "Central and Peripheral Actions of Amphetamine in ADHD," ages 7–12 ("substantial Hispanic minority"), $73,750; Stephen P. Hinshaw, University of California, "Pharmacologic and Psychosocial Intervention for ADHD," $139,946; Stephen P. Hinshaw, "Peer Status, Social Behavior, and Intervention for ADHD," ages 6–11

Also see note 18 below, listing new multisite, multimodel projects developed starting in 1992 by NIMH.

18. See Rieger and Leshner, 1992. The recipients in 1992 were: Lilly Hechtman, Montreal Children's Hospital, "Methylphenidate and Multimodal Treatment in ADHD," $129,366; Howard B. Abikoff, Long Island Jewish

Medical Center, "Methylphenidate and Multimodel Treatment in ADHD," ages 7–10, $200,305; Howard B. Abikoff (second grant), $88,016; James M. Swanson, University of California, "Multisite Multimodal Treatment Study of ADHD/ADD," $276,599; Keith C. Conners, Duke University, "Multi-Modal Treatment of ADD," $124,792; Laurence Greenhill, Research Fund for Mental Hygiene, New York City, "Multimodel Treatment of ADHD in an Urban Setting," $184,013.

Also see note 17 above, giving a longer list of individual NIMH-funded studies in which stimulants are being given to children.

19. See bibliography. The affiliations of the authors are Jacqueline Faye Jackson, Ph.D., Research Associate, Institute of Human Development, University of California, Berkeley; Maisha Bennett, Ph.D., President, Association of Black Psychologists; Harold Dent, Ph.D., Outreach Director, National Center for Minority Special Education Research and Outreach; Halford Fairchild, Ph.D., Past President, Association of Black Psychologists; Reginald Jones, Ph.D., Director, National Center for Minority Special Education Research and Outreach; Patricia Rhymer Todman, Ph.D., Associate Professor, University of the Virgin Islands.

20. "Antidepressants Found . . . ," 1992; "Targeted Drug Therapy . . . ," 1992.

21. Baker, 1993.

22. Breggin, 1991a.

23. Documentation is provided in Breggin, 1991a.

24. Tardiff, 1988, 1992; also see Eichelman and Hartwig, 1990.

25. Tardiff, 1988, p. 1050.

26. See Weiner, 1991, p. 548.

27. Breggin, 1991a.

28. Lewis, 1989; Tardiff, 1988, 1992.

29. Such as tardive dyskinesia, tardive dystonia, tardive akathisia, tardive psychosis, and tardive dementia. The rates for these disorders exceed 50 percent in longer-term use (Breggin, 1991a).

30. Monahan, 1990.

31. We learned about the study when we were sent a Department of Probation memorandum about it (Stone, R., 1991). Ginger Ross Breggin then interviewed the grant recipient, Gail Wasserman, by telephone on November 19, 1992. She reported that the first phase was completed and the study is ongoing.

Chapter 6

1. My articles and book chapters provide a survey of ongoing surgery at the time, as well as a general critique of the clinical and political implications (Breggin, 1972a&b, 1973a,b&c, 1975a&c, 1977a&b, 1980, 1981b, 1982,

1983a). A brief summary and citations of some of the extensive news coverage of the anti-psychosurgery campaign can be found in Breggin (1980). A compendium of articles about the controversy was published by Valenstein, 1980. While Valenstein grew bolder in criticizing psychosurgery after its relative demise, he was a major impediment to the campaign against it. Brought in by the psychosurgeons to their panels and public appearances, he substituted for the real critics of psychosurgery.

2. In 1982 Heidi Hansen and her colleagues from Denmark summarized the effects of the most modern forms of psychosurgery:

> The patient's options for action are reduced by a weakening of initiative and ability to structure his situation; emotionality fades, is organized more shallowly and is more dependent upon the immediate situation. Contact with other people becomes more flattened and the immediate bearing more mechanical. (p. 115)

3. Mark and Ervin sometimes claimed their psychosurgery was a treatment for violence induced by epilepsy. That epilepsy can cause violence remains unsubstantiated. Also, Mark, Ervin, and Sweet repeatedly call their operation "psychosurgery" rather than brain surgery for epilepsy, and—as in this quote—they suggested that it might work on patients without any brain disease.

4. Bird, 1968.

5. Quoted in Mason, 1973. Also see Scheflin and Opton, 1978, p. 285.

6. Also identified as Leonard K. in some of their publications. "Thomas" is a pseudonym. Every other detail of the story is accurate, and nothing has been disguised.

7. For an example of citing no serious side effects, see Mark, Sweet, and Ervin, 1972. Mark and Ervin made the spurious claim that epilepsy causes violence. Moreover, according to the medical records I have reviewed, Thomas R. was never seen to have epileptic seizures prior to his surgery; but Mark and Ervin assert that one unnamed physician once witnessed a single psychomotor seizure. Brain wave studies (EEGs) before his surgery (for example, in the medical records on March 24, 1966) showed no abnormalities. Also, as pointed out in note 3 above, Mark, Ervin, and Sweet suggest their surgery might work on patients with no demonstrable disease, and they often referred to it as psychosurgery rather than neurosurgery for epilepsy. Furthermore, operations for epilepsy must focus on a specific, localized idea of the brain that is malfunctioning, while Mark always operated on the same place, a nerve center in the temporal lobe called the amygdala. It is a frequent site for psychosurgical operations. In *Violence and the Brain,* Mark and Ervin point out that lesions in the amygdala of an animal's brain tend to produce a taming effect in the animal.

8. The device was in the early stages of development; thus, unlike several later patients, Thomas could not wander freely about the ward while being unknowingly stimulated and recorded. But while in the experimental room, he would be unaware of whether or not they were stimulating his brain.

9. For a further analysis of Delgado's writings, see Breggin, 1982.

10. See *Medical News*, September 25, 1967.

11. The period following discharge was described in a lengthy letter written to me by his mother, Mrs. G., on February 10, 1972, and confirmed in recent interviews.

12. Breggin, 1973b.

13. Mark claims that Thomas had "15 years of episodic hallucinations," but this is not confirmed in the records, in my interviews with Thomas's mother, his wife, or his wife's psychiatrist, or even in Mark's publications. As already documented, Mark's reports detail how the "delusions" developed following psychosurgical stimulation and destruction of his brain. Rodin's report seems to confirm this.

     After reviewing Thomas's records, in the May 1974 *Psychology Today* MIT professor of psychology Stephen Chorover supported my observations on the results of Thomas's surgery. Mark was again given the opportunity to respond in a lengthy rebuttal. The neurosurgeon detailed his theoretical and political disagreements with his critics, but made no attempt to contradict anything that Chorover and I were saying about Thomas's fate.

14. Department of Justice, 1973.

15. "Impact of Malpractice Suit on Psychosurgery Minimized," *Clinical Psychiatry News,* May 1979. The suit is *Kille* v. *Mark,* 1973.

16. From his Department of Veterans Affairs medical record, dated January 1, 1993.

17. Struck, 1986.

18. The story of the California controversy is told in Chavkin, 1978; Scheflin and Opton, 1978; and Schrag, 1978.

19. In mid-1972 William Sweet urged Congress to support a series of biomedical violence-prevention centers aimed at identifying people who might imperil society due to their genetic and brain defects (Chavkin, p. 94).

20. Opposition to the violence centers was broad-based: participants included psychologist and attorney Edward M. Opton, Jr., psychiatrists Lee Coleman and Phil Shapiro, civil rights and women's groups, African-American activists, and many psychiatric survivors, including Leonard Frank and Wade Hudson.

21. Other examples of the age-old "bad blood" theory of mental illness are cited in Breggin, *Toxic Psychiatry.*

22. Andy (1971) wrote to me that the age range began at seven. His assistant, Jurko (1971), wrote to me that the age range was five to twelve, and that most of the patients were institutionalized.

23. See Gonzalez, 1980. In fact, the University of Mississippi set up a special committee of Andy's peers to evaluate his surgery, and the group declared it "experimental." Since Andy did not use experimental protocols, the surgery was halted (Breland, 1973).

24. *Kaimowitz* v. *Michigan Department of Mental Health,* 1973. The most extensive description of the case was written by the losing attorney, Samuel

Shuman (1977), who was outraged by the verdict and my role in it. Shuman's book contains a valuable appendix, including the court's opinion in the case. A brief analysis of the case can be found in Robitscher, 1980, and Breggin, 1975, and chapters by several authors in Valenstein, 1980.

25. The code is reproduced in *Trials of War Criminals,* 1946–1949 (pp. 181–182), and in Katz, 1972 (pp. 305–306).

26. I discuss the FDA in Breggin, 1991a and 1993a.

27. Later the Department of Health and Human Services decided to establish guidelines for psychosurgery insurance coverage under Medicare and Medicaid. The proposed guidelines were leaked to me, and I gave them to Glenn Frankl, who wrote two stories for the *Washington Post* (April 8 and May 10, 1980). The publicity forced the issue to be referred to the federal Office of Health and Technology Assessment (OHTA), which "evaluates the safety and efficacy of new and unestablished medical technologies that are being considered for coverage under Medicare." In 1985 in Report #9, "Sterotactic Cingulotomy as Means of Psychosurgery," the OHTA concluded that there were insufficient studies to assess the outcome and dangers of modern psychosurgery, and that it must remain experimental "rather than accepted clinical practice." Nonetheless, some surgeons continue to perform psychosurgery as if it were a routine part of medical practice.

28. The commission set up a "research project" under Ballantine that excluded input from several known skeptics about psychosurgery, including a well-known MIT professor of psychology. The project did not have a control group. The single "control" case in the whole study was an accidental one—a patient who had burr holes put in his head but who turned out to be physically unsuitable for the surgery. His head was then closed up without an operation. Nonetheless, the patient claimed a miraculous cure and absolutely refused to believe he had not been operated upon. In psychiatry, even more than in general medicine, placebo can be enormously powerful. Also, as I discovered in reviewing several patient records, Ballantine gave his post-surgery patients huge amounts of narcotics that surely helped them feel better initially.

29. Breggin, 1980.

30. For the original charges, see Rowland, 1978, and for the decision see Elshire, 1979.

31. James Wirth, clinical director of inpatient services in the department of psychiatry, was recently deposed in a malpractice suit against Johns Hopkins and some of its doctors. He wasn't sure how many Johns Hopkins patients were given shock each year, "but it's in the hundreds." In another deposition in the same ongoing malpractice suit, Johns Hopkins psychiatrist John Richard Lipsey testified that "perhaps 20%" of all inpatients in psychiatry "are getting ECT." Neither Wirth nor Lipsey is being sued in the case; they are experts in defense of the hospital and the defendant doctors.

32. Jenike et al., 1991. Also see Jenike, 1988, 1990.

33. Simmons, 1991; Mindus and Nyman, 1990; and Sachev et al., 1992. Also

see bibliographies contained in the latter two articles and in other citations in this chapter.

Chapter 7

1. William Shirer's massive *Rise and Fall of the Third Reich* (1960) gave many Americans their most complete picture of Nazi Germany, but did not mention the killing of mental patients, let alone psychiatry's larger role in the Holocaust. Yet Shirer himself was among the first to write about the psychiatric murders in his earlier book *Berlin Diary* (1941), before extensive confirmation surfaced at the Nuremberg Trials. The first book by an American to fully confront psychiatry's role in Nazi Germany was self-published by a former mental patient—psychiatric survivor Lenny Lapon (1986). He could not get his excellent work commercially published. Robert Lifton's *Nazi Doctors* (1986) fails to look deeply enough into psychiatry's unique responsibility. Benno Müller-Hill, professor and director at the Institute for Genetics in Cologne, Germany, began researching the subject, and quickly "realized that the official history of human genetics and psychiatry in Germany between 1933 and 1945 was a fraud" (Müller-Hill, 1992, p. 6). Jeffrey Masson and I have been planning a book on the role of psychiatry in Nazi Germany but have found it difficult to get an American publisher, although we have an English one. I did manage to publish a couple of magazine stories on the subject in the 1970s, but never a professional article until recently (Breggin, 1992h & 1993b).

2. Proctor, 1988; Pross and Aly, 1991; Müller-Hill, 1988, 1991a&b; and *Trials of War Criminals,* 1949.

3. Proctor, 1988; Lauter and Meyer, 1982; and Müller-Hill, 1988.

4. Meyer, 1988; Müller-Hill, 1988, p. 65; and Pross and Aly, 1991.

5. Pross and Aly, 1991.

6. Mitscherlich and Mielke, 1949, p. 100; Sosnowski, 1962.

7. Fisher, 1993.

8. Fisher, 1993.

9. Pross and Aly, 1991, p. 30.

10. Pross, 1991.

11. Müller-Hill, 1991a, p. 461 and p. 465.

12. Friedlander, 1992; Proctor, 1988; Meyer, 1988; Sereny, 1983.

13. Sereny, 1983, pp. 53–54; Wiesenthal, 1967, p. 314.

14. Lauter and Meyer, 1982.

15. Alexander, 1949; Müller-Hill, 1988.

16. Müller-Hill, 1991b.

17. Sereny, 1983.

18. Mitscherlich and Mielke, 1949, observed that "in the concentration camps

prisoners were selected by the same medical consultants who were simultane ously sitting over the destiny of mental institution inmates."

19. See Chroust, 1992. Also, Müller-Hill, 1988; *Trials of War Criminals,* 1949.

20. Müller-Hill, 1988, p. 41.

21. Chroust, 1992; also, Mitscherlich and Mielke, 1949.

22. Quoted in Mitscherlich and Mielke, 1949, p. xi.

23. Cited in Pross and Aly, 1991, p. 7.

24. Meyer, 1988; *Trials of War Criminals,* 1949, pp. 65 and 67.

25. Weiss (1987, p. 1) defines eugenics as "a political strategy denoting some sort of social control over reproduction" through which "this supposed science seeks to regulate human procreation by encouraging the fecundity of the allegedly genetically superior groups in society and simultaneously discouraging and even prohibiting so-called inferior types from having children."

26. Lauter and Meyer, 1982; Meyer, 1988; Müller-Hill, 1988; Proctor, 1988; and Weiss, 1987.

27. Proctor, 1988, p. 20.

28. Weinreich, 1946, pp. 32–33; also see Wistrich, 1982, p. 26.

29. Proctor, 1988, p. 60; also see Popenoe, 1934.

30. Interpretation of the Sterilization Law, 1934.

31. *Eugenical Sterilization* also cites a publication by W. W. Peter in which Hitler's sterilization program is justified as a political and social necessity. In the article, Peter (1934) states, "The present load of social irresponsibles are liabilities which represent a great deal of waste" (p. 190). Neither the large report nor Peter's article cited any professional criticism of Hitler's eugenical program, and they would have been hard pressed to find any.

32. The 1907 Indiana act was considered a eugenic model and aimed "to prevent procreation of confirmed criminals, idiots, imbeciles, and rapists." The law stated that "heredity plays a most important part in the transmission of crime." It *required* state institutions to develop special medical committees to determine which inmates should be involuntarily sterilized.

33. Reilly, 1991, p. 98.

34. Reilly, 1991, p. 95.

35. Proctor, 1988; Müller-Hill, 1988.

36. Kallmann's article was followed in the *Eugenical News* by one by Rudolph Binder (1938), openly praising Hitler and Germany's sterilization of an estimated 300,000 people. Binder complained that "These useless, hopeless and harmful people receive the best of care" (p. 116).

37. Armstrong, 1993, p. 75.

38. Baker, 1974, pp. 61 and 365.

39. "Euthanasia," 1942.

40. Kater, 1992.

41. Pross and Aly, 1991, p. 15.

42. Müller-Hill, 1988, p. 12.

43. Müller-Hill, 1988, p. 11; Pross and Aly, 1991; Proctor, 1988, p. 112.

44. Welsing, 1991, gives an ominous warning, appropriate to today's insecure economy:

> The specific fear of white genetic annihilation, while present in the global white collective, becomes more prominent and is more frequently acted upon in times when whites have lost a war and/or when there is serious economic insecurity. [p. 227]

45. Breggin, 1979.

46. Breggin, 1991a, reviews the resurgence of electroshock and the brain-damaging effects of psychiatric drugs. Concerning organized psychiatry's views on involuntary treatment and state hospitals, also see American Psychiatric Association, 1984.

47. E.g., Humphrey, 1992. As Proctor (1988, p. 183) said of Germany, "Humanistic propaganda notwithstanding, the argument for the destruction of life not worth living was at root an economic one."

Chapter 8

1. Fernando, 1993.

2. Savitt, 1978.

3. Savitt, 1978.

4. Savitt, 1978.

5. Bradford and Blume, 1992.

6. Rymer, 1992.

7. Bradford and Blume, 1992, p. 181.

8. Bradford and Blume, 1992.

9. Claiborne, 1992.

10. Bradford and Blume, 1992.

11. Claiborne, 1992.

12. Trueheart, 1993.

13. Claiborne, 1992.

14. Trueheart, 1993.

15. Auchmutey, 1992.

16. Blustein, Bonnie, August 30, 1993, correspondence.

17. Auchmutey, 1992.

18. Jones, 1993.

19. Associated Press, June 16, 1993.

20. Associated Press, June 16, 1993.

21. Priest, 1993.

22. Leary, 1993.

23. Leary, 1993.

24. Castaneda, 1992.

25. Horne, 1992–1993. The article cites references.

26. As noted in Chapter 2, the association may have been between low intelligence and incarceration (Tardiff, 1988, p. 1038).

27. Quoted from a 1970 newspaper article in Katz, 1972, p. 345. Even staunch supporters of behavioral genetics soon concluded that XYY men are not especially aggressive and don't contribute to "society's problem with aggressive crimes" (Mednick and Christiansen, 1977, p. 187).

28. Katz, 1972, p. 342, quoted from Bauer, January 22, 1970. All the citations in this section, including the partial text of the newspaper articles, can be found in Katz, pp. 342–346.

29. Bauer, January 22, 1970.

30. Bauer, February 13, 1970; Bauer, May 4, 1970.

31. The characterization is by Bauer (May 4, 1970). The actual consent form read, "The chromosome study ordinarily costs about $100 and, once performed in a lifetime, need ordinarily never be done again. However, no fees will be charged to you." The form is reproduced in Katz, 1972 (p. 345).

32. Ramm, 1989.

33. Cited in Miller, 1991, p. 236.

34. Blustein, Bonnie, August 30, 1993, correspondence.

35. Miller, J. G. 1991 & 1992.

36. Corea, 1977, pp. 206–17.

37. Cited in Corea, 1977, p. 155.

38. Corea, 1977, p. 177.

39. Lewin, 1992; DeWitt, 1992.

40. Baltimore teens made up 23 percent of the city's births and D.C. teens represented 18 percent in 1990. See Valentine and Goldstein, 1992.

41. Valentine and Goldstein, 1992.

42. Judges also feel empowered to enforce sterilization on child abusers (Editorial, February 12, 1993). A judge recently offered a woman and her husband, both child abusers, the alternative of jail or sterilization of the woman by tubal ligation. The alternative of vasectomy was not presented to the man.

43. Dugger, 1992.

44. Simon, 1993.

45. Thompson, 1993.

46. Goodwin, 1992a.

47. Goodwin, 1992b.

48. Justice Department, 1992.

49. The metaphor of the "weed" is not new in the arena of biomedical social control. In describing the origins of eugenics in the nineteenth century and the impulse to sterilize "the problem people" of England, Gena Corea, 1977, noted that one doctor wrote, "We would sterilize these people for the same reason we would weed a garden" (p. 145).

50. Miller, J. G., 1992.

51. See the National Center on Institutions and Alternatives, 1992. Also reported in Terry, 1992.

52. Editorial, August 4, 1993. Crack is the preferred form of the drug in the inner city, though many whites also use it. Nevertheless, that the law singles out crack users, and that the arrest rate of blacks for using it is high, at least in part reflect institutionalized racism.

53. According to the *Washington Post,* an Environmental Protection Agency (EPA) task force report shows that "among urban children 5 years old and younger, the percentage of blacks who have excessive levels of lead in their blood far exceeds the percentage of whites at all income levels" (Weisskopf, 1992).

54. Our schools are essentially segregated. In our forty-seven largest cities, only one in four public school children is white. Many urban schools are going bankrupt, and there are huge disparities in school budgets from district to district. Children are "tracked" with a disproportionate number of black and Hispanic students being suspended or placed in special education classes. Columnist Courtland Milloy, 1993a, declares that "the public school students in the city are being subjected to a particularly insidious brand of intellectual genocide."

55. The seminal 1987 study by the United Church of Christ Commission for Racial Justice identified race as the single most important factor in the location nationwide of hazardous-waste facilities (*Sierra,* 1993). More recently the *National Law Journal* reported that identification by the EPA of Superfund sites in minority communities took 20 percent longer, and fines for these polluters were half the amounts fined when pollution occurred in white neighborhoods (*Sierra,* 1993).

56. Despite civil rights advances, there is still blatant economic discrimination in the United States. Whether it is something as small as a quick meal at Denny's, or something as important as buying a car, obtaining a loan, renting an apartment, getting a job, or financing a home, black Americans are often relegated to the ranks of second-class citizens (for banking, see Editorial, June 11, 1993). In Montgomery County, Maryland, a black person who is apartment-hunting will encounter discrimination 56.5 percent of the time (Nelson, 1993). Discrimination includes being charged higher rent and fees to discourage rental (called a "race tax") as well as being told fewer units are available. Congressman Henry B. Gonzalez said, "To see that lending discrimination is alive and well in

Congress's own back yard is very demoralizing." It must also be demoralizing to a young black man to consider the hurdles he must leap to support a family.

57. For a discussion of this and other issues surrounding genocide, see Kuper, 1981.

58. See Kuper, 1981, for the complete text.

59. See Molotsky, 1992.

Chapter 9

1. The psychology of self-determination is described in Breggin, 1980a and 1993a.

2. See Breggin, *Toxic Psychiatry,* 1991a, for a discussion of biopsychiatry and each of these vulnerable groups.

3. Womack, 1992.

4. Odum, 1992. Some students were surprised by the high rates of self-destructive and dangerous behavior; but others thought that the figures were too low. It was likely that many students didn't confess to their most incriminating activities.

5. For the combination of awareness and impotence in today's youth, see Kozol, 1991; Gaines, 1991; and Gatto, 1991.

6. Gaines, 1991.

7. Rimer, 1993.

8. MacFarquhar et al., 1993, located fifteen "individual assistance approach" programs in twelve states. They identified thirteen characteristics: (1) services tailored to the youth, not the youth tailored to the services; (2) youth and family centered; (3) flexible funding for flexible programming; (4) unconditional care policy (never abandoning the client); (5) team planning; (6) the goal of "normalization" in contrast to accepting institutionalization; (7) community care; (8) intensive case management; (9) extensive funding adequate to the task; (10) striving for least-restrictive alternatives; (11) accountability; (12) services based on outcome data; (13) specifically trained and supported staff. We believe that a focus on *meeting basic needs* is one of the most important elements. It is implied but not isolated in MacFarquhar et al.'s review. It dovetails with the concept that conflict in general is best resolved through the mutual satisfaction of basic needs (Breggin, 1992a).

A good overview with an analysis of the Alaskan program (AYI) can be found in Katz-Leavy et al., 1992. Also see Burchard and Burchard, 1991; Burchard and Clarke, 1990; and VanDenBerg, 1988 & 1989.

9. Armstrong, 1993.

10. This view of love is most fully explored in *Beyond Conflict* (Breggin, 1992a).

11. Breggin, 1991a, 1992a, Breggin and Breggin, 1994; Mosher and Burti, 1989.

12. The commission on children reached consensus on a remarkable number of proposed government policies: the need for tens of billions of dollars of tax refunds and tax breaks for the poor to help eradicate extreme poverty; government child support when fathers cannot be forced to pay their share; Head Start educational programs for all children who need them; and the increased availability of prenatal and child health care services. It recommended that America do much more for its children and for the poor families in which they live. It cited racism as a fundamental problem.

The point is not to argue about the pros and cons of the conclusions reached by the National Commission on Children. Despite the commission's conservative origins, some consider its proposals too radical, while others believe them insufficient.

13. Rich, August 1, 1993.

14. Watts College of Child Development, c/o Ernest H. Smith, M.D., Community Division Pediatrics, Martin Luther King Hospital, P.O. Box 7883, Culver Street, CA 90233-7883. It is a cooperative, volunteer "spiritual college of the mind."

15. For how to locate the American Academy of Psychotherapists, see Appendix.

16. Such as Gerald Coles, *The Learning Mystique,* or Peter Breggin's *Toxic Psychiatry,* with its extensive bibliography and resources appendix.

17. For how to locate State Protection and Advocacy Offices, see Appendix.

Legal Aid Societies can be located through the local phone book or through the National Legal Aid and Defender Association, 1625 K Street, NW, Suite 800, Washington, DC 20006. Phone: (202) 452-0620.

18. Reiss and Roth, 1993.

19. National Research Council, 1993.

Bibliography

Abrams, R. (1945). Kaufbeuren, Bavaria, July 2. 10-page U.S. Army press release. Unpublished.

Abrams, R. (circa 1973). Personal interviews with Peter Breggin, supplemented with photographs of the Kaufbeuren state mental hospital and crematorium taken by Abrams in 1945. Unpublished.

Achenbach, J. (1992, May 6). "Mind over gray matter? Psychiatrists debate power of the pill." *Washington Post,* p. B1.

Adams, R.D., and M. Victor (1993). *Principles of Neurology.* New York: McGraw-Hill Book Company.

Adler, T. (1992, May). "Goodwin to take post amid campaign jitters." *APA Monitor,* p. 1.

Agnew, B. (1993, November). " 'Prevention Research Initiative' gets pretty basic." *Journal of NIH Research* 5:33–34.

Alcohol, Drug Abuse, and Mental Health Administration (undated, circa early 1992). "Violent Behavior: Etiology and Early Intervention—ADAMHA 1994 Planning Document." Unpublished.

Alexander, F. G., and M. D. Selesnick (1966). *The History of Psychiatry.* New York: Harper and Row.

Alexander, L. (1945, July 20). *Neuropathology and neurophysiology, including electroencephalography, in wartime Germany.* CIOS Item 24, Medical. Combined Intelligence Sub-Committee, G-2 Division SHAEF (Rear) APO 413. Declassified report.

Alexander, L. (1949). "Medical science under dictatorship." *New England Journal of Medicine,* 241, 39–47.

Alexander, L. (1953). *Treatment of Mental Disorders.* Philadelphia: W. B. Saunders Company.

All Things Considered (1992, July 6). Official Transcript from National Public Radio, 2025 M Street NW, Washington, D.C. 20036.

American Psychiatric Association (1979). *Task force report on electroconvulsive therapy.* Washington, D.C.: APA.

American Psychiatric Association (1980). *Task force report 18 on tardive dyskinesia.* Washington, D.C.: APA.

American Psychiatric Association (1984). *Task force report on the homeless mentally ill.* Washington, D.C.: APA.

American Psychiatric Association (1987). *Diagnostic and statistical manual of mental disorders, Third Edition, revised.* Washington, D.C.: APA.

American Psychiatric Association (1989). *Treatments of psychiatric disorders: A task force report of the American Psychiatric Association.* Washington, D.C.: APA.

American Psychiatric Association (1992, April). *Fact sheet: Patient/therapist sexual contact.* Washington, D.C.: APA.

American Psychological Association (1992, May/June). "Mental health community react to Goodwin's resignation." *Science Agenda,* p. 1.

Anderson, C. (1992, July 30). "NIH, under fire, freezes grant for conference on genetics and crime." *Nature,* 358:357.

Anderson, J. (1973, June 11). "The Washington merry-go-round." *Washington Post,* p. B11.

Andy, O. J. (1966). "Neurosurgical treatment of abnormal behavior." *American Journal of Medical Sciences,* 252:232–238.

Andy, O. J. (1970). "Thalamotomy in hyperactive and aggressive behavior." *Confinia Neurologica,* 32:322–325.

Andy, O. J. (1971, May 28). Letter to Peter Breggin.

Angier, N. (1993, October 22). "Study finds a genetic flaw that may explain some male violence." *The New York Times,* p. A14.

Annas, G. J., and S. Elias (eds.) (1992). *Gene Mapping: Using Law and Ethics as Guides.* New York: Oxford University Press.

"Antidepressants found to prevent depression-related 'anger attacks.'" (1992, September). *Clinical Psychiatry News,* p. 6.

Armstrong, C. W. (1927). *The Survival of the Unfittest.* London: The C. W. Daniel Company.

Armstrong, L. (1993). *And They Call It Help: The Psychiatric Policing of America's Children.* New York: Addison-Wesley Publishing Co.

Associated Press (1974, May 22). "Bond will ask study of mental treatment." *St. Louis Globe-Democrat,* p. 1.

Associated Press (1990, July 27). "Most American Indians from 1 group, geneticist says." *Washington Post,* p. A24.

Associated Press (1992, June 27). "New federal center to address causes of violence, accidents." *Washington Post,* p. A2.

Associated Press (1992, September 14). "Penalties lower for pollution in minority areas." *Washington Post,* p. A9.

Associated Press (1993, Junc 2). "New Texas school plan faces challenge." *Washington Post,* p. A5.

Associated Press (1993, June 16). "In some states, AIDS found top killer of young adults." *Washington Post,* p. A3.

Athens, L. (1989). *The Creation of Dangerous Violent Criminals.* New York: Routledge.

Auchmutey, J. (1992, September 6). "Ghosts of Tuskegee." *Atlanta Journal/Atlanta Constitution,* p. M1.

Babington, C. (1992, September 5). "U-Md. cancels conference on genetic link to crime: NIH pulled funds over proposed content." *Washington Post,* p. A1.

Baker, B. (1993, July). "Limited data suggest fluoxetine safe for children." *Clinical Psychiatry News,* p. 18.

Baker, J. R. (1974). *Race.* New York and London: Oxford University Press.

Ballantine, H. T. (1985). "Neurosurgery for behavioral disorders." In R. H. Wilkins and S. S. Rengachary (eds.). *Neurosurgery.* New York: McGraw-Hill, pp. 2527–2537.

Barkley, R. (1981). *Hyperactive Children: A Handbook for Diagnosis and Treatment.* New York: Guilford Press.

Barnes, D. M. (1992, November). "From the editor—Anatomy of an attempted murder: How to kill research on violent behavior." *The Journal of NIH Research,* 4:10.

Bass, A. (1993, February 8). "Controversy places research in peril." *Boston Globe,* p. 37.

Battista, C. (1993, June). "Conference seeks to raise issues of racial/ethnic identity." *Psychiatric Times,* p. 12.

Bauer, D. (1970, January 22). "Maryland tests for criminal potential." *Washington Daily News,* p. 7.

Bauer, D. (1970, February 13). "XYY tests stop." *Washington Daily News,* p. 5.

Bauer, D. (1970, May 4). "Criminal-prone tests resumed." *Washington Daily News,* p. 1.

Baughman, Jr., F. A. (1992, October). "Says drug companies too powerful." *Clinical Psychiatry News,* p. 5.

Baughman, Jr., F. A. (1993, May 12). "Treatment of attention-deficit hyperactivity disorder." *Journal of the American Medical Association,* 269:2368.

Baur, E., E. Fischer, and F. Lenz (1923). *Menschliche Erblichkeitslehre und Rassenhygiene.* 2nd edition. Munich: J. F. Lehmann.

Begley. S. (1993, June 28). "The puzzle of genius." *Newsweek,* p. 46.

Bell, D. (1992). *Faces at the Bottom of the Well.* New York: Basic Books.

Bennett, M. H. (1993, February). "President's message: Actions on the 'Federal Violence Initiative.' " *Psyche Discourse* 24:No. 2, pp. 4–8.

Bernat, J. L., and F. M. Vincent (1987). *Neurology: Problems in Primary Care.* Oradell, NJ: Medical Economics Books.

Bielski, V. (1992, July 15). "Mean genes." *SF [San Francisco] Weekly,* p. 12.

Bielski, V. (1993, October). "Bad to the bone?" *California Lawyer,* p. 73.

Binder, R. (1938). "Germany's population policy." *Eugenical News,* 23-24: 113–116.

Binding, K., and A. Hoche (1920). *Die Freigabe der vernichtung lebensunwerten Lebens: Ihr Mass und ihre Form.* Leipzig: F. Meiner.

Bird, D. (1968, August 14). "More stress urged on causes of civil disorders." *The New York Times,* p. 19.

Black Economic Research Center. (1974, Fall). "Black land loss: The plight of Black ownership." *Southern Exposure*, 2:112–121.

Bohman, M., C. R. Cloninger, S. Sigvardsson, and A. L. von Knorring (1982). "Predispositions to petty criminality in Swedish adoptees: I. Genetic and environmental heterogeneity." *Archives of General Psychiatry*, 39:1233–1241.

Bondurant, J. V. (1988). *The Conquest of Violence: The Gandhian Philosophy of Conflict*. Princeton, NJ: Princeton University Press.

Boneau, C. A. (1992). "Observations on psychology's past and future." *American Psychologist*, 47:1586–1596.

Boswell, T. (1992, June 17). "Cutting athletics: Save now, pay later." *Washington Post*, p. D1.

Bower, B. (1988, July 30). "Alcoholism's elusive genes." *Science News*, 134:74.

Bradford, P. V., and H. Blume (1992). *Ota Benga: The Pygmy in the Zoo*. New York: St. Martin's Press.

Breggin, G., and P. Breggin (1992, spring). "Feminist paradigms and conflict resolution." *ICAR Newsletter* (Institute for Conflict Analysis and Resolution, George Mason University), p. 1.

Breggin, P. (1972a, February 24). "The return of lobotomy and psychosurgery." *The Congressional Record*, pp. E1602-E1614. For current availability of the document, see Breggin (1982).

Breggin, P. (1972b). "Lobotomy is still bad medicine." *Medical Opinion*, 8:3236.

Breggin, P. (1972c). "Lobotomies: An alert." *American Journal of Psychiatry*, 129:98–99.

Breggin, P. (1973a, November 26). "Psychosurgery." *Journal of the American Medical Association*, 226:1121.

Breggin, P. (1973b, November-December). "Follow-up Report on Thomas R." *Rough Times*, p. 8. Also distributed as a Report from the Center for the Study of Psychiatry in 1973.

Breggin, P. (1973c). "The second wave of psychosurgery." *M/H* (*Mental Health*), 57:10–13.

Breggin, P. (1975a). "Psychosurgery for political purposes." *Duquesne Law Review*, 13:841–862.

Breggin, P. (1975b). "Psychiatry and psychotherapy as political processes." *American Journal of Psychotherapy*, 29:369–382.

Breggin, P. (1975c). "Psychosurgery for the control of violence: a critical review." Chapter IV in Fields, W., and W. Sweet (eds.): *Neural Bases of Violence and Aggression*. St. Louis: Warren H. Green Publisher.

Breggin, P. (1977a). "If psychosurgery is wrong in principle . . . ?" *Psychiatric Opinion*, November/December 1977, p. 23.

Breggin, P. (1977b). "La seconde vague. A propos dc la lobotomie." In Verdiglione, A. (ed.): *La Folie II: Actes Due Colloque De Milan, 1976*. Paris: Giangiacomo Feltrinelli.

Breggin, P. (1979). *Electroshock: Its Brain-Disabling Effects*. New York: Springer Publishing Company.

Breggin, P. (1980). "Brain-disabling therapies." In Valenstein, E. (ed.): *The Psychosurgery Debate*. San Francisco: W. H. Freeman.

Breggin, P. (1981a). "Disabling the brain with electroshock." In Dongier, M., and E. D. Wittkower (eds.): *Divergent Views in Psychiatry*. Hagerstown, Maryland:Harper and Row.

Breggin, P. (1981b). "Psychosurgery as brain-disabling therapy." In Dongier, M. and E. D. Wittkower (eds.): *Divergent Views in Psychiatry*. Hagerstown, Maryland: Harper and Row.

Breggin, P. (1982). "The return of lobotomy and psychosurgery" [with a new introduction]. In Edwards, R. B. (ed.), *Psychiatry and Ethics*. Buffalo: Prometheus Books, pp. 350–388. Originally published in the *Congressional Record*, February 24, 1972, E1602–E1612. Reprinted in *Quality of health care—human experimentation: hearings before Senator Edward Kennedy's Subommittee on Health*, U.S. Senate, Washington, D.C., U.S. Government Printing Office, 1973.

Breggin, P. (1983a). "What cost leukotomy?" *American Journal of Psychiatry*, 140:1101.

Breggin, P. (1983b). "Iatrogenic helplessness in authoritarian psychiatry." In Morgan, R. F. (ed.) : *The Iatrogenics Handbook*. Toronto: IPI Publishing Company.

Breggin, P. (1983c). *Psychiatric Drugs: Hazards to the Brain*. New York: Springer Publishing Company.

Breggin, P. (1984). "Electroshock therapy and brain damage: the acute organic brain syndrome as treatment." *Behavioral and Brain Sciences*, 7:24–25.

Breggin, P. (1985). "Shock treatment III: Resistance in the 1980s." Chapter 4 in Morgan, R. F. (ed.) : *Electric Shock*. Toronto: IPI Publishing.

Breggin, P. (1986). "Neuropathology and cognitive dysfunction from ECT." [Presented at the Consensus Development Conference on Electroconvulsive Therapy, sponsored by NIMH and NIH, 1985.] *Psychopharmacology Bulletin*, 22:476–479.

Breggin, P. (1990a). "Brain damage, dementia and persistent cognitive dysfunction associated with neuroleptic drugs: evidence, etiology, implications." *Journal of Mind Behavior*, 11:425–464.

Breggin, P. (1990b, March). "The scapegoating of American children." *The Rights Tenet*, p. 3. [Newsletter of the National Association for Rights Protection and Advocacy.] Reprinted from the *Wall Street Journal*, November 7, 1989, p. A30.

Breggin, P. (1991a). *Toxic Psychiatry: Why Therapy, Empathy and Love Must Replace the Drugs, Electroshock and Biochemical Theories of the 'New Psychiatry'.* New York: St. Martin's Press.

Breggin, P. (1991b). "Psychotherapy in the shadow of the psycho-pharmaceutical complex." *Voices* [the journal of the American Academy of Psychotherapists], 27:15–21.

Breggin, P. (1992a) *Beyond Conflict: From Self-Help and Psychotherapy to Peacemaking.* New York: St. Martin's Press.

Breggin, P. (1992b, March 15). "We could learn a thing or two from chimpanzees." *The New York Times,* p. A16.

Breggin, P. (1992c, August 31). "The real crime is neglecting inner-city youth." *Washington Post,* p. A18.

Breggin, P. (1992d, summer). "News and views on psychiatry: The violence initiative—A racist biomedical program for social control." *The Rights Tenet,* pp. 3–8.

Breggin, P. (1992e, September 18). "U.S. hasn't given up linking genes to crime." *The New York Times,* p. A34.

Breggin, P. (1992f, September 23). *Report from the Center for the Study of Psychiatry: The federal violence initiative.* Bethesda, Maryland: Center for the Study of Psychiatry.

Breggin, P. (1992g, September 25). Testimony before the Violence Initiative Panel of the Congressional Black Caucus Legislative Weekend. Washington, D.C.: Center for the Study of Psychiatry.

Breggin, P. (1992h). "How and why psychiatry became a death machine." In Rolland, C., H. Freidlander, and B. Müller-Hill (eds.). *Medical science without compassion. Past and present (Proceedings, Cologne, September 28-30, 1988),* pp. 389–426. Hamburg: Hamburger Stiftung für Sozialgeschichte des 20.

Breggin, P. (1992i). "A case of fluoxetine-induced stimulant side effects with suicidal ideation associated with a possible withdrawal reaction ('crashing')." *International Journal of Risk and Safety In Medicine,* 3:325–328.

Breggin, P. (1992j, March). "The return of ECT." *Readings: A Journal of Reviews and Commentary in Mental Health,* 7(1):12–17.

Breggin, P. (1992k, February 11). "The president's sleeping pill and its makers." *The New York Times,* p. A18.

Breggin, P. (1992l, Winter/Spring). "News and views on psychiatry: Prozac, suicide and violence: An analysis with reports from the Prozac Survivors Support Group, Inc." *The Rights Tenet,* pp. 4–6.

Breggin, P. (1993a). "News and views on psychiatry: The FDA—More harm than good?" *The Rights Tenet,* pp. 3–5.

Breggin, P. (1993b). "Psychiatry's role in the holocaust." *International Journal of Risk and Safety in Medicine,* 4:133–148.

Breggin, P., and G. Breggin (1993a, March). "A biomedical programme for urban violence control in the US: The dangers of psychiatric social control." *Changes: An International Journal of Psychology and Psychotherapy* 11(1):59–71.

Breggin, P., and G. Breggin (1993b, April). "The federal violence initiative: Threats to black children (and others)." *Psych Discourse* [journal of the Association of Black Psychologists], 24(4):8–11.

Breggin, P., and G. Breggin (1993c, June 2). The hazards of biologizing social problems: Testimony before the NIH panel on violence research. Bethesda, MD: Center for the Study of Psychiatry.

Breggin, P., and G. Breggin (1993d, September 21). Report and recommendations to the NIH panel on violence research. Bethesda, MD: Center for the Study of Psychiatry.

Breggin, P., and G. Breggin (1994). *Talking Back to Prozac.* New York: St. Martin's Press.

Breggin, P., and G. de Girolamo (1987). "G. Ellettroshock: tra rischioiatrogeno e mito terapeutico." *Quaderni Italiani di Psichiatrica,* 6:497–540.

Breland, Jr., A. E., Chief Division of Neurology, and Chairman, Committee on Surgical Therapy of Behavioral Disorders, The University of Mississippi Medical Center, Jackson (1973, August 27): "Memorandum to the members of the committee concerning Current Status of Psychosurgery."

Bridges, P. (1992). "Psychosurgery revisited." *Journal of Neuropsychiatry,* 2:326–330.

Brimelow, P. (1993, February 1). "Gambler Dan." *Forbes,* pp. 86–87.

Bronowski, J. (1965). *Science and Human Values.* New York: Harper & Row.

Brown, C., and A. M. Lago (1991). *The Politics of Psychiatry in Revolutionary Cuba.* New Brunswick, NJ: Transaction Publishers.

Brown, M.H. (1972, January 22). "Brain surgery can help rehabilitate criminals." *Los Angeles Times,* Part II, p. 4.

Brown, P. (1988). *Transfer of Care.* London: Routledge, Chapman, and Hall.

Brown, S.-L., and H. M. van Praag (eds.) (1991). *The Role of Serotonin in Psychiatric Disorders.* New York: Bruner/Mazel.

Brunner, H. G., M. Nelen, X. O. Breakefield, H. H. Ropers, and B. A. van Oost (1993, October 22). "Abnormal behavior associated with a point mutation in the structural gene for monamine oxidase A." *Science,* 262:578–580.

Buckley, S. (1993, May 18). "Montgomery test scores soar for Black, Latino students." *Washington Post,* p. B1.

Burchard, J., and S. Burchard (1991). *Annual Independent Review of Alaska Youth Initiative.* Burlington: Department of Psychology, University of Vermont.

Burchard, J. D., and R. T. Clarke (1990). "The role of individualized care in the service delivery system for children and adolescents with severely maladjusted behavior." *Journal of Mental Health Administration,* 17(1):48–60.

Burton, J. (ed.) (1990a). *Conflict: Human Needs Theory.* New York: St. Martin's Press.

Burton, J. (1990b). *Conflict: Resolution and Prevention.* New York: St. Martin's Press.

Bush, G. M. (1993, October 12). "Inner-city groups want conference canceled." *Press-Telegram,* p. B1.

Butterfield, F. (1992a, October 23). "Dispute threatens U.S. plan on violence." *The New York Times,* p. A12.

Butterfield, F. (1992b, November 13). "Study cites biology's role in violent behavior." *The New York Times,* p. A12.

Cameron, D., and E. Frazer (1987). *The Lust to Kill.* New York: Polity Press.

Carey, G. (1991, May 15). *Genetics and Violence.* A commissioned paper for the Panel for the Understanding and Control of Violence of the National Academy of Sciences, National Research Council. Unpublished.

Carnegie Council on Adolescent Development. (1989). *Turning Points: Preparing American Youth for the 21st Century.* New York: Carnegie Corporation.

Castaneda, R. (1992, December 10). "CDC cuts seen hurting AIDS efforts in District." *Washington Post,* p. D3.

Caudill, H. M. (1962). *Night Comes to the Cumberlands.* Boston: Little Brown and Company.

Charles, G. (1993, October 28). "Etats-Unis: Le nouvel ordre biologique." *L'Express,* pp. 92–98.

Chavkin, S. (1978). *The Mind Stealers.* Boston: Houghton Mifflin.

Chira, S. (1993, July 14). "Is small better? Educators now say yes for high school." *The New York Times,* p. 1.

Chorover, S. (1974, May). "The pacification of the brain." *Psychology Today,* pp. 59–69.

Chroust, P. (1992). "The letters of Friedrich Mennecke: Documents of a medical committer" [sic]. In Rolland, C., H. Friedlander, and B. Müller-Hill, (eds.). *Medical science without compassion. Past and present (Proceedings, Cologne, September 28–30, 1988),* pp. 201–223. Hamburg: Hamburger Stiftung für Sozialgeschichte des 20.

Claiborne, W. (1992, April 5). "The skeleton in the museum's closet." *Washington Post,* p. F1.

Clift, E. (1974, Fall). "Black land loss: 6,000,000 acres and fading fast." *Southern Exposure,* 2:108–111.

"Clinton proposes budget drop for NIMH, rise for substance abuse." (1993, June). *Psychiatric Times,* p. 10.

Cloninger, C. R., and Gottesman, I. I. (1987). "Genetic and environmental factors in antisocial behavior disorders." In Mednick, S. A., T. E. Moffitt, and S. A. Stack (eds.) *The Causes of Crime: New Biological Approaches,* pp. 92–109. New York: Cambridge University Press.

Coate, R. A., and J. Rosati (1988). *The Power of Human Needs in World Society.* Boulder: Lynne Rienner Publishers.

Cohen, D. (ed.) (1990). "Challenging the therapeutic state: Critical perspectives on psychiatry and the mental health system." *Journal of Mind and Behavior,* 11:(2– 3)247–274.

Cohen, R. (1993, November 23). "Dealing with illegitimacy." *Washington Post,* p. A21.

Coleman, L. (1984). *The Reign of Error: Psychiatry, Authority and Law.* Boston: Beacon Press.

Coles, G. (1987). *The Learning Mystique: A Critical Look at "Learning Disabilities."* New York: Pantheon Books.

"Confidence wanes in search for genetic origins of mental illness." (1989, March). *The Psychiatric Times,* p. 7.

Corea, G. (1977). *The Hidden Malpractice: How American Medicine Mistreats Women.* New York: Jove/HBJ Book.

de Cuevas, Jr. (1992, September-October). "Our children are in trouble." *Harvard Magazine,* 95:46–53.

Currie, E. (1985). *Confronting Crime.* New York: Pantheon Books.

Currie, E. (1993a, January). "In search of the violence initiative." *Journal of NIH Research,* 5:20–21.

Currie, E. (1993b, March). "Elliot Currie responds." *Journal of NIH Research,* 5:16.

Currie, E. (1993c). *Reckoning: Drugs, the Cities, and the American Future.* New York: Hill and Wang.

Daly, C. J. (1992, December 25). "With the slamming of a taxi door, race issue reverberates in Boston." *Washington Post,* p. A4.

Day One (1993, July 5). Transcript No. 118 of TV feature on violence. ABC-TV News.

David, R. (1992a, November 10). "All the lonely children." Speech delivered at the Annual Moira J. Whitehead Lecture, Pittsburgh, Pennsylvania. Unpublished.

David, R. (1992b). "The health crisis in African American communities: Rethinking the diagnosis and prescription." *Harvard Journal of African American Public Policy,* 1:1–12.

Delgado, J. (1969). *Physical Control of the Brain—Toward a Psychocivilized Society.* New York: Harper Colophon.

Delgado, J., V. Mark, W. Sweet, F. Ervin, G. Weiss, Y. Bach, G. Rita, and B. Hagiwara (1968). "Intracerebral radio stimulation and recording in completely free patients." *Journal of Nervous and Mental Diseases,* 147:329–339.

Department of Health and Human Services (1991). *Healthy People 2,000: National health promotion and disease prevention objectives.* Washington, D.C.: DHHS publication no. (PHS) 91-50212.

Department of Health and Human Services (1992). *Response to Peter Breggin's Statement at the Black Caucus.* 12-page undated, unsigned, and unpublished document obtained through Freedom of Information. It was probably for distribution to the press.

Department of Justice (1973). In-house memo by Ann Sadowsky to the Director of Law Enforcement Administration of DOJ. Available in *Hearings on S. 974 before the subcommittee on health of the senate committee on Labor & Public Welfare,* 93rd Congress, 1st session, pt. 2, pp. 385–386, 1973.

Department of Justice (1992). *Operation Weed and Seed: Reclaiming America's Neighborhoods.* Washington, D.C.: Department of Justice.

DeWitt, C. B. (director of NIJ) (circa 1992). The program on human development and criminal behavior. Washington, D.C.: U.S. Department of Justice, National Institute of Justice.

DeWitt, K. (1992, December 5). "Teenagers split on birth control plan." *The New York Times,* p. 7.

DiIulio, Jr., J. J. (1993, November 13). "Save the children." *The New York Times,* p. 23.

Dugger, C. (1992, September 8). "Troubled children flood ill-prepared care system." *The New York Times,* p. 1.

Duster, T. (1990). *Backdoor to Eugenics.* New York: Routledge.

Earls, F. (1991). "A developmental approach to understanding and controlling violence." In Fitzgerald, H.E. et al. (eds.). *Theory and Research in Behavioral Pediatrics,* 5:61–88. New York: Plenum Press.

Eckholm, E. (1993, January 31). "Teen-age gangs are inflicting lethal violence on small cities." *The New York Times,* p. 1.

Editorial (1992, March 9). "The speech police." *Wall Street Journal.*

Editorial (1992, March 21). "The Fred Goodwin case." *Washington Post,* p. A22.

Editorial (1993, June 11). "Sterilization—and unfit mothers." *The New York Times,* p. A32.

Editorial (1993, Feb. 12). "Banks and blacks in Washington." *Washington Post,* p. A20.

Editorial (1993, July 7). "Mandatory madness." *Washington Post,* p. A20.

Editorial (1993, August 4). "Same drug, different penalties." *Washington Post,* p. A16.

Edwards, D. (1993, July 7). "Congress swamped the courts." *Washington Post,* p. A21.

Eichelman, B., and A. Hartwig (1990). "The Carolina Nosology of Destructive Behavior (CNDB)." *Journal of Neuropsychiatry,* 2:288–296.

Eisler, R. (1988). *The Chalice and the Blade.* New York: Harper & Row.

Eisler, R., and D. Loye (1990). *The Partnership Way.* New York: HarperCollins.

Elshire, H.D. (1979, March 17). "Decision. By the Chairperson, Board of Medical Quality Assurance: In the Matter of the Accusation Against: Murray Hunter Brown, M.D., Before the Division of the Medical Quality, Board of Medical Quality Assurance, Department of Consumer Affairs, State of California." No. D-2200.

Ervin, F. R., V. H. Mark, and J. Stevens (1969). "Behavioral and affective responses to brain stimulation in man." In Zubin J., and C. Ghagass (ed.). *Neurobiological Aspects of Psychopathology,* pp. 54–56. New York: Grune and Stratton.

Escobar, G. (1993, February 6). "Treatment of D.C. Latinos called 'appalling' by panel." *Washington Post,* p. 1.

Escobar, G., and N. H. Greenberger (1993, September 9). "One team's road trip to sorrow." *Washington Post,* p. A1.

Esmail, A., and S. Everington (1993, March 13). "Racial discrimination against doctors from ethnic minorities." *British Medical Journal,* 306:691–692.

"Euthanasia" (1942). *American Journal of Psychiatry,* 99:141–143.

Fasnacht, B. (1993, September 3). "Child and adolescent disorders get fine-tuning in *DSM-IV.*" *Psychiatric News,* p. 8.

Fausto-Sterling, A. (1985). *Myths of Gender: Biological Theories about Women and Men.* New York: Basic Books.

Fernando, S. (1993, March). "Psychiatry and racism." *Changes: An International Journal of Psychology and Psychotherapy,* 11(1):46–58.

Finkelstein, N.G. (1992, September 18). "How we inspired the Nazis." *The New York Times,* p. A34.

Fireside, H. (1979). *Soviet Psychoprisons.* New York: W. W. Norton.

Fisher, M. (1993, January 19). "German doctor's Nazi past debated." *Washington Post,* p. A14.

Foreman, J. (1985, November 21). "Mass. neurosurgeon suggests quarantine for AIDS carriers." *Boston Globe,* p. 30.

Foucault, M. (1973). *Madness and Civilization.* New York: Vintage.

Fowler, M. (1992). *Educator's manual:* A project of the CH.A.D.D. National Education Committee. Plantation, FL: CH.A.D.D.

Frank, L. (1978). *The History of Shock Treatment.* Available from Leonard Frank, 2300 Webster Street, San Francisco, CA 94115.

Frank, L. (1990). "Electroshock, brain damage, memory loss, and brainwashing." *Journal of Mind and Behavior,* 11:489–512.

Franklin, J. (1984). *The Mind fixers.* Baltimore, MD: *The Evening Sun.* A reprint of articles published July 23–31, 1984.

Freedman, D. X. (1992). "Editorial: Violence (and a message for the 90s?)." *Archives of General Psychiatry,* 49:485–486, 1992.

Freeman, W. (1959). "Psychosurgery." In Arieti, S. (ed.) *American Handbook of Psychiatry*, pp. 1521–1540. New York: Basic Books.

French, M. (1985). *Beyond Power*. New York: Ballantine Books.

Friedenberg, A. (1973, September 18). "Breggin condemns psychosurgery." *Student Life* (Washington University), p. 1.

Friedenberg, E. Z. (1986, March). "Solving crime." *Readings: A Journal of Reviews*, pp. 20-22.

Friedlander, H. (1992). "From euthanasia to the final solution." In Rolland, C., Friedlander, H., and B. Müller-Hill (eds.). *Medical science without compassion. Past and present (Proceedings, Cologne, September 28–30, 1988)*, pp. 91–116. Hamburg: Hamburger Stiftung für Sozialgeschichte des 20.

Gaines, D. (1991). *Teenage Wasteland: Suburbia's Deadend Kids*. New York: Harper Perennial.

Gandhi, M.H. (1957). *Gandhi: An Autobiography*. Boston: Beacon Press.

Gatto, J. (1991). *Dumbing Us Down: The Hidden Curriculum of Compulsive Schooling*. New York: New Society Publishers.

Gelernter, J., D. Goldman, and N. Risch (1993, April 7). "The A1 allele at the D2 dopamine receptor and alcoholism." *Journal of the American Medical Association,* 269(13):1673–1677.

Gelles, R. J., and C. P. Cornell (1990). *Intimate Violence in Families*. Second edition. Newbury Park, CA: Sage Publications.

Giardina, D. (1992, October 31). "Appalachian mirror." *The New York Times*, p. 21.

Gibbs, N. (1993, July 12). "Truth, justice and the Reno way." *Time*, pp. 20–27.

Gil, G. (1989, June 15). "Visit by controversial speakers is canceled." *Louisville Courier Journal*, p. 1.

Gilliam, D. (1992, July 29). "Science or social control?" *Washington Post,* p. B1.

Gilliam, D. (1993, January 16). "The dream is falling on deaf ears." *Washington Post*, p. B1.

Goffman, E. (1961). *Asylums*. Garden City, N.Y.:Doubleday.

Golden, G.S. (1991, March). "Role of attention deficit hyperactivity disorder in learning disabilities." *Seminars in Neurology*, 11(1):35–41.

Goleman, D. (1992a, September 15). "New storm brews of whether crime has roots in genes: Experts express doubt that any strong link exists." *The New York Times*, p. C1.

Goleman, D. (1992b, December 15). "New light on how stress erodes health." *The New York Times*, p. C1.

Goleman, D. (1993, June 22). "Studying the pivotal role of bystanders." *The New York Times,* p. C1.

Gonzalez, D. (1993, May 26). "Salvaging of futures: It's one life at a time." *The New York Times*, p. B3.

Gonzalez, E. R. (1980, November 21). "Medical News—Psychosurgery: waiting to make a comeback?" *Journal of the American Medical Association,* 244:2245–2251.

Goodall, J. (1986). *The Chimpanzees of Gombe.* Cambridge: Harvard University Press.

Goodman, A. G., T. W. Rall, A. S. Nies, and P. Taylor (1991). *The Pharmacological Basis of Therapeutics, 8th edition.* New York: Pergamon Press.

Goodman, E. (1993, June 19). "Breaking the silence." *Washington Post,* p. A21.

Goodwin, F. K., and K. R. Jamison (1990). *Manic-Depressive Illness.* New York: Oxford University Press.

Goodwin, F. K. (1992a, February 11). Partial transcript of address to the National (Advisory) Mental Health Council, pp. 115–120. Provided by DHHS to U. S. Congressman John Conyers.

Goodwin, F. K. (1992b, May 5). "Conduct disorder as a precursor to adult violence and substance abuse: Can the progression be halted?" Washington, D.C.: Address to the American Psychiatric Association. Recorded by Mobiltape Company, Inc., 25061 W. Avenue Standford, Suite 70, Valencia, CA 91355. Transcript made from the audio by the Center for the Study of Psychiatry.

Goodwin, F. K. (1992c, May 5). "Conduct disorder as a precursor to adult violence and substance abuse: Can the progression be halted?" Washington, D.C.: Address to the American Psychiatric Association. Transcript provided by the Department of Health and Human Services under the Freedom of Information Act.

"Goodwin stumbles." (1992, March 5). *Nature, 356,* 6.

Gordon, T. (1970). *P.E.T.: Parent Effectiveness Training.* New York: Peter H. Wyden, Inc.

Gould, S. J. (1981). *The Mismeasure of Man.* New York: W.W. Norton, 1981.

Graedon, J., and T. Graedon (1985). *The People's Pharmacy.* New York: St. Martin's Press.

Grahame-Smith, D.G., and J. K. Aronson (1992). *Oxford Textbook of Clinical Pharmacology and Drug Therapy.* Oxford: Oxford University Press.

Green, A. (1989). "Physical and sexual abuse of children." In Kaplan, H., and B. Sadock (eds.) *Comprehensive Textbook of Psychiatry.* Baltimore: Williams and Wilkins, pp. 1962–1970.

Green, C. (1993, May). "Starting stimulant medication: Child Development Unit notes for parents." From the Child Development Unit, The Children's Hospital, England.

Greenberger, S. S. (1993, July 11). "Science friction: The struggle of female researchers at NIH." *Washington Post,* p. C3.

Greenspan, S., and A. Cunningham (1993, July 25). "The kids who would be killers." *Washington Post,* p. C1.

Gubin, S. (1993, March). "Prozac: The miracle drug?" *Sojourner,* pp. 5H–6H.

Hacker, A. (1991). *Two Nations: Black and White, Separate, Hostile, and Unequal.* New York: Charles Scribner's Sons.

Hansen, H., R. Andersen, A. Theilgaard, and V. Lunn (1982). *Stereotactic psychosurgery: A psychiatric and psychological investigation of the effects and side effects of interventions. Acta Psychiatricia Scandinavica.* Supple. 301, Volume 66, Munksgaard, Copenhagen, p. 1–123.

Hazlett, D. (1993, March 10). "Attention disorder not linked to socioeconomic condition." *Valley News Dispatch* (Pennsylvania), p. A12.

Herman, E., and E. Newberger (1992, March 11). Letter from the American Orthopsychiatric Association to Louis W. Sullivan, Secretary, Department of Health and Human Services concerning address by Frederick Goodwin to the Mental Health Leadership Forum on February 25, 1992.

Hernton, C. C. (1965). *Sex and Racism in America.* New York: Doubleday.

Herskovits, M. (1941). *The Myth of the Negro Past.* Boston: Beacon Press.

Higley, J., P. Mehlman, D. Taub, S. Higley, S. Suomi, M. Linnoila, and J. Vickers (1992). "Cerebrospinal fluid monamine and adrenal correlates of aggression in free-ranging rhesus monkeys." *Archives of General Psychiatry,* 49:436–441.

Higley, J., W. Thompson, M. Champoux, D. Goldman, M. Hasert, G. Kraemer, J. Scanlan, S. Suomi, and M. Linnoila (1993, August). "Paternal and maternal genetic and environmental contributions to cerebrospinal fluid monamine metabolites in rhesus monkeys (*Macaca mulatta*)." *Archives of General Psychiatry,* 50:615–623.

Hilts, P. (1992, September 5). "U.S. puts a halt to talks tying genes to crime." *The New York Times,* A1.

Hitler, A. (1940). *Mein Kampf.* New York: Reynal & Hitchcock.

Hoche, A. (1939). *Jahresringe: Innenansicht eines Menschenlebens.* Munchen: J.F. Lehmann.

Hooper, L. (1992, October 13). "Study shows long-term care to be more effective in treating depression." *Wall Street Journal,* p. B7.

Horgan, J. (1993, June). "Eugenics revisited." *Scientific American,* p. 123–131.

Horne, G. (1992–3, Winter). "Race backwards: Genes, violence, race and genocide." *CovertAction,* 43:29–35.

Hubbard, R., and E. Wald (1993). *Exploding the Gene Myth.* Boston: Beacon Press.

Humphrey, D. (1992). *Dying with Dignity: Understanding Euthanasia.* New York: Carol Publishing Group.

Huxley, J. (1989). "The Galton lecture for 1962: Eugenics in evolutionary perspective." In Keynes, M., and G. A. Harrison (eds.). *Evolutionary studies: A centenary celebration of the life of Julian Huxley. Proceedings of the twenty-fourth annual symposium of the Eugenics Society, London, 1987,* pp. 207–239. London: Macmillan.

Institute for Philosophy and Public Policy. (1992). *Genetic factors in crime: Findings, uses and implications. October 9–11, 1992* [a conference brochure]. College Park, Maryland: University of Maryland.

"Interpretation of the sterilization law." (1934). *Journal of the American Medical Association*, 102:630–631.

Isikoff, M. (1992, February 22). "HHS official apologizes for 'male monkey' remarks." *Washington Post*, p. A5.

Issac, R.J., and V. C. Armat (1990). *Madness in the Streets*. New York: Free Press.

Jackson, J. F., M. Bennett, H. Dent, H. Fairchild, R. Jones, and P. R. Todman (1993, January 21). Letter to Ralph L. Rosnow, Chairman, Committee on Standards in Research, and Elizabeth Baldwin, Research Ethics Officer, Science Directorate, American Psychological Association, Washington, D.C.

Jenike, M. (1988, July). "Obsessive-compulsive disorders: Treatment with drugs, ECT, and psychiatric surgery." *Psychiatric Times*, p. 1.

Jenike, M. (1990, April). "Obsessive-compulsive disorder." *HMS [Harvard Medical School] Health Letter*, pp. 4–7.

Jenike, M., L. Baer, H. T. Ballantine, R. L. Martuza, S. Tynes, I. Giriunas, L. Buttolph, and N. H. Cassem (1991) "Cingulotomy for refractory obsessive-compulsive disorder." *Archives of General Psychiatry*, 48:548–555.

Jennings, V. (1993, August 11). "Retaliation was the rule, NIH workers tell panel." *Washington Post*, p. A13.

Jensvold, Margaret, M.D., v. Louis W. Sullivan, M.D. Civil Action No. L-90-3123. The United States District Court for the District of Maryland.

Jonas, J.M. (1992, October). "Dr. Jeffrey M. Jonas, director of CNS clinical development at Upjohn, replies" [to Fred Baughman, Jr.]. *Clinical Psychiatry News*, p. 5.

Jones, J. H. (1993). *Bad Blood: The Tuskegee Syphilis Experiment*. New York: Free Press.

Jordan, M. (1992, December 18). "Local child abuse and neglect cases reach a record number." *Washington Post*, p. A2.

Judson, G. (1992, December 26). "Battle with poverty in Hartford schools." *The New York Times*, p. 26.

Jurko, M. F. (1971, May 31). Letter to Peter Breggin concerning Dr. Jurko's work with psychosurgeon O. J. Andy.

Kaimowitz v. *Department of Mental Health*. (1973, July 10). Civil Action No. 73-19434-AW (Wayne County, Michigan, Circuit Court). See Shuman (1977) for the entire opinion. Excerpts quoted in Breggin (1975a).

Kallmann, F. J. (1938). "Heredity, reproduction and eugenic procedure in the field of schizophrenia." *Eugenical News*, 23:105–113.

Kanner, L. (1942). "Exoneration of the feeble-minded." *American Journal of Psychiatry*, 99:17–22.

Kansas City Star (1973, June 15). "Director vacillates over lobotomies," p. 3.

Kantrowitz, B. (1992, December 14). "A 'silver bullet' against teen pregnancies?" *Newsweek,* p. 43.

Kaplan. A. (1992, December). "PTSD in children exposed to violence." *Psychiatric Times,* p. 2.

Karel, R. (1991, June 7). "Members react to campaign discrediting Prozac, psychiatry." *Psychiatric News,* p. 18.

Kater, M. H. (1989). *Doctors Under Hitler.* Chapel Hill, NC: University of North Carolina Press.

Kater, M. H. (1992). "The crisis of physicians and medicine in Nazi Germany." In Rolland, C., H. Friedlander, and B. Müller-Hill (eds.). *Medical science without compassion. Past and present (Proceedings, Cologne, September 28–30, 1988),* pp. 61–90. Hamburg: Hamburger Stiftung fur Sozialgeschichte des 20.

Katz, J. (1972). *Experimentation with Human Beings.* New York: Russell Sage Foundation.

Katz-Leavy, J. W., I. S. Lourie, B. A. Stroul, and C. Zeigler-Dendy (1992, July). *Individualized services in a system of care.* CASSP Technical Assistance Center, Center for Child Health & Mental Health Policy, Georgetown University Child Development Center, 3800 Reservoir Road, N.W., Washington, D.C. 20007.

Kaufman, M. (1993, August 21). "A museum's Eskimo skeletons and its own." *The New York Times,* p. 1.

Kennedy, F. (1937). "Sterilization and eugenics." *Journal of Obstetrics and Gynecology,* 34:519–520.

Kennedy, F. (1942). "The problem of social control of the congenital defective: Education, sterilization, euthanasia." *American Journal of Psychiatry,* 99:13–16.

Kelves, D. J. (1985). *In the Name of Eugenics.* New York: Alfred A. Knopf.

Kevles, D. J., and L. Hood (eds.) (1992) *The Code of Codes: Scientific and Social Issues in the Human Genome Project.* Cambridge, MA: Harvard University Press.

Kille v. *Mark,* Civil No. 681,998 (Super. Ct., Suffolk Co., Mass., filed Dec. 3, 1973).

Kolata, G. (1992, January 20). "Maker of sleeping pill hid data on side effects, researchers say." *The New York Times,* p. A1.

Kolata, G. (1993, January 26). "Carbon monoxide gas is used by brain cells as neurotransmitter." *The New York Times,* p. C3.

Kopp, M. (1936). "Legal and medical aspects of eugenic sterilization in Germany." *American Sociological Review,* 1:761–770.

Koshland, Jr., D. E. (1989, October 13). "Sequences and consequences of the human genome." *Science,* 246:389.

Koshland, Jr., D. E. (1990, October 12). "The rational approach to the irrational." *Science,* 250:189.

Kosterlitz, J. (1987, April 4). "Health focus: Drugs for Sale." *National Journal,* p. 850.

Kotlowitz, A. (1991). *There Are No Children Here.* New York: Anchor Books.

Kotulak, R. (1993, April 15). "Reshaping brain for better future." *Chicago Tribune,* p. 1.

Kotulak, R. (1993, December 12). "Tracking down the monster within us." *Chicago Tribune,* p. 1.

Kotulak, R. (1993, December 13). "How brain chemistry unleashes violence." *Chicago Tribune,* p. 1.

Kotulak, R. (1993, December 14). "Why some kids turn violent." *Chicago Tribune,* p. 1.

Kotulak, R. (1993, December 15). "New drugs break spell of violence." *Chicago Tribune,* p. 1.

Kozol, J. (1991). *Savage Inequalities—Children in America's Schools.* New York: Crown Publishers.

Kramer, M. (1992, June 1). "Straight talk about sex." *Time,* p. 36.

Krauthammer, C. (1993, July 23). "Media hype about the 'gay gene.'" *Washington Post,* p. A23.

Krauthammer, C. (1993, November 19). "Subsidized illegitimacy . . ." *Washington Post,* p. A29.

Krieger, L. M. (1990, March 18). "Gene link theories prompt backlash." *San Francisco Examiner,* p. E16.

Kropotkin, Petr. (1914). *Mutual Aid: A Factor in Evolution.* Boston: Porter Sargent Publishers.

Kruesi, M., J. Rapoport, S. Hamburger, E. Hibbs, W. Potter, M. Lenane, and G. Brown (1990, May). "Cerebrospinal fluid monamine metabolities, aggression, and impulsivity in disruptive behavior disorders of children and adolescents." *Archives of General Psychiatry,* 47:419–426.

Kruesi, M., E. Hibbs, T. Zahn, C. Keysor, S. Hamburger, J. Bartko, and J. Rapoport (1992, June). "A 2-year prospective follow-up study of children and adolescents with disruptive behavior disorders: Prediction by cerebrospinal fluid 5-hydroxyindoleacetic acid, homovanillic acid, and autonomic measures?" *Archives of General Psychiatry,* 49:429–435.

Kuper, L. (1981). *Genocide: Its Political Use in the Twentieth Century.* New Haven: Yale University Press.

La Fond, J. Q., and M. L. Durham (1992). *Back to the Asylum.* New York: Oxford University Press.

Landers, S. (1992, May). "NIMH's chief would broaden research plan." *NASW News,* p. 1.

Langbein, H. (1992). "Experiments on humans in Dachau and Auschwitz: Observations and reflections of an eyewitness." In Rolland, C., H. Friedlander, and B. Müller-Hill (eds.). *Medical science without compassion.*

Past and present (Proceedings, Cologne, September 28–30, 1988), pp. 39–58. Hamburg: Hamburger Stiftung für Sozialgeschichte des 20.

Lapon, L. (1986). *Murderers in white coats: Psychiatric genocide in Nazi Germany and the United States.* Psychiatric Genocide Research Institute, P.O. Box 80071, Springfield, MA 01138-0071.

Lauter, J., and J.-E. Meyer (1982). "Mercy killing without consent. Historical comments on a controversial issue." *Acta Psychiatrica Scandinavica,* 65:134–141.

Leary, W. (1992, March 8). "Struggle continues over remarks by mental health official." *The New York Times,* p. A34.

Leary, W. (1993, January 12). "Spread of AIDS is spurred by racism, U.S. panel says." *The New York Times,* p. A14.

Leifer, R. (1969). *In the Name of Psychiatry.* New York: Science House.

Leonard, H., S. Swedo, M. Lenane, D. Rettew, D. Cheslow, S. Hamburger, and J. Rapoport (1991). "A double-blind desipramine substitution during long-term clomipramine treatment in children and adolescents with obsessive-compulsive disorder." *Archives of General Psychiatry,* 48:922–927.

Leonard, H., S. Swedo, M. Lenane, D. Rettew, S. Hamburger, J. Bartko, J. Rapoport (1993). "A 2- to 7-year follow-up study of 54 obsessive-compulsive children and adolescents." *Archives of General Psychiatry,* 50:429–439.

Lewin, T. (1992, December 4). "Baltimore school clinics to offer birth control by surgical implant." *The New York Times,* p. A1.

Lewis, D. (1989). "Adult antisocial behavior and criminality." In Kaplan, H. I., and B. J. Sadock (eds.) *Comprehensive Textbook of Psychiatry,* Baltimore: Williams & Wilkins, pp. 1400–1405.

Lewis, N. (1992, December 23). "Delinquent girls take a violent turn." *Washington Post,* p. A1.

Lewontin, R. C. (1992). *Biology as Ideology.* New York: HarperPerennial.

Lewontin, R. C., S. Rose, and L. Kamin, (1984). *Not in Our Genes: Biology, Ideology, and Human Nature.* New York: Pantheon Books.

Liebow, E. (1967). *Tally's Corner.* Boston: Little, Brown and Company.

Lifton, R. (1986). *Nazi Doctors: Medical Killing and the Psychology of Genocide.* New York: Basic Books.

MacFarquhar, K. W., P. W. Dowrick, and T. R. Risley (1993, January). "Individualizing services for seriously emotionally disturbed youth: A Nationwide Survey." *Administration and Policy in Mental Health,* 20:165–174.

Manders, D. W. (1992, October). "The curious continuing ban of L-Tryptophan." *Townsend Letters for Doctors,* p. 880.

Marcus, A. D. (1991, April 9). "Prozac firm fights drug's use as defense." *Wall Street Journal,* p. B8.

Mark, V. H. (1974, February 25). "The continuing polemic of psychosurgery." *Journal of the American Medical Association,* 227(8):943.

Mark, V. H. (1974, July). "A psychosurgeon's case for psychosurgery." *Psychology Today,* Vol. 8:No. 2, pp. 31ff.

Mark, V. H., and F. R. Ervin (1968, August). "Is there a need to evaluate the individuals producing violence?" *Psychiatric Opinion,* 5:34, pp. 32–34.

Mark, V. H. and F. R. Ervin (1970). *Violence and the Brain.* New York: Harper & Row.

Mark, V. H., F. R. Ervin, and W. H. Sweet (1971). "Deep temporal lobe stimulation in Man." Paper delivered at a conference in Bar Harbor, Maine; pp. 485–505. The pagination suggests it was reproduced for the conference proceedings.

Mark, V. H., W. H. Sweet, and F. R. Ervin (1967, September 11). "The role of brain disease in riots and urban violence." *Journal of the American Medical Association,* 201:217.

Mark, V. H., W. H. Sweet, and F. R. Ervin (1972). "The effect of amygdalotomy on violent behavior in patients with temporal lobe epilepsy." In Hitchcock, E., L. Laitinen, and K. Vaernet (eds.). *Psychosurgery,* pp. 139–155. Springfield, Illinois: Charles C. Thomas.

Mark, V. H., H. Barry, T. McLardy, and F. R. Ervin (1970). "The destruction of both anterior thalamic nuclei in a patient with intractable agitated depression." *Journal of Nervous and Mental Disease,* 150:266–272.

Marshall, E. (1993, October 1). "NIH told to reconsider crime meeting." *Science,* 262:24.

Mason, B. J. (1973, February). "Brain surgery to control behavior: Controversial operations are coming back as violence curbs." *Ebony,* Vol. XXVIII, No. 4, p. 63.

Massey, D. S., and N. A. Denton (1991). *American Apartheid: Segregation of the Underclass.* Cambridge: Harvard University Press.

Masson, J. M. (1984). *Freud: The Assault on Truth.* Boston: Faber and Faber.

Masson, J. M. (1988). *Against Therapy: Emotional Tyranny and the Myth of Psychological Healing.* New York: Antheneum.

Maugh II, T. H. (1989, November 16). "Mental illness theory—Study raises doubts." *Los Angeles Times,* p. A15.

McGuinness, D. (1989). "Attention deficit disorder: The emperor's new clothes, animal "pharm," and other fiction." In Fisher, S., and R. P. Greenberg (eds.). *The limits of biological treatments for psychological distress,* pp. 151–188. Hillsdale, NJ: Lawrence Erlbaum Associates.

Meddis, S. V. (1993, July 23–25). "Is the drug war racist?" *USA Today,* p. 1.

Medical News. (1967, September 25). *Journal of the American Medical Association,* 201:28.

Mednick, S. A., P. Brennan, and E. Kandel (1988). "Predisposition to violence." *Aggressive Behavior,* 14:25–33.

Mednick, S. A., and K. O. Christiansen (eds.) (1977). *Biosocial Bases of Criminal Behavior.* New York: Gardner Press.

Mednick, S. A., W. F. Gabrielli, and B. Hutching. (1984). "Genetic influences in criminal convictions: Evidence from an adoption study." *Science,* 224:891–893.

Mednick, S. A., and K. Van Dusen (1983, August 15). "Proposal: Early identification of the chronic offender." Submitted to the U.S. Department of Justice, Office of Juvenile Justice and Delinquency Prevention by the Social Research Institute, University of California, with the signed approval of the Institute Director, Ward Edwards, and the Senior Vice President of Academic Affairs, Cornelius J. Pings.

Medvedev, Z. A., and R. A. Medvedev (1979). *A Question of Madness: Repression by Psychiatry in the Soviet Union.* New York: W.W. Norton.

Mehler, B. (1989). "Foundation for fascism: the new eugenics movement in the United States." *Patterns of Prejudice,* 23(4):17–25.

Melillo, W. (1993, June 11). "Britain denies Upjohn approval for Halcion: 'Concern must be for patients,' official says." *Washington Post,* p. A3.

Mencimer, S. (1993, January 31). "D.C.'s new death row." *Washington Post,* p. C1.

Mercer, B. (1990, December 28). "100 years later, tragedy lingers at blood-stained wounded knee." *Washington Post,* p. A6.

Messner, S., and K. Tardiff (1986). "Economic inequality and levels of homicide: An analysis of urban neighborhoods." *Criminology,* 24:297–317.

Meyer, J.-E. (1988). "The fate of the mentally ill in Germany during the Third Reich." *Psychological Medicine,* 18:575–581.

Miller, J. G. (1991). *Last One Over the Wall: The Massachusetts Experiment in Closing Reform Schools.* Columbus: Ohio State University Press.

Miller, J. G. (1992). Personal communication to Peter Breggin. Miller is Director of the National Center for Institutions and Alternatives (CIAA), Alexandria, Virginia.

Miller, J. J. (1992, winter). "The violent gene." *Diversity and Division II,* pp. 9–13.

Milloy, C. (1993a, March 17). "Teaching failure by example." *Washington Post,* p. D1.

Milloy, C. (1993b, July 4). "Imprisoning mind and body." *Washington Post,* p. B1.

Mindus, P., and H. Nyman (1990). "Normalization of personality characteristics in patients with incapacitating anxiety disorders after capsulotomy." *Acta Psychiatrica Scandinavica,* 83:283–291.

Mitscherlich, A., and F. Mielke. (1949). *Doctors of Infamy.* New York: Henry Schuman.

Molotsky, I. (1992, December 5). "Poet of the south for the inauguration." *The New York Times,* p. 8.

Monahan, J. (1990, October 11). *The John D. and Catherine T. MacArthur Foundation Research Network on Mental Health and the Law.* Charlottesville,

VA: University of Virginia School of Law. The date designates approval by the board. Unpublished.

Mosher, L., and L. Burti (1989). *Community Mental Health.* New York: W.W. Norton.

Mosse, G. L. (1985). *Toward the Final Solution: A History of European Racism.* Madison, WI: University of Wisconsin Press.

Müller-Hill, B. (1988). *Murderous Science: Elimination by Scientific Selection of Jews, Gypsies, and Others. Germany 1933–1945.* London: Oxford University Press.

Müller-Hill, B. (1991a). "Psychiatry in the Nazi era." In Block, S., and P. Chocoff (eds.). *Psychiatric Ethics,* pp. 461–472. New York: Oxford University Press.

Müller-Hill, B. (1991b.) "Bioscience in totalitarian regimes: The lesson to be learned from Nazi Germany." In Roy, D. J., B. E. Wynne, and R. W. Old (eds.). *Bioscience-Society,* pp. 67–76. New York: John Wiley & Son.

Müller-Hill, B. (1992). Introduction. In Rolland, C., H. Friedlander, and B. Müller-Hill (eds.). (1992). *Medical science without compassion. Past and present (Proceedings, Cologne, September 28–30, 1988),* pp. 5–12. Hamburg: Hamburger Stiftung fur Sozialgeschichte des 20.

Müller-Hill, B. (1993, April 8). "The shadow of genetic injustice." *Nature,* 362:491–492.

Murray, C. (1993, October 29). "The coming white underclass." *Wall Street Journal,* p. A14.

Mydans, S. (1993, May 2). "Gangs go public in new fight for respect." *The New York Times,* p. A1.

Myerson, A., J. Ayer, T. Putnam, C. Keeler, and L. Alexander (1936). *Eugenical Sterilization: Report of the Committee of the American Neurological Association for the Investigation of Eugenical Sterilization.* New York: Macmillan.

Nasrallah, H., J. Loney, S. Olson, M. McCalley-Whitters, J. Kramer, and C. Jacoby (1986). "Cortical atrophy in young adults with a history of hyperactivity in childhood." *Psychiatric Research,* 17:241–246.

National Advisory Mental Health Council (1993, October). "Health care reform for Americans with severe mental illnesses." *American Journal of Psychiatry,* 150:1447–1465.

National Center for Children in Poverty (1990). *Five million children—A statistical profile of our poorest young citizens.* New York: Columbia University.

National Center on Institutions and Alternatives (NCIAA) (1992, April 17). *Hobbling a generation: Young African American males in the criminal justice system of America's cities: Baltimore, Maryland.* NCIAA, 635 Slaters Lane, Suite G-100, Alexandria, VA 22314.

National Commission on Children (1991a). *Beyond rhetoric: A new American agenda for children and families.* Washington, D.C.: National Commission on Children.

National Commission on Children (1991b). *Speaking of kids—A National survey of children and parents.* Washington, D.C.: National Commission on Children.

National Commission for the Protection of Human Subjects on Biomedical and Behavioral Research (1977). *Report and recommendations: Psychosurgery.* Department of Health, Education and Welfare, Pub. No. (OS) 77-0002. Washington, D.C.: U.S. Government Printing Office.

"National effort to combat depression begins." (1993, May). *Psychiatric Times,* p. 3.

National Research Council (1993). *Losing Generations: Adolescents in High-Risk Settings.* Washington, D.C.: National Academy Press.

Nelkin, D., and L. Tancredi (1989). *Dangerous Diagnostics: The Social Power of Biological Information.* New York: Basic Books.

Nelson, C. (1993, April 21). "County leads area in housing discrimination." *Gazette,* p. A8.

Newman, A. (1993, January). "Theory linking D2-receptor gene, alcoholism is dealt a serious blow." *Clinical Psychiatry News,* p. 2.

Null, G. (1993, February/March). "Prozac, Eli Lilly and the FDA." *Townsend Letter for Doctors,* No. 115/116, pp. 177–187.

Oaks, D. (1992, May 1). "Psychiatric survivors & allies hold counter-conference & protests across the street from American Psychiatric Association huge annual meeting." *Dendron,* p. 1.

Odum, M. E. (1992, December 17). "Survey of Va. students shows many engage in risk behavior." *Washington Post,* p. C4.

Office of Minority Health (1989, October). *Assessment of minority homicide and violence issues in public health service programs.* Washington, D.C.: U.S. Department of Health and Human Services. Prepared by ROW Sciences, Inc., 5515 Security Lane, Suite 500, Rockville, MD 20852.

Ourand, J. P. (1993, May 12). "More than 100 NIH employees seek legal help." *Gazette,* p. A5.

Palca, J. (1992, August 7). "NIH wrestles with furor over conference." *Science,* 257:739.

Pam, A. (1990). "A critique of the scientific status of biological psychiatry." *Acta Psychiatrica Scandinavica* 82:(supplement 362), pp. 1–35.

"Paradigms of power: The case of Eli Lilly." (1992, December 7). *The Nation,* p. 690.

Paul, S. M. (1993, March 9). "Why I'm leaving government for a drug firm." *Wall Street Journal,* p. A18. Reprinted in *Psychiatric Times* (1993, May), p. 8.

Payer, L. (1992). *Disease-Mongers.* New York: John Wiley & Sons, Inc.

Pelham, Jr., W. E. (1993). "Recent developments in pharmacological treatment for child and adolescent mental health disorders." *School Psychology Review,* 22:158–161.

Peter, W. W. (1934). "Germany's sterilization program." *American Journal of Public Health,* 24:187–191.

Petrunik, M. (1982). "The politics of dangerousness." *International Journal of Law and Psychiatry,* 5:225–253.

Phillips, R. (1992, April 3). "Answering the challenge to our profession." *Psychiatric News,* p. 3.

Physicians' Desk Reference (PDR) (1993). Montvale, NJ: Medical Economics Company.

Popenoe, P. (1930). "Eugenic sterilization in California." *American Journal of Psychiatry,* 10:117–133.

Popenoe, P. (1934). "The German sterilization law." *Journal of Heredity,* 25:257–260.

Priest, D. (1993, January 12). "U.S. is urged to view AIDS as racial issue." *Washington Post,* p. A3.

Proctor, R. (1988). *Racial Hygiene: Medicine Under the Nazis.* Cambridge: Harvard University.

Proctor, R. (1992). "Genomics and eugenics: How fair is the comparison?" In Annas, G. J., and E. Sherman (eds.). *Gene Mapping: Using Law and Ethics as Guides,* pp. 57–93. New York: Oxford University.

Pross, C. (1991). "Breaking through the postwar coverup of Nazi doctors in Germany." *Journal of Medical Ethics,* 17 (Supplement):13–16.

Pross, C. (1992). "Nazi physicians: Criminals, charlatans or pioneers? The commentaries of the Allied experts at the Nuremberg Medical Trial." In Rolland, C., H. Friedlander, and B. Müller-Hill (eds.). *Medical science without compassion. Past and present (Proceedings, Cologne, September 28–30, 1988),* pp. 253–284. Hamburg: Hamburger Stiftung für Sozialgeschichte des 20.

Pross, C., and G. Aly (1991). *The value of the human being: Medicine in Germany 1918–1945.* 52-page exhibit booklet published by the Arztekammer Berlin in Connection with the Bundesarztekammer. Berlin: Arztekammer Berlin.

Putnam, F. W. (1990). "Foreword." In Donovan, D. M., and D. McIntyre, *Healing the Hurt Child.* New York: W. W. Norton.

Ramm, D. (1989, Fall). "Overcommitted." *Southern Exposure,* 17(3):14–17.

Rapoport, J. L. (1989). *The Boy Who Wouldn't Stop Washing.* New York: E. P. Dutton.

Raspberry, W. (1993, August 27). "Triage for juveniles." *Washington Post,* p. A25.

Regier, D. A., and A. I. Leshner (1992, February). *Request for applications: cooperative agreement for a multi-site, multimodel treatment study of attention-deficit hyperactivity disorder (ADHD)/attention-deficit disorder (ADD).* MH-92-03. Washington, D.C.: Department of Health and Human Services; Public Health Service; Alcohol, Drug Abuse and Mental Health Administration; and NIMH.

Reilly, P. R. (1991). *The Surgical Solution: A History of Involuntary Sterilization in the United States.* Baltimore: Johns Hopkins University Press.

Reinhold, R. (1993, July 17). "Officials report ties of plotters to hate groups." *The New York Times,* p. 6.

Reiss, A., and J. Roth (eds.) (1993). *Understanding and Preventing Violence,* Washington, D.C.: National Academy Press.

Rensberger, B. (1992, March 1). "Science and sensitivity." *Washington Post,* p. C3.

Reuter. (1992, September 16). "Blacks less likely to get kidney drug." *Washington Post,* p. A17.

Rhein, R. (1993, November). "Whew! A healthy budget boost for NIH." *Journal of NIH Research,* 5:36–40.

Rich, S. (1992, February 28). "Federal health official resigns, citing controversy over remarks." *Washington Post,* p. A4.

Rich, S. (1993a, March 27). "Poverty is blamed for 9-point deficit in 5-year-olds' IQs." *Washington Post,* p. A3.

Rich, S. (1993b, August 12). "Challenging a theory on welfare." *Washington Post,* p. A3.

Richman, L. S. (1992, August 10). "Struggling to save our kids." *Fortune,* pp. 34–40.

Rimer, S. (1992, June 18). "Job offers make clear what riots blurred: Idealism of Los Angeles young." *The New York Times,* p. A20.

Rimer, S. (1993, July 29). "Felons and farmers lock arms in the flood." *The New York Times,* p. A1.

Robitscher, J. (1980). *The Powers of Psychiatry.* Boston: Houghton Mifflin.

Rodgers, J. E. (1992). *Psychosurgery: Damaging the Brain to Save the Mind.* New York: HarperCollins.

Rodin, E. (1972, August 9). Memo to Jacques S. Gottlieb: Results of discussions [with Vernon Mark and others in Boston] held in regard to aggressive surgery. Exhibit AC-4 in *Kaimowitz* v. *Department of Mental Health* (1973).

Rodin, E. (1973, March 27). "A neurological appraisal of some episodic behavioral disturbances with special emphasis on aggressive outbursts." Exhibit AC-3 in *Kaimowitz* v. *Department of Mental Health.* Date is from the exhibit stamp. The document is undated.

Rolland, C., H. Friedlander, and B. Müller-Hill (eds.). (1992). *Medical science without compassion. Past and present (Proceedings, Cologne, September 28–30, 1988),* Hamburg: Hamburger Stiftung für Sozialgeschichte des 20.

Rosanoff, A. (1938). *Manual of Psychiatry and Mental Hygiene.* New York: John Wiley & Sons.

Rosenfeld, A. (1968, June 21). "The psycho-biology of violence." *Life,* pp. 67–71.

Rowland, R. G. (1978, July 21). "Accusation. By the Executive Director, Board of Medical Quality Assurance: In the Matter of the Accusation against: Murray Hunter Brown, M.D., Before the Division of the Medical Quality, Board of Medical Quality Assurance, Department of Consumer Affairs, State of California." No. D-2200.

Rothgeb, C. L. (1993, June 3). Letter to Ginger Ross Breggin regarding Norman Paul's finances from the Coordinator of Freedom of Information in the Department of Health and Human Services, 5600 Fishers Lane, Rockville, MD 29857.

Rubenstein, R. (1975). *The Cunning of History: Mass Death and the Future of America.* New York: Harper & Row.

Rugeley, C. (1993, June 21). "Richards signs last of legislation to reform psychiatric hospitals." *Houston Chronicle,* p. A1.

Rymer, R. (1992, September 6). "Darwinism, Barnumism and Racism." *The New York Times Book Review,* p. 3.

Sabshin, M. (1992, March 10). "To aid understanding of mental disorders." *The New York Times,* p. A24.

Sachdev, P., P. Hay, and S. Cummings (1992). "Psychosurgical treatment of obsessive-compulsive disorder." *Archives of General Psychiatry,* 49:582–583.

Saltus, R. (1993, February 8). "Evidence that genes play a role in violence is weak." *Boston Globe,* p. 37.

Santarelli, D. E. (1974, June 18). "Guideline G 6060.1a. Use of LEAA funds for psychosurgery and medical research." Washington, D.C.: U. S. Department of Justice, Office of the National Institute of Law Enforcement and Criminal Justice.

Savitt, T. L. (1978). *Medicine and Slavery: The Diseases and Health Care of Blacks in Antebellum Virginia.* Urbana: University of Illinois Press.

"Says obsessive-compulsive disorder might be the most biologically-based mental illness." (1989, July). *Clinical Psychiatry News,* p. 1.

Scheflin, A., and E. M. Opton, Jr. (1978). *The Mind Manipulators.* New York: Paddington Press.

Schell, W. G. (1901). *Is the Negro a Beast?* Moundsville: Gospel Trumpet Publishing Company.

Schrag, P. (1978). *Mind Control.* New York: Pantheon Books.

Schwartz, A. (1993, September 29). "A rough place to visit." *Washington Post,* p. A21.

Schwartz, J. (1993, July 7). "Second patient dies in connection with test of hepatitis B drug." *Washington Post,* p. A16.

Schwartz, J., and B. Cohn (1991, April 1). " 'The drug did it: A tough sell in court." *Newsweek,* p. 66.

Schweitzer, A. (1933). *Out of My Life and Thought.* New York: Holt, Rinehart and Winston.

Scull, A. T. (1977). *Decarceration.* Englewood Cliffs, N.J.: Prentice-Hall.

Scully, D. (1980). *Men Who Control Women's Health: The Miseducation of Obstetrician-Gynecologists.* Boston: Houghton Mifflin Company.

Seeman, P., H.-C. Guan, and H. H. van Tol (1993, September 30). "Dopamine D4 receptors elevated in schizophrenia." *Nature,* 365:441–445.

Seidelman, W. E. (1989 November/December). "In memoriam: Medicine's confrontation with evil." *Hastings Center Report,* pp. 5–6.

Seidelman, W. E. (1992). An inquiry into the spiritual death of Dr. Hippocrates. In Rolland, C., H. Friedlander, and B. Müller-Hill (eds.). *Medical science without compassion. Past and present (Proceedings, Cologne, September 28–30, 1988),* pp. 427–443. Hamburg: Hamburger Stiftung für Sozialgeschichte des 20.

Selden, S. (1991). "Selective traditions and the science curriculum: Eugenics and the biology textbook, 1914–1949." *Science Education,* 75:493–512.

Seligman, D. (1992). *A Question of Intelligence: The IQ Debate in America.* New York: Carol Publishing Group.

Sereny, G. (1983). *Into That Darkness.* New York: Vintage Books.

Shirer, W. (1941). *Berlin Diary.* New York: Alfred A. Knopf.

Shirer, W. (1960). *The Rise and Fall of the Third Reich.* New York: Simon and Schuster.

Shufeldt, R. W., M.D. (1907). *The Negro: A Menace to American Civilization.* Boston: Richard G. Badger.

Shuman, S. (1977). *Psychosurgery and the Medical Control of Violence.* Detroit: Wayne State Press.

Sierra. (1993, May/June). "A place at the table." *Sierra,* p. 51.

Simmons, H. G. (1991, January 3). "Lobotomies rare, but need closer scrutiny." *Toronto Star.*

Simon, R. (1993, July/August). "Should white families be allowed to adopt African American children?" *Health,* p. 22.

Sipchen, B. (1992, April 24). "A cure for violence?" *Los Angeles Times,* p. E1.

Smith, B. D. (1993, August 1). "Relaxed, firm dads save school events." *The New York Times: Education Life supplement,* p. 5.

Smith, R. (1993, March 13). "Deception in research, and racial discrimination in medicine." *British Medical Journal,* 306:668–669.

Sosnowski, K. (1962). *The Tragedy of Children under Nazi Rule.* Warszaw: Zachodnia Agencja Prasowa.

Spotts, J. V., and C. A. Spotts (1980). *Use and abuse of amphetamine and its subsitutes.* Rockville Maryland: National Institute on Drug Abuse. DHEW Publication No. (ADM) 80–941.

Spradley, J., and M. Martin-Foucher (1949). "New treatment in psychiatric disorders." *Diseases of the Nervous System,* 10:235–238.

Squires, S. (1990, November 15). "Brain function yields clues to hyperactivity." *Washington Post,* p. D1.

Stevens, J. R., V. H. Mark, F. Ervin, P. Pacheco, and K. Suematsu (1969). "Deep temporal stimulation in man: Long latency, long lasting psychological changes." *Archives of Neurology,* 21:159–169.

Stolberg, S. (1993, October 22). "Researchers link gene to aggression." *Los Angeles Times,* p. A36.

Stone, R. (1991, August 30). Department of Probation Intradepartmental Memorandum to Manhattan Family Intake and Investigation Program Officers. Re: Research Project. From Robert Stone, Branch Chief.

Stone, R. (1992a, October 9). "HHS 'Violence Initiative' caught in a crossfire." *Science,* 258:212.

Stone, R. (1992b, November 20). "NRC panel provides a blueprint." *Science,* 258:1298.

Stone, R. (1993, June 11). "Panel finds gaps in violence studies." *Science,* 260:1584–1585.

Struck, D. (1986, February 2). "Social and behavioral science: Scientists return to search for biological causes of criminal behavior." *The Sun.*

Styron, W. (1993, January 4/11). "Prozac days, halcion nights." *The Nation,* p. 1.

Suomi, S. (1991). "Adolescent depression and depressive symptoms: Insights from longitudinal studies with rhesus monkeys." *Journal of Youth and Adolescence,* 20:273–287.

Sullivan, L. (1992a, July 10). "Remarks to NAACP National Health Summit, Nashville, Tennessee." Press Handout. Washington, D.C.: Department of Health and Human Services.

Sullivan, L. (1992b, October 22). "Remarks to the American Academy of Child and Adolescent Psychiatry annual meeting." Press Handout. Washington, D.C.: Department of Health and Human Services.

Sullivan, L. (1993, March). "Off-the-mark criticism." *Journal of NIH Research,* 5:16.

Swanson, J. M., D. Cantwell, M. Lerner, K. McBurnett, L. Pfiffner, and R. Kotkin (1992, fall). "Treatment of ADHD: Beyond medication." *Beyond Behavior,* 4(1):13–22.

Sweet, W., R. Ervin, and V. Mark (1969). "The relationship of violent behavior to focal cerebral disease." In Garantinni S., and E. B. Sigg (eds.). *Aggressive Behavior,* pp. 336–352. Amsterdam: Excerpta Medica Foundation.

Szasz, T. (1963). *Law, Liberty and Psychiatry.* New York: Macmillan.

Szasz, T. (1974). *The Myth of Mental Illness.* New York: Harper & Row.

Talbott, J. A., R. E. Hales, and S. C. Yudofsky (1988). *Textbook of Psychiatry.* Washington, D.C.: American Psychiatric Press.

Talbott, J., and K. Tillotson (1941). "The effects of cold on mental disorders; a study of 10 patients suffering from schizophrenia and treated with hypothermia." *Diseases of the Nervous System,* 2:116–126.

Talan, J. (1992, October 19). "U.S. study on urban strife draws an expert's fire." *Boston Globe,* p. 3.

Talan, J. (1993, October 11). "Study with monkeys finds intolerance, violence, aggression might be genetic." *Saint Paul Pioneer Express,* p. C5.

Tanouye, E. (1993, April 15). "Critics see self-interest in Lilly's funding of ads telling the depressed to get help." *Wall Street Journal,* p. B1.

Tarasoff v. *Regents of the University of California,* 551 P.2d334 (1976).

Tardiff, K. (1988). "Violence." In Talbott, J. A., R. E. Hales, and S. C. Yudofsky (eds.). *Textbook of Psychiatry,* pp. 1037–1057. Washington, D.C.: American Psychiatric Press.

Tardiff, K. (1992). "The current state of psychiatric treatment of violent patients." *Archives of General Psychiatry,* 49:493–499.

"Targeted drug therapy best for curbing aggression." (1992, September). *Clinical Psychiatry News,* p. 2.

Ternon, Y. (1992). "The participation of physicians in genocide: Reality of the past; threat to the future." In Rolland, C., H. Friedlander, and B. Müller-Hill (eds.). *Medical science without compassion. Past and present (Proceedings, Cologne, September 28–30, 1988),* pp. 445–459. Hamburg: Hamburger Stiftung für Sozialgeschichte des 20.

Terry, D. (1992, September 13). "More familiar, life in a cell seems less terrible." *The New York Times,* p. A1.

Thomas, S. F. (1990, October 24). "Give attention deficit disorders their due." *Education Week,* p. 1.

Thompson, A. G. (1993, July/August). "Should white families be allowed to adopt African American children?" *Health,* p. 22.

Timnick, L. (1977, November 9). "Chemical found in schizophrenics' blood." *Los Angeles Times,* p. 1.

Touchette, N. (1992, November). "Cowering inferno: Clearing the smoke on violence initiative research." *Journal of NIH Research,* 4:31–33.

Touchette, N. (1993, January). "Seeking second opinions on violence research." *Journal of NIH Research,* 5:35–36.

Touchette, N. (1993, November). "NIH panel sidesteps concern about violence research." *Journal of NIH Research,* 5:29–31.

Toufexis, A. (1993, April 19). "Seeking the roots of violence. The search for biological clues to crime is igniting brutal political controversy." *Time,* pp. 52–53.

Toups, C. (1991, April 29). "Bitter pill for the maker of Prozac." *Insight,* pp. 54–55.

Trials of war criminals before the Nuernberg Military Tribunal, Volumes I and II (October 1946–April 1949). Washington, D.C.: U.S. Government Printing Office.

Trueheart, C. (1993, July 6). "The Eskimos finally go home." *Washington Post,* p. C1.

Turner, J. (1986, February 8). "World Health Organization: Antibiotic conference cancelled for second time." *Lancet,* p. 333.

"Twin studies unravel relationship between genes and environment." (1992, December). *Psychiatric Times,* p. 20.

Urban Strategies Group. (1992, September). "A call to reject the federal weed and seed program in Los Angeles."

Valenstein, E. (ed.) (1980). *The Psychosurgery Debate.* San Francisco: W. H. Freeman.

Valentine, P. W., and A. Goldstein (1992, December 4). "Baltimore to try Norplant to reduce teen pregnancy." *Washington Post,* p. A1.

VanDenBerg, J. (1988). "Alaska's services for children with emotional problems: A bright new hope." *Coping,* 111:12–17.

VanDenBerg, J. (1989, November). *AYI program background.* Available from Division of Mental Health and Developmental Disabilities, Box H-04, Juneau, AK 99811-0620.

Vatz, R. E. (1993, March 1). "Attention-deficit disorder mythology." *Wall Street Journal,* p. A15.

Vobejda, B. (1992a, July 8). "Child poverty rose during the prosperous '80s." *Washington Post,* p. A3.

Vobejda, B. (1992b, December 10). "Home alone, glued to the TV." *Washington Post,* p. A3.

von Mises, L. (1947). *Planned chaos.* Irvington-on-Hudson, NY: Foundation for Economic Education.

Vrba, R. (1992). "Personal memories of actions of SS doctors of medicine in Auschwitz I and Auschwitz II (Birkenau)." In Rolland, C., H. Friedlander, and B. Müller-Hill (eds.). *Medical science without compassion. Past and present (Proceedings, Cologne, September 28–30, 1988),* pp. 15–29. Hamburg: Hamburger Stiftung für Sozialgeschichte des 20.

Wagner, R. (1992, April). "The Congress' Black Caucus disputed ADAMHA director's NIMH appointment." *Psychiatric Times,* p. 1.

de Waal, F. (1989). *Peacemaking Among Primates.* Cambridge: Harvard University Press.

Wasserman, D. [principle investigator] (undated, probably June 1991). Untitled application for funding of a conference on genetic factors in crime.

Weiner, J. M. (ed.) (1991). *Textbook of Child and Adolescent Psychiatry.* Washington, D.C.: American Psychiatric Press.

Weinrich, M. (1946). *Hitler's Professors.* New York: Yiddish Scientific Society.

Weiss, S. (1987). *Race Hygiene and National Efficiency.* Los Angeles: University of California Press.

Weisskopf, M. (1992, January 16). "Minorities' pollution risk is debated." *Washington Post,* p. A25.

Welsing, F. C. (1991). *The Isis Papers.* Chicago: Third World Press.

Wender, P. H. (1973). *The Hyperactive Child.* New York: Crown Publishers.

Wender, P. H. (1987). *The Hyperactive Child, Adolescent and Adult.* New York: Oxford University Press.

Wertham, F. (1969). *A Sign for Cain.* New York: Paperback Library.

West, C. (1993). *Race Matters.* Boston: Beacon Press.

Wheeler, D. (1992a, June 24). "An escalating debate over research that links biology and human behavior." *Chronicle of Higher Education,* p. A7.

Wheeler, D. (1992b, September 2). "U. of Md. conference that critics charge might foster racism loses NIH support." *Chronicle of Higher Education,* p. A9.

Wheeler, D. (1992c, September 16). "Meeting on possible links between genes and crime canceled after bitter exchange." *Chronicle of Higher Education,* p. A7.

Wheeler, D. (1992c, November 4). "Looking beyond the causes of violence, researchers investigate ways to prevent it." *Chronicle of Higher Education,* p. A7.

Wheeler, D. (1992d, November 4). "Ambitious federal plan for violence research runs up against fears of misuse." *Chronicle of Higher Education,* p. A7.

White, J. E. (1993, June 7). "Philosopher with a mission." *Time,* pp. 60–62.

Wiesenthal, S. (1967). *The Murderers Among Us.* London: Heinemann.

Will, G. F. (1993, November 18). "Underwriting family breakdown." *Washington Post,* p. A23.

Wilson, A. N. (1990). *Black-on-Black Violence.* New York: Afrikan World Infosystems.

Wilson, A. N. (1992). *Understanding Black Adolescent Male Violence.* New York: Afrikan World Infosystems.

Wilson, J. Q., and R. J. Herrnstein (1985). *Crime and Human Nature.* New York: Simon & Schuster.

Wistrich, R. (1982). *Who's Who in Nazi Germany.* New York: Macmillan.

Wolff, C. (1992, July 24). "Police council member charges officers beat her and family." *The New York Times,* p. B1.

Womack, A. (1992, December 8). "Surburban teens said to drink more than city teens." *Washington Post,* p. C6.

Yette, S. F. (1971). *The Choice: The Issue of Black Survival in America.* Silver Spring, MD: Cottage Books. Originally published by G. P. Putnam's Sons, New York.

Yllo, K., and M. Bograd (1988). *Feminist Perspectives on Wife Abuse.* Newbury Park: Sage Publications.

Yudofsky, S., and F. Ovsiew (1990). "Neurosurgical and related interventions for the treatment of patients with psychiatric disorders." *Journal of Neuropsychiatry,* 2:53–55.

Zametkin, A. J., T. E. Nordahl, M. Gross, A. C. King, W. E. Semple, J. Rumsey, S. Hamburger, and R. M. Cohen (1990, November 15). "Cerebral glucose metabolism in adults with hyperactivity of childhood onset." *New England Journal of Medicine,* 323:1361–1366.

Zametkin, A. J., L. L. Liebenauer, G. A. Fitzgerald, A. C. King, D. V. Minkunas, P. Herscovitch, E. M. Yamada, and R. M. Cohen (1993, May). "Brain metabolism in teenagers with attention-deficit hyperactivity disorder." *Archives of General Psychiatry,* 50:333–340.

Index

drug withdrawal, 188
  symptoms, 85, 111
DSM-III-R, 72–76, 78, 81, 84, 88
Dukes, M.N.G., 52
Duster, Tony, 28
Dutch study on genetics and violence, 61, 69, 70

Earls, Felton, 41–42, 112
educational campaign, 17
Edwards, Don, 175, 176
Elders, Joycelyn, 173
electroshock treatment, 139, 154, 155, 156
Elias, Sherman, 50
Eli Lilly
  advertising prescription drugs, 30
  at the APA, 28–29
  Bush, Quayle, and FDA, 34–35
  federal government role in promoting, 33
  influencing justice system, 36–37
  logo, 29, 30, 33
  National Mental Health Association, 30–31
  NIMH breakthrough, 31–33
  research funding, 34, 105–6
emotional disability, 90
empathy, 187, 188, 192, 194, 195, 196
EMS (eosinophilic myalgia syndrome), 35–36
England eugenics movement, pre-World War II, 50, 150
enrichment programs, 93, 94
environmental factor
  alcoholism, 62
  antisocial personality disorder, 171
  child development, 91–94
  human behavior, 56
  influencing suffering and distress, 183–84
  monkey research, 56
  NRC report, 200
  schizophrenia, 60
  stress-related illness, 113
epilepsy
  causing aggression, 124
  causing violence, 134
Erickson, Dale, 133
Ervin, Frank, 116–18, 119, 120–27
Eskimos
  Alaska Youth Initiative, 187
  display of Minik and family, 164–65
ethics
  concern over Ritalin NIMH study, 107
  high-tech abuse, 113

intrusive research techniques, 25, 102–3, 113
  science and medicine bias, xiii
  sibling research, 113
  Tuskegee Study, 166, 167
ethnicity
  antisocial personality disorder, 171
  sibling research ethics, 113
  violence predictor, 24
eugenics
  academia theories, 66–67
  Final Solution resulting from, 146
  pre-World War II England, 50, 150
  pre-World War II Germany, 146
  psychiatry, 146
  racism in America, 171–72
  violence control, 47–70
euthanasia
  extermination camp outgrowth, 141–42
  German children, 139–40
  German mentally defective, 138–39
  status, 156
  United States, 151
Evening Sun, The, 4
exclusion, 179
exhibit. *see* display
extermination. *see also* murder
  concentration camps, 141–42, 154–55
  crematoriums, 138, 141
  gas chamber, 141, 142
  German centers, 139, 140, 141

FAES. *see* Foundation for Advanced Education in the Sciences
family conflict, 89
family service programs
  countering foster home care, 173
family therapy
  ADHD in child, 77, 79–81
  what to look for, 197
fathering ADHD child, 78, 79–80
FDA. *see* Food and Drug Administration
federal agencies
  NRC report sponsorship, 24
  psycho-pharmaceutical complex, 28
federal government
  biomedical control programs, 96–114
  drug treatment of children, 3–4, 72, 107
  Eli Lilly promotion, 33
  grants to, 33
  and public health issues, 21
  sterilization, 172
  violence initiative, xii, xiv, 1–22
Fields, Ruby, 39

About the Authors

Peter R. Breggin, M.D., is an internationally known psychiatrist in private practice in Bethesda, Maryland. He is the founder and director of the nonprofit Center for the Study of Psychiatry, which includes *Children First!*, the only membership organization devoted to protecting children and families from biopsychiatric intrusions into their lives. He is also professor of conflict resolution at George Mason University, and the author of many books and articles, most recently *Toxic Psychiatry* (1991), *Beyond Conflict* (1992), and with Ginger Breggin, *Talking Back to Prozac* (1994), all published by St. Martin's Press.

Dr. Breggin's reform work began in the 1950s as a Harvard College student when he directed the Harvard-Radcliffe Mental Hospital Volunteer Program. He received his medical training at Case Western Reserve, and his psychiatric training at Harvard and the State University of New York, Upstate Medical Center. Before going into private practice in 1968, he was a full-time consultant with the National Institute of Mental Health. During the 1970s, he won recognition for organizing a successful campaign against the return of lobotomy and then went on to write the first medical books about the brain-damaging effects of electroshock and psychiatric drug treatment.

Dr. Breggin continues to influence the mental health professions through his private practice, workshops, publications, research, and medical-legal activities. His reform efforts have been extensively covered in the general and scientific press from *The New York Times* and *Time* magazine to *Science* magazine and the *New Scientist*. Among many media appearances, he has been a psychiatric expert on "60 Minutes," "20/20," and "Dan Rather Reports."

Ginger Ross Breggin is Director for Research and Education at the Center for the Study of Psychiatry. In 1992 she initiated and spearheaded the national campaign against the federal violence initiative, including opposition to funding for a conference on genetic factors in crime, and has recently helped to set up *Children First!* She is the co-author of *Talking Back to Prozac*. Her background is in public relations, writing, and investigative journalism. She works closely with Dr. Breggin in all of the center's activities, and has coauthored articles in the fields of mental health and conflict resolution. She is also an award-winning photographer and a mother.